Magda Lamb is an author, painter, visual artist, illustrator, and activist. The mother of two daughters, she enjoys film, theatre, illustrating, painting, reading, and gardening. She studied Art and Graphic Design in London.

ONLY OBLIVION

MAGDA LAMB

AIA PUBLISHING

Only Oblivion
Magda Lamb
Copyright © 2021
AIA Publishing, Australia
ABN: 32736122056
http://www.aiapublishing.com

Any references to real people and events in this book are purely my personal opinion, written from my subjective perspective and are not statements of fact. Others may recall people, events, and circumstances differently. My intention is to share my perspective as a matter of public interest and education.

ISBN: 978-1-922329-18-9
Cover design by Rose Newland

To my daughters

Acknowledgments

A huge thanks to my daughters, to Hol and Dave, and to the special friends in my life, Marisa, Charlie, Emma, Maria W., Gella, Cath, and Shelley.

To JT and Isabel, I thank you for your counsel and for all you've done to help. To all friends of Lois W (the cofounder of Al-Anon), and especially to my amazing discussion group, thank you.

A massive thank you to my splendid editor, Tahlia Newland, and all at AIA Publishing.

Chapter One

"He who learns must suffer. And even in our sleep, pain that cannot forget falls drop by drop upon the heart, and in our own despair, against our will, comes wisdom to us by the awful grace of God." Aeschylus

What I need is a drink. A chilled, crisp glass of Chablis, or a tangy glass of Merlot, Chianti—any house red for that matter—followed by another, and then some more, until the bottle is gone. Then I'll pour a few shots of Tanqueray gin for good measure. Yes, that's just what I need. A few shots of Tank and a splash of Indian Tonic Water with lime wedges will take the edge off and help me unwind, relax, sleep. Yet here I am drying myself out; I'm looking out my window, sipping flat Lucozade straight from a plastic bottle. The only side effects I have by abstaining is an aching body, fatigue, and a mood that's so very low, I feel lower than a snake's belly.

So far, my drinking days have been going on for almost five years. I had it under control. No, I didn't. Obviously, I did not. I thought it wasn't a problem—after all I was functioning in the daytime, getting work and daily chores done, never drinking before 8 pm, never getting blind drunk, and I'd never drink anywhere other than at home.

I think I might have inherited my family addict gene. My late mother was addicted to prescription drugs for as long as I can remember, as was her mother. My late paternal grandfather was a brandy loving gambler, and my aunt Maeve was an alcoholic—a full-blown blackout drinker for most of her life.

Up until now I thought it was okay to self-medicate daily with alcohol, but it has dawned on me that this is a crazy way to live my life each and every day. I don't want to turn into an alcoholic like my aunt Maeve. I realise it's time to quit this habit without the help of doctors, rehabs, counsellors or religion. It has to come from within.

Due to either rogue landlords or illegal evictions, I've moved from houses to flats five times in as many years. I've had a few stints of living in my car between moves. One time I lived in my poky London art studio, sleeping on the concrete floor, for two months. I'd hoped to find stability when I moved to the South West with Sylvia and Frida, my two daughters, who've now graduated. But once again, I'm homeless, living in my car.

I'm parked between coaches and lorries near the Downs, people watching. Joggers, dog walkers and university students walk on by. They don't notice me. I feel invisible. I try reading, then re-reading the same paragraph. But I can't focus.

This timeless entity is monotonous: birdsong, distant laughter, and dogs barking that keep me alert, as well as coaches and lorry engines firing up, traffic passing, and the frequent blast of loud music booming from passing cars.

I habitually double-check that I've locked my doors. Afternoon sun heats up my car like an oven, so I move my parking space every hour to the next shadow of branches. I make sketches of the majestic trees—they're living giants and kind companions, providing shade from the sun and shelter from May rain.

I don't own a decent smart phone, and without one there's nothing to distract me from my jumbled mind. I'm conserving my phone battery in case Sylvia or Frida call me.

Random thoughts race through my head. I ask myself why someone like me, well read, educated, a loving mother, a single parent, ended up like this.

The Lucozade supply is buried under my coat and pillow in the footwell, out of the heat. It's better to sip and not drink too quickly, because of the problem of having nowhere to pee publicly in broad daylight.

The local superstore has customer toilets, and a few pubs have facilities. Also, there's a Starbucks a short drive away that have toilets and WiFi, plus electric-socket points. That's useful to charge my computer and phone, but their closing times vary; they're not open twenty-four hours.

I've automatically kicked into survival mode.

The activity on the Downs quietens when the sun begins to set. No more dog walkers or busy traffic, just a few student stragglers returning to Halls. After dark the Downs is a deserted terrain.

While there's enough light for me to see what I'm doing, I prepare to camp for the night. I move my car away from the parked trucks and coaches and strategically hang my North Face jacket by the roof-grip handle hook, adjusting it into a makeshift curtain. Cases and bags pack the boot of my car to the roof. I transfer bags from the rear seat to the front-passenger seat and footwell, but leave my driver's seat clear, just in case I need to make a quick get-away in the night. My bed is the rear seat with my pillow and a sleeping bag. There's not much room. Seatbelts dig into me, and I can't straighten my legs; I have to bend my knees to fit on the seat.

Night-time falls. I play classical music on my Macbook's iTunes. The screen glows brilliantly in the darkness. It might draw unwanted attention to me should a car or the cops drive by. In a panic I slam it shut. I'm not doing anything wrong, unless sitting in your own car vulnerable and homeless is classed as loitering. I can't risk being hassled; it's too much bother and shame.

The day has dragged. I bemoan aloud, 'God? Why have you abandoned me?' No answer. I mutter prayers to the God I discarded five years ago. Again, he doesn't answer.

I wait patiently with stoical acceptance until sleep finds me.

A choir of birds singing their morning song wake me early. I'm startled at first—don't know where the hell I am. I didn't sleep well. The bulky seatbelts are hideously uncomfortable. My body aches. I'm parked on a slope, so it feels weird. When I had to pee in the night, I had to hide behind my car and squat in the gutter. I'll get used to it. I've got hand sanitizer that gets super runny in the heat. With no sink to wash in, this morning I used baby wipes for face, hands, neck, feet, and underarms. I completed my beauty ablutions with a facial cleanser, then brushed my hair and plaited it into a tidy braid that dangles down my back. I gargled mouthfuls of warm bottled water to brush my teeth and spat the white foam onto the grass verge. I don't want to look like a homeless person, so I'm keeping myself looking presentable. It's a very basic wash and whistle. It will have to do.

The fundamental things I take for granted are no longer available: no bed, bathroom, or toilet; no kitchen to rustle up a cup of morning tea, coffee, or toast; no WiFi, art easel, palette, oil paint, brushes, or art materials. Also, I'm adjusting to not having electricity. I'm without news and weather updates. I'll have to rely on my car radio for those.

There's no privacy to change my clothing, and no clean clothes, unless I hike to the launderette. Absolutely every damn thing requires effort executed with military precision. And then there's the effort I have to make to remain inconspicuous. Blending in; that's another hurdle in itself.

Frida bought me a crystal for my last birthday. It's black with silver bits and cool to the touch. I hold it in my right hand and apply it to my forehead, running it from my right temple to my left. After I repeat the movement a few times, I drop it carefully inside my driver's door pocket; that's where I keep it, so I know where to find it.

I roll a cigarette and start to smoke. My stomach growls with hunger. I need breakfast to settle my stomach, and I need to check if Nick has emailed me. Frida put me in touch with Nick. He's one of the founders of an organisation that helps tenants with crooked landlords, including winning back stolen deposits from rogue landlords. Maybe he'll get my two grand back from my most-recent crooked ex-landlord who had illegally evicted me.

There's a Costa Coffee a short distance away. I park in the library's small car park and walk. The coffee shop is busy with customers working on their laptops. I order a panini and a flat white and check my emails—nothing new in my inbox.

I log into online banking; my funds are not healthy, but at least I can cover my car insurance direct debit. My income is zero, but I have credit available on my credit cards—emergency funds. I'm in limbo about my deposit theft. Once the landlord dispute is over, I have sufficient funds to get myself to Ireland.

It's a job to stay hydrated in this scorcher of a day—the mercury hits thirty-six degrees. I sweat buckets, and my car feels like a furnace. I haven't showered in a few weeks, so I ring a friend, Connie, to ask if she'd permit me to use her shower if I offer to pay. After three attempts I realise that she blanked my calls; our short friendship is over. Most Londoners I've met are so direct that they'll let you know if they don't like you, but not the dwellers of the South West I've met so far. They're difficult to read. I'm okay about it; I hate feeling at anyone's mercy, anyway.

I figured I'd join the local council's fitness centre for free membership. They have pay-per-day rates for the use of their swimming pool and gym—complete with shower.

Today I use the centre for the first time. Rather than draw attention to myself by purchasing a swim ticket, I walk through the crowded reception area, holding a blue bath towel under my arm. I follow signs to the pool showers and changing rooms to pass myself off as a swimmer. I find a tall, metal locker and place my backpack inside, but keep hold of my towel and plastic bag of bits including a washbag. A shower is available. Inside the cubicle I hang my plastic bag of stuff on the door hook— clean clothes, talcum powder and trainers—and strip down. I've dropped a dress size.

After I press the white 'Water On' button, lashings of warm water cascade over my aching body. Using my shampoo and shower gel, I get rid of the filth and smell of stale sweat and grease from my hair. I crouch beneath the soothing waterfall and watch the soap suds disappear, swirling their way down the plug hole. When the water stops, I press the button again. The water re-starts, and I repeat this a few more times, staying in the water long after the suds run clear. I dry off, dress in clean clothes and discreetly leave the fitness centre.

I feel so refreshed, clean as a whistle.

When I drive back to the Downs, I park in a different spot— it draws less attention when I vary my parking spots. I call Frida.

'At last! I tried calling you! Was your phone off?' she speaks quickly. It's good to hear her voice.

'My phone was shut in the locker—I got myself a shower at that fitness centre. My signal probably dropped out.'

'If you want to mix it up a bit,' she continues, 'and not get your face too well known there, you can use the shower here if my housemates go out. Sylvia mentioned you can shower at hers, but her moody housemates are always in the bathroom at her place. She can barely get in there herself!'

'Thanks that sounds like a plan. What have you been up to?' I ask.

'Really been busy,' she replies. 'I've started cycling to work. I bought a cheap Raleigh bike. It's really scary cycling on the roads! Oh, and my job probation period at the spa is nearly up. That means I'll be able to get you a day pass to use the spa facilities and swanky showers.'

'Okay!' I reply. It appears I now have a few showers from which to choose.

'I haven't got a shift at the spa tomorrow. How about we meet for lunch?'

I readily agree. 'Yeah, let's do lunch. Tomorrow it is.'

We arrange to meet at one of our favourite little independent cafés.

Chapter TWO

Our lunch is enjoyable, and conversation relaxed. We chat small talk, not mentioning the elephant in the room. I hide my anxiety, not saying how the arrival of strangers on the Downs makes me feel edgy. A number of rusty camper vans coughing out black exhaust fumes have been arriving to camp.

The influx of visitors are hippy looking with dishevelled, matted hair and ragged clothes. I keep seeing the same camper van, one messily sprayed with CND symbols and smiley logos on the rusty bodywork.

The occupants are two young-looking women. The younger one is beanpole thin and can't be older than sixteen. The other is chubby and smiley; she's not a lot older. They dress similarly: matted hair; rows of neck beads; faded, dirty, cut-down denim short-shorts and espadrille sandals. Every so often the chubby one hops out of the camper van. She takes turns hopping into the different lorries with its truck driver for ten minutes or so, then she re-appears and walks back to her camper van while counting a bunch of notes. She doesn't see me. I'm invisible.

The other day I overheard a lady in a coffee shop say that just before the Glastonbury Festival kicks off, the camper visitors descend upon the Downs for an extended pit stop. She said they stop off to catch up with cronies or earn some cash in hand. They don't seem to make any trouble. Then they leave for the festival and are not seen again until the following year.

Frida and I order the day's special and one piece of cake to share.

'Have you spoken to anyone who might help out?' The elephant in the room has left. Frida tilts her head to one side, waiting for me to answer.

'No, I'm not sure there is anyone.'

We share more good-natured banter before we bid farewell until Frida's next day off.

I think of Prem, a friend in London; we've been friends for seventeen years. I haven't seen her in five years, but we've kept in touch with text messages. Her gran's ashes were scattered somewhere on the Downs. I return to the Downs, find a shady spot, and call her. She picks up the phone on the second ring.

'Prem?' I strain to hear her.

'That is so weird,' she exclaims. 'I was literally about to call you! How are you?'

'Oh, that's nice. I've been better. How are you?' For once I don't say something like, 'I'm fine,' or 'Everything's hunky dory.' I relay what's happening, the simplified version.

'Oh God! Five weeks homeless! Poor you! So you've been living in your car all this time?'

I reassure her that it's temporary and that my intention is to relocate at the first opportunity, just as soon as the landlord dispute is settled.

'What about in the meantime?' she asks, then pauses before continuing in her well-spoken accent. 'Listen, I've just thought of something; I'm going to email you a link. These people might be able to help you. My mum told me about them.'

A website link is better than no help. I feel isolated, despite being in contact with Frida and Sylvia. I go to a café to check my emails.

There's one from Prem. I click on the link she has sent. The homepage gives info about an international Christian community in the English countryside. A photo gallery shows picturesque views of woodland with a farmhouse in the heart of the setting. It says how Rodney and his wife, Marlene, founded it as an experiment in communal living. It goes onto say it offers respite for people who are in need of support or who feel they are experiencing a crisis.

There's an online application form for anyone interested who feel they might benefit from joining the community for an introductory visit. I complete the form, to the best of my ability. I hover over the send box, then one click, and it's sent.

~

Three days after sending the online application, I hear from Rodney. He asks me to meet him the next day. Now I wait for him while standing in scorching sunshine at the edge of College Green.

In the distance I see a man dressed in camouflage-green combat trousers, a green t-shirt and sunglasses walking straight towards me. He smiles broadly as he gets nearer.

'Magda? I'm Rodney.' His hand reaches out to shake mine. 'I'm sorry I'm late.' He takes off his sunglasses for a moment to wipe his sweaty forehead.

'Hello,' I reply. He's only five minutes late.

He points across the road to a small café. 'Shall we go there for a little chat?'

I nod and follow him across the busy road and towards the café.

We find a table and sit opposite one another. Rodney offers to buy ice-cold Coca Cola and two portions of carrot cake. He places a fork and piece of cake in front of me. My stomach can't face the cake. I take small, polite nibbles while he asks me a few questions about my predicament.

'I just need to know a little about yourself. Your application form didn't tell us much. Is that okay with you?' he asks.

'I didn't know what to write on that; sorry,' I reply.

'Don't worry. This is just an informal chat. Tell me, do you have a problem with addiction?'

'No, my mother was addicted to prescription drugs; she died years ago.' I stumble over my words. I figure that on-and-off moderate alcohol abuse isn't classed as an addiction.

'Have you been convicted of any violent crime?'

'No'

'Are you taking any prescribed medication?'

'No'

'Can you afford £75 a week towards the community purse without it causing hardship?'

'No'

'Are you claiming any welfare benefits?'

'No'

'Do you work?'

'I was a marketing analyst. I lost the job when I relocated to the South West, so I'm back to being a visual artist, unwaged.'

'Who's your next of kin?'

'My daughter.'

'What do you think you can contribute to our community?'

'I hope to offer help and friendship.' I'm not sure if I'm giving the right answers. I mention the deposit dispute and illegal eviction.

Rodney explains how the community residents are easy

going and friendly. He doesn't go into detail. The commune, he says, offers respite and residency for up to a maximum of six residents at any one time. There are also two full-time, live-in staff.

Rodney tells me he'll hold a house meeting the following morning to see if the votes are in my favour. It's up to the current residents who will determine if I am accepted to join the commune for an introductory week or not. He promises to text me the voting results outcome tomorrow.

Chapter Three

I've given up hope of hearing back, but then a message arrives saying I'm welcome to join them.

I'm apprehensive. Might the community be a bunch of misfits? Will they think I'm the misfit? I spend the next four days worrying, not knowing what to expect. One thing I do know is that it will make a change to be able to stretch my legs when I try to sleep. I look forward to company and civilisation.

Rodney emails with the community ground rules attached.

The number one rule in the book is no alcohol or non-prescribed drugs on or off site. It goes on to say the community is an alcohol-and-drug-free zone, because some people who are part of the community are struggling with addiction. The rules have a zero tolerance to all violence, verbal intimidation, or bullying. Any kind of pornography and gambling are banned. It says if the rules are broken, the guilty person will be asked to leave. The structure of the community day is outlined, explaining mealtimes, daily chores and so forth.

Absences from mealtimes or over-night stays are forbidden without forty-eight hours prior consent.

The rules are straight-forward common sense. Other

regulations that are not in the printed rule book, per se, but expected to be abided by are: no paid work outside the community as it would disrupt the commune's timetable; all residents are to respect each person's privacy and not to disturb other residents in their private living quarters without consent; lastly, romantic relationships between either community residents or visiting volunteers are not permitted.

Compared to the crisis I'm experiencing, the rules sound as easy as falling off a log. Also, it's reassuring to know these rules are in place for good reasons, for the safety of the community.

I drive out in the early evening. July end-of-the-day sunlight bobs out from a cloudy sky for short spells, brightening the countryside, but not easing my trepidation. They would have eaten their Sunday roast by now, and they know I'm on my way. I take a deep breath and continue my journey. When I come to a gravel, single-track lane, I know I'm nearly there. The gravelled lane curves around to meet the front patio area of the farmhouse. An assortment of ivy and climbing plants cling haphazardly onto its walls. From the outside, the extended two-story brick Victorian farmhouse looks blended by time—the house is modest, unremarkable, but the oblong side extension, with its pitched roof and patio, is massive. Different coloured brickwork indicate that the single-story extension was added later.

I park my car, my hands sweaty with nerves, and walk towards the farmhouse. The gravel crunches under my feet. A patio door is wide open, showing two men standing in the doorway in deep conversation. They stop talking, look my way and smile.

'Magda?' one of them asks.

'Yes. Hi,' I reply.

'Welcome! Did you find us okay?'

'Yes, thanks; I did.' I step through the patio doors into what's called the garden room. It doubles up as a diner/reception room, and the evening sitting room for residents' use. Opposite the enormous patio doors, huge windows show off the back-yard perennials. Crammed bookcases line the exposed-brick walls, and black wooden pillars rise from the oatmeal-coloured flagstone floor. A fridge and kettle hide in the corner, and a Welsh dresser stores crockery, cutlery, cereals, and snacks. Old armchairs and coffee tables surround the fire. A mighty wooden table that looks like some battle-worn Viking longboat owns the garden room, accompanied by a reclaimed church pew positioned along an exposed brick wall. The mismatched dining chairs on the other side are neatly tucked underneath.

Rodney appears through another door. 'You found us! Great. Let's introduce you everyone,' he says. 'This is my wife, Marlene.'

The woman with salt-and-pepper hair in a messy bun offers her hand to shake mine.

'And I see you've already met Vinnie and Cedric.'

I force a smile and nod.

Vinnie's hair is tied back into a ponytail. He taps his long fingers incessantly on every surface within his reach and speaks so softly that it's hard to hear him when he talks. He nods to acknowledge me, as does Cedric, who seems out of place and stands with an awkward stance.

'Felicity will be back later,' Rodney says.

At that moment the kitchen door opens.

'And this is Ethan,' Cedric says.

Ethan peers over the rim of his mug. He has black, wavy hair and a diagonal scar that runs just above his right eyebrow, half of which is missing. When he lowers the mug, I see his face properly, but it doesn't reveal anything.

'Before it gets dark,' Rodney says, 'let me show you around.'

He takes me on a whistle-stop tour of the commune. Outside are green houses, vegetable plots, chickens in a coop, a barn-converted workshop, and a diminutive bespoke structure with an elvish arch doorway. It resembles an unripe wooden pumpkin, spirited away from Hansel and Gretel's wood, and it serves as prayer space with bales of hay for seats.

The residents' living quarters are wooden shepherds' huts situated opposite the main farmhouse on the inner edge of the woodland. There's one each for Vinnie, Felicity, and Ethan and a large log cabin for the married-couple live-in staff. The huts have wood burners, and pretty curtains drape inside the little windows. Cedric's room is adjacent to the garden room, with Rodney's office next door. Rodney leads the way to what will be my home for my one week stay.

The rusty, old Bedford van perches on a mound under a tree. It's navy blue and has floral curtains at the windows. Rodney slides open its noisy door, and I peep inside. A hotchpotch of brown carpet squares covers the floor. A makeshift bed replaces the front seats, and a wood burner sits next to the sliding door with a basket of kindling, newspapers and chopped logs next to it. The musky smell of mildew permeates. It's cosy, shabby and strangely homely.

'What do you think?' Rodney asks.

'It's amazing,' I reply.

'I know it's basic, but you'll be able to enjoy some rest and respite, and you'll eat well too. Good, fresh food every day!'

'Thank you,' I reply. Rodney's kindness, and the hospitality brightens my day no end.

'What made you want to create this community?' I ask.

'It was God's plan, a calling,' he replies without hesitation, then he claps both hands and rubs them together. 'Let's get you some tea.'

We set off down the hilly footpath.

Marlene brings me a plate of left-over roast dinner, still warm. I feel bad because I'm making more washing-up, but no one seems to mind. I sit alone at the communal dining table—it would easily seat twelve—and take in my surroundings. For a minute I have a sinking feeling that all eyes are on me, but then a conversation starts. Vinnie asks if anyone has heard from Felicity. No, no one has heard from her. I approach Cedric, who's sitting in an armchair.

'Sorry, but is it all right to pop outside?' I ask.

'Sure,' he replies.

I step outside and sit on the wall of a low-brick flowerbed. A vintage armchair with an assortment of textile patches sewn on the armrests sits in the middle of the patio, and beside it a basket of laundry occupies a handcrafted wobbly wooden bench.

I sense someone behind me and look up to see Ethan flicking a lighter.

He sits next to me and smiles. 'You okay?' He retrieves his rollie from behind his ear and absentmindedly plucks eyebrow hair.

'Yes, thanks,' I reply.

He glances away while he speaks, blowing out plumes of smoke. 'That's mine, over there,' he says, pointing to his shepherd hut—the one under a tree. I hear a trace of private-school English.

'How long have you been here?' I ask.

'Three months; since April.'

He stubs out his dog-end and blurts out, 'Darling! Let's have tea!' But then he feels in his pocket for his iPhone and draws it out to inspect it.

I'm a bit perplexed as to why he's called me darling.

'I can't get a good signal here!' he mutters, then he waves his iPhone around for half a minute, signal searching before giving up.

At 9 pm Rodney and Marlene bid everyone goodnight. They shut the kitchen door, which is now out of bounds until morning. The large garden room is open all night for the residents' use.

The night is turning chilly, and it occurs to Vinnie to offer to light my wood burner. He shows me how to stack the logs and place the kindling and newspaper balls around them, then he lights a piece of paper and blows steadily on the glowing kindling until the fire catches. After a minute, satisfied that the fire's coming to life, he closes the burner's iron doors.

We return to the garden room and discuss books; he's currently reading Stephen King. I learn he arrived at the community almost a year ago, but he doesn't go into detail as to why.

It's late, almost midnight. Vinnie rubs his eyes. 'I think I'll turn in now.'

'Yes, do. Thanks for everything,' I reply.

'No worries; see you in the morning. If you hear a car, it'll be Felicity.'

I leave the garden room as quiet as a mouse. I can't see a thing, and I've forgotten my way to the Bedford. I try to find my way in the darkness, and when I get as far as the chicken coop, I realise it's not this far up. I backtrack towards the lights of the garden room that illuminate the darkness.

Back in the garden room, I'm wondering if I should ask for help when I hear the sound of a car driving up. A door slams. The security light activates, and the patio door slowly slides open. I stand to greet the woman who walks in.

'Hi, you're Magda?' she asks in a whisper.

'Yes, and you must be Felicity?' I reply.

'Yes, it's lovely to meet you. Everything okay?'

She must wonder why I'm rattling around alone at this late hour.

'Actually, I can't find my way back to the Bedford.'

She smiles. 'Oh, don't worry, I'll show you to the way.'

'Have you had a good day?' I ask as I follow her out.

'Not great; I lost my phone, but I'm home at last. I'm sure you'll like it here. It's actually going to be nice to have another female resident around here to balance it out.'

I realise how I'd been foolishly walking round in circles practically within spitting distance of the Bedford. Felicity yanks open the sliding door. The wood burner's still going.

'Okay. See you in the morning,' she says. 'You know what time breakfast is?'

'Yes, thank you! See you there.'

She heaves the door shut, and here I am. Safe and warm.

I kick off my shoes and change into pyjamas. I've lived and slept in the same pair of jeans for almost seven weeks, so it's a relief. I climb into my little bed. I'm tired, but my mind is racing. It's bliss to be able to stretch my legs.

It's eerily quiet. I'm used to nearly seven weeks of noisy traffic and sirens blaring past my car all day and night. I'd forgotten what peace sounds like. I switch off the lamp. Pitch dark. I find the quietness odd, so I open iTunes on my Mac to listen to Johnny Cash until I fall asleep.

Chapter Four

Iwake in the night a few times, startled and unable to place where I am for a few seconds. Waking up in strange surroundings disorientates me. Once I twig where I am, my panic subsides, and I finish my sleep.

I'm looking forward to today. My sides don't hurt this morning; the absence of car seatbelts digging into me makes a change. My neck pain is better. My back feels wrecked. As for my legs, they still ache after being folded for so long. I have the luxury of showering to come. I'll be able to brush my teeth at a real sink. There are cups of tea to look forward to in place of the coffee-shop kerfuffle.

I can drop my guard and relax because there's nothing to fear here. Maybe I'll speak to Sylvia and Frida today. It'll be easier with them knowing I'm in a land of civilisation and safe for now.

The sound of birds, bleating goats and nature take the place of city noises. I have new friends I can talk to, instead of berating God. These simple things are like seventh heaven.

I quickly dress for breakfast. The weather's cooler, cloudy and overcast. In the broad light of day I can see the footpath that leads me to back to the farmhouse. I'm not the last person to arrive for breakfast. Vinnie's already busy in the kitchen, kneading bread on the counter, chatting to Felicity. There's a chores rota stuck to the wall; it's designed to provide structure for day-to-day living.

Ethan appears at the patio door. 'Darling! Is there any coffee left?' he calls out to Felicity.

She pours him a mug.

Ethan stays at the patio door and lights a cigarette. He smokes while rearranging his hair with his free hand, then looks up at the cloudy sky. 'Did you sleep okay in the Bedford, darling?' he asks,

'Yes, fine, thanks.'

While Felicity clears away after breakfast, Rodney enters the garden room. He reminds Felicity to remember the shopping list. Ethan and I are on gardening chores.

Just as we're about to make a start, Rodney calls out, 'By the way, Ethan, how was your lunch yesterday with your friend?'

Ethan had had permission to leave the commune for a few hours.

'It was nice,' Ethan replies.

'What is your friend's name?' Rodney asks.

'Trina.'

Rodney seems curious to know more, but Ethan changes the subject by asking where the gardening gloves are.

Ethan and I spend the morning digging up weeds and chatting. After a few hours we stop for a tea break.

'I wonder what the weather will be like tomorrow,' I say.

'Rain, I think.' Ethan fidgets, paces, and sits on the low wall. He lights his roll up and pushes his hair out of his eyes. 'I'm an alcoholic,' he announces out of the blue. He looks down at his muddy boots, then looks up at me and adds, 'I've been sober three months!'

'Really! Well done; that's great!' I reply.

'Thank you.' He seems less edgy after telling me he's an alcoholic and seeing I'm not fazed.

He pauses, as if he wants to say more, then rubs his forehead and says, 'More tea?'

'Great idea.'

'Ethan?' Felicity calls out.

He looks up. 'Yes, darling?'

'About yesterday? Your lunch? Any gossip?'

'Nothing happened between Trina and me, I swear! We're just mates! Nothing more!' he replies, open eyed and indignant.

'Really?'

'What have I got to offer? Look at me! I have nothing to offer anyone!'

'Okay, I believe you!' Felicity says. 'I know you haven't got a proper home, or a job, but you should work on your self-esteem!'

'Yeah. Maybe.'

Chapter Five

The rain patters on the roof of the Bedford all night. After dressing I head for the garden room for breakfast.

Ethan's already in the kitchen; he pops his head around the door and calls out, 'I've made eggs, darling. Come and eat.'

I sit at the table and pour coffee. My legs still ache. I absentmindedly joggle them.

We chat like we're best friends, bonding over scrambled eggs. When we've finished eating, we step outside. Rain soaks the low wall that functions as our seat.

Ethan lights his roll up. 'Have you ever paid for sex?' he blurts out.

I'm taken aback, but I don't show it. It seems a bizarre question. 'No, I haven't. Have you?'

'Me? Nah! You got to be kidding! Of course not!' His eyes dart around. Perhaps he's trying to shock me or be avant-garde. At least he isn't perpetuating the sex industry or human trafficking. 'What about drugs?' he continues. 'You tried heroin? Crack?'

I look at him blankly.

'Banged up, ever?'

I know this means he's asking if I've ever injected. 'No, never. Have you?'

'Nah! Never banged anything up. I smoked crack once or twice. And the odd bump of coke; it's alcohol that's my drug of choice.' He says it with a trace of cockney in his voice.

'Look at this!' He shows me his iPhone. I see the homepage of a rehabilitation facility website that shows a mansion with impressive grounds. 'This is where I'm going!'

He goes onto tell me he's applied for six weeks government funding for treatment in this rehab. He doesn't know when funding will be approved. Also, he doesn't have a plan, or a home, following the treatment. From what I can tell, he's close to the community residents, but his family seem distant, and he never mentions having friends outside the commune bubble. I'm unsure why he wants rehab. His recovery seems to be going well.

Later, after collecting kindling, Ethan leads the way up the hilly footpath to the Bedford. While the fire catches, we drink tea, sitting on the floor side by side in front of the fire, talking like we've known each other for years.

'You'll never guess what, darling,' Ethan says.

'What's that?'

'Look,' he says, pulling up his sleeve, 'this is over four grand! My ex-girlfriend, Koemi, bought it for me. I used to hide it under the floorboards of my old flat whenever I was on a relapse, and then forget where I'd hid it; that's how come I've held onto it this long. She gave me a taste for the high life. She's a millionaire—inherited it. She paid for everything! The seven years we were together, she paid for world travel, my designer clothing, shopping, Cristal Champagne, the works! She provided me with an education on how it is to live rich.'

It sounds a far cry from where he is today, living here and

relying on welfare benefits. I don't see the big deal of his past high living, but I nod. 'That's really nice.'

'Me and Koemi split up nine years ago, after seven years together,' he says. 'And I think you should meet Denise, my mum's friend!'

'Oh,' I reply.

'Yeah! When I was seventeen and she was fifty, I had a quick fling with her. Y'know a fun-time drunken thing!' He says it as if it's the most natural thing in the world. 'I hate getting arrested; I've been nicked dozens of times. I hate the cells.' He pauses before continuing, 'You ever cheated?'

'No, I haven't. Have you?'

'Cheat? *Me*? Never in my life. If there's one thing I *hate* it's a cheat and a liar! Oh, that's two things!'

I look into the fire.

'I'm proud to say that I have never cheated,' he says. 'I don't do flings, one- night stands, online dating or blind dates, and I've only ever had three girlfriends in my entire life, all meaningful relationships.'

I'm not sure if he's trying to shock or impress me, and if he is, why?

He stands up to leave and goes to give me a goodnight peck on my cheek, but I back away. He emits a loose sexual energy around me and Felicity, like an adolescent. I think he's an unconventional type, who wants to be accepted, liked. I see a depth to his character, and there is something complicated about him that doesn't quite add up.

Chapter Six

Although I'd been curious about what had brought the others to the community, I only know about Ethan. He's here for addiction recovery, and he'd be homeless without it.

In the morning's feelings meeting, Ethan shares his thoughts: 'Yesterday I heard good news, my HIV tests came back negative. Since then, I've been feeling a bit guilty because of my past sexual misconduct and the way I'd seek out sex in sordid places. Anyhow, that's history. My AA sponsor said I should stop skipping my AA meetings.'

Everyone nods knowingly. When it's my turn to speak, I have nothing to say. It's not like anyone would be interested in my feelings.

The week flies by, mostly raining. Rodney, to my surprise, kindly offers me another week at the commune because the rain has spoilt my experiencing the outdoors at its best. Of course, I accept.

Ethan and I talk a lot, and I feel I get to know him quite well. One day he shows me inside his hut. Everything has its place. I notice a single flower in a small glass and a miniature shrine, complete with little tea-light candles and a tiny statue of

Buddha. He's never mentioned Buddhism to me, which seems odd seeing as we're becoming so friendly. He tries to kiss my cheek, but again I turn away.

I notice different sides to his character. Sometimes Ethan's buzzing to get to an AA meeting, but then he'll scrap the plan. Other times his accent changes from well-spoken to cockney for no apparent reason.

At sunrise on the day before I leave, a bitter breeze chills the air. The fact that I leave with nowhere to go hangs over my head, but I hide my anxiety.

To make lunch special and give me a bit of a send-off, we eat outside, surrounded by the smell of freshly mown grass. I'm not quite sure what's to celebrate in my returning to live on the streets, but the table resembles a summer picnic, and we all look happy.

'Ethan will go into mourning when you leave,' Marlene says.

'I wouldn't go that far,' I reply.

The atmosphere has changed. My new friends are already adjusting to my departure. Maybe they're wondering who's going to replace me, or when they'll be given marching orders of their own.

Later, Ethan and I make tea for a Netflix evening. I strive more than he to concentrate—for a change. He shows me YouTube clips of spiritual gurus he finds inspirational.

'When I get out of rehab, let's attend a guru retreat abroad!' he says.

I shrug. 'Maybe.'

The past week has seen spectacular skies at night. The absence of city light pollution makes a wonderful display of stars. Tonight is exceptional.

Ethan lights the wood burner in the Bedford. We sit together on the floor in front of the fire that's whooshing to life.

'Darling, I'm serious about us going away for a spiritual retreat, think about it. Please?' he asks.

'We'll see,' I reply.

He promptly plants a kiss on my cheek. 'I had to do that! I'm going to miss you.'

'Me too.' It's true; I like him, especially because he's an optimist.

'Before you I wondered if I'd ever feel this way about someone when not, y'know, under the influence,' he adds.

I return the compliment. 'That's a lovely thing to say. You're special yourself.'

Comfortable silence fills the lull when we stop talking, leaving just the crackling of the fire. We're in a cocoon of otherworldly tranquillity with the miracle of rehab around the corner.

Chapter Seven

I strip my bed, load it in the washing machine and start the wash cycle, then I vacuum the hotchpotch carpet and pack. Today I leave.

Ethan saunters into the garden room. 'Coffee, anyone?'

Vinnie raises his index finger to indicate he'd like one, as do I.

'Cedders?' Ethan calls out to Cedric.

'I'm good, thanks,' Cedric replies.

Ethan tells me his sister, Phoebe, is on her way to visit him. She's on a short vacation from her overseas home, and he hasn't seen her in ages. He's asked Rodney for permission if she can stay overnight, and he's agreed.

I go to Felicity's hut. She's sitting at a small table. It's rare to see her sit down; she never shies away from the chores.

'I thought I'd give you my mobile number?' I say.

'Sure!' She grabs a pen, then she looks at me. 'Are you going to be okay?'

'I guess so,' I reply.

'Make sure you say goodbye to everyone.'

I walk down the wooden steps of her hut, hoping we'll stay friends.

Ethan walks across the lawn and intercepts me. 'You talking to Felicity?' he asks. 'Whatever you do, don't say anything bad about me to anyone. This is my home; I'm homeless without this place.' He holds an unlit roll-up cigarette in his left hand and pushes his hair back, over and over again. He looks edgy.

I look at him quizzically. 'Why would I do that?' I'm curious why Phoebe is sleeping here tonight, rather than Ethan being invited to the relative's house where she's staying.

'Nothing, never mind.' He walks off.

When Phoebe arrives by car, Ethan dashes out to meet her. She greets him casually, but he's hyper, overexcited, and keen to take her for a walk in the woodland.

I finish packing my car and say my final goodbyes. I'm about to head off when I hear the loud vroom of a car. It's Ethan. Phoebe is in the passenger seat.

He stops close to where I'm standing and jumps out, the engine still running. He hugs me for a split second. 'Take care! Good luck!' He gives me a friendly slap on my back, jumps back in the driver's seat and speeds off.

Chapter EiGht

I leave the countryside in the distance and with trepidation head to Bristol, where I'll spend a few nights parked near the Downs. I psych myself up for what I know is ahead.

The deposit dispute has been dragging on for ten weeks. When it's resolved I'll secure housing with my deposit refund, or I'll go to Ireland. I'd forgotten how painful car seatbelts feel when they dig into my sides every night. My legs start to ache where I can't stretch. Vinnie, Felicity and Cedric are the only ones who send text messages to wish me well during these first days of adjustment. There's no word from Ethan until the fourth day when he sends me a short text message, to say 'Hi.' Every other day after that, he sends a short text.

I'm in a coffee shop late one afternoon when my phone rings. It's Felicity.

'Hi, Magda?'

'Wow, Felicity! How's things?' I ask.

'I've left. Packed and left, for good,' she replies.

'What? Why?'

'I know; it's sudden. I thought I'd tell you. Anyhow, I'll call you soon. I've got to go; I'm in a mad rush.'

I'm surprised she's left so abruptly. It makes me think how the dynamics can change overnight in a commune.

Cedric and I arrange to have coffee. He looks at me with concern when he spots me.

'How are things at the commune?' I ask.

'Oh, it's really different without you and Felicity. And I'm next to leave. I've been offered a job in London. I tried to get Ethan to think about job hunting, or to start saving up to leave the commune. Live independently. You know? He won't though! Did you know he's quit AA meetings?'

'No. We don't have much contact,' I reply.

'Have you met the other Ethan?' he asks. 'When his accent changes and he goes … kind of all street. Street Ethan. Even the way he walks changes.'

I think back to the Ethans I saw: Ethan the campy clown, the worrier, the posh Bertie Wooster doppelgänger, happy-go-lucky, giddy flirt, the shocking, tender, anxious, and the show-off, the chaotic, contradictor and the captivating. I shrug, uninterested.

'Well, he claims he's aware he's doing it and that it's a habit from street life he's had to learn, what with scoring drugs and the delinquent living in the hood,' Cedric adds.

I can't think how to respond, but I remember what Felicity had said to him about self-esteem. It seems he isn't comfortable in his own skin.

My daily routine gets me down. Everything is a tremendous amount of effort: to pee, wash, eat, check my emails.

Taking my car through the carwash and keeping it clean somehow makes living in it not as bad. I might be living in a car, but at least it's a clean one.

Every time I speak with Frida and Sylvia, which is a few times a week, I hide my worries, but I wish I had good news. I made some sketches as gifts for them. It's not a lot to offer, but sometimes a creative person in pain has no option but to create.

Chapter Nine

A text message arrives from Ethan: *Are you free to meet? ASAP?* It's late evening. I'm sitting in a diner, on the phone to Felicity. I don't know what's so urgent; I haven't seen him since I left the community. He doesn't wait for a reply, just calls instead.

'It's okay if you're busy. Umm … there's stuff going on here.' He hesitates.

'What's wrong?' I ask.

'I've just found out. I'm evicted. I mean, well, they're shutting the doors. Closing down the community. Everyone's out. We've been given two months' notice. I'll be homeless.'

'You're kidding?'

'No. I'm not. You know The Orangery?'

I know it. It's a pub half-way between where I am, Bristol, and where he is, Gloucestershire.

'Please. Can you be there to meet up in an hour?'

I frown. 'Errr … yeah. Okay. I'll see you there.'

I send Felicity a text: *New update. Community is closing. Everyone's been given eviction notice.*

She replies: *You're kidding. Why?*

Me: *I don't know. Ethan's just told me.*

Felicity: *OMG. What a shock.*

When I arrive, Ethan's already there waiting, with his elbow resting on the open car window. He seems glad to see me. He reaches out to hug me, but instead of hastily letting go, as he did that day I'd left the commune, he pulls me closer. His hug tightens.

'Let's go for coffee and talk,' he says when he releases me. 'No, it's late for caffeine. Just follow me.'

I'm not sure if he knows where he is going, but I tailgate his car. Eventually, we reach a quaint village in the middle of nowhere and his driving slows, then stops. I climb into his car and listen while he vents his frustration about the eviction, and no rehab funding, either. He's agitated, but he's chosen me to confide in, and so I feel a closeness or chemistry between us. Being in one another's company again is like no time has elapsed.

I understand why he's so anxious. We're both on stormy waters. I think maybe, if we hang on to each other, we'll survive.

'We have a special connection,' he says.

'Yes, we do.'

'I'm not ready for a real kind of relationship, but can we be together? As a couple?' He sits still—for a change.

I nod. 'Yes. Okay, we can do that.'

'There are two conditions, though. One is there must be absolute fidelity on both sides and no one else on the scene, ever. *No* cheating.'

'Of course. Fidelity always.'

'Secondly, never allow me to pick up a drink. If I try, you have to stop me. No matter what.'

'I promise I'll stop you picking up a drink, and that there'll be fidelity,' I reply, agreeing to our pledge.

'Good,' he says, then a moment later adds, 'Oh, I'm going away this bank holiday weekend!'

'That's nice; who with?'

'My cousins,' he replies without a moment's hesitation.

'Oh. Where are you going?'

'Dorset. Camping.'

'That'll be nice.' I say.

He frowns. 'Ermm … So that's not true. I'm kind of seeing someone right now. I'm going with her. Trina. Not my cousins.'

'Oh!' I say, slightly bewildered due to the pledge we'd made just moments before. I recognise the name. Trina. He'd mentioned they were platonic friends. I'm sure he was telling the truth. I wonder what's changed.

'We're in separate tents and that. I'm going to finish it kindly with her,' he says.

I wonder what's to finish if nothing's started, but I just say, 'Oh. Are you?'

A black cloud descends. One that Ethan is oblivious to. It floats down and darkens our magical night, at least mine.

'By the way, whatever you do,' he warns, 'don't message me while I'm away. iPhones are terrible for showing texts. I don't want her to suspect anything.'

'Okay.' His camping trip is in thirty-six hours' time. I push my doubts aside, but they linger at the back of my mind.

After he leaves, I go for a long drive, thinking I'll never hear from Ethan again. However, an hour before he leaves for his trip, he sends me a thoughtful text message, which dampens some doubts away.

Chapter Ten

Nick emails and says I'll have to write a statement for the deposit tribunal before my case is heard by the panel. I focus my mind and finish it in one long sitting. He also tells me my name's been added to the list of union volunteers, as we've been asked to participate in Banksy's 'Dismaland' exhibition.

I've convinced myself our romance was meaningless to Ethan, so I don't plan to call him again. But on Monday morning my phone rings, and I see it's Ethan.

'Hi, Magda. It's me!' he says. 'I've just got back. How are you?'

'I'm fine. How was your weekend?'

'Fun. It was fun!'

'Great, so what's new?' It's an invite for him to come clean.

A cagey answer replaces his usual chitchat, almost like a riddle. 'Not much. Weather was good. … Listen, I've been thinking. What would you say about you and me applying together to a different community? There must be loads! It'll be a laugh!'

'Umm.' I scratch my head. 'I don't know.'

'Think about it! I've got another call. I'll phone you right back.'

Only he doesn't call straight back. It's the next day when he phones and says he'd like to meet later at The Orangery.

We meet in the car park and walk together to the bar. I feel uncomfortable being inside a saloon with him. Upside-down bottles of golden whisky and other spirits reflect in the bar mirrors; the reflections seem to double their quantity. The stench of ale wafts through the deserted saloon lounge.

Ethan orders two glasses of Coca-Cola. His drug of choice is everywhere; his mood is edgy. He catches sight of his reflection in the mirrors and fiddles with his hair. He doesn't make eye contact with me, nor does he mention the camping trip, rehab, his AA sponsor, or why he's quit AA.

What he does divulge is that a new replacement resident has arrived at the commune. 'He's a recovering addict; he's on a benzo script.' By which he means Valium. 'It looks like I've sold him some of my unwanted clothes. Four-hundred quids worth. Maybe I'll buy an iPad to treat myself for being four months sober!'

The liquid gold catches his eye. 'Let's go; I don't like it here. Follow me.' It's a relief to walk out into the night air. It doesn't occur to him to call his sponsor. He's in good recovery now, so I guess he doesn't need to.

'There's an Indian restaurant up the road,' he says.

We walk around in circles until eventually we find it, but it's closed, so we arrange to meet on Friday.

It's strange to not be sure of the day of the week. I double check to see I've got the right day. Yes, today is Friday. Just before I set off, Ethan texts: *Hope you're not on your way yet. I'm at my aunt's house in Hampshire. Family drama. Stressing me out. Having cravings. Sorry!*

It's the first craving he's mentioned since I've known him.

He's had the whole day to call or message me. I reply: *Oh no! I hope you're okay?*

He replies: *I'll be fine. I'll sleep it off.*

I'm not sure what triggered his craving, or if he's really at his aunt's house.

Chapter Eleven

Dismaland, Banksy's immersive art exhibition where I'm volunteering, runs for thirty-six days. It's located in Weston-super-Mare on the coast. In the evenings I layer up my clothing against the chilly coastal weather.

We're fortunate Banksy has offered our organisation, the tenants union, the opportunity to spread the word of solidarity and highlight our cause. We are the voice for tenants in the private-rental sector. Our agenda is to collect data and get our petitions signed by as many as we can of the one-hundred-and-fifty thousand visitors over the exhibition period. Our plan is to use the data we collect to stand up for tenant's rights and show the government there's need for change in the private-rental sector.

The activist area is a huge green tent called the guerrilla tent. Next to our pitch, in the same tent, are the *Strike!* magazine activists. In our corner we have a large counter with the name 'Comrades Advice Bureau' emblazoned in yellow lettering over the red backdrop. Our petitions, merchandise and literature lie displayed on the counter. The Dismaland paid staff and us volunteers strike up friendships.

There are three sessions—morning, afternoon, and evening. The end of each session is called a changeover during which Dismaland closes to the public for an hour, and we have meal breaks. It's also a good time to explore the exhibition—when it's free from crowds.

At night-time, the lights of Dismaland illuminate the entire satirical theme park exhibition. Giant outdoor sculptures and exhibits draped in twinkling lights decorate the warped fairy tale. The exhibition is thought provoking and atmospherically, audibly, and visually remarkable.

Each day is busy. I stand during my long, triple shifts, but the distractions ease my body pain. It seems fitting that I, a homeless activist who sleeps in her car, am doing work like this. My life has some purpose. I'd forgotten what it is to be happy.

On my last Dismaland shift, some of us comrades exchange emails. Everyone's planned what they're doing next—everyone apart from me.

Four months have passed since the dispute began, and today I have news. With Nick's help I've won back most of my deposit. It's a relief, but I still feel flat by homelessness and boredom. Since seeing more of Ethan, however, I feel less lonely.

Chapter Twelve

Ethan's eviction is looming. He should be at his wits' end. He's mentioned a large, remote Christian community that Rodney's recommended to him—not that he's interested.

We love being in one another's company. It's strange to find myself in a relationship when I hadn't been looking for one. I can count the years on my fingers and toes since my last calamity of a relationship.

Every night we speak for hours on the phone. He whispers in hushed tones so as not to wake the resident in the next hut to his. He said he'd purchased new bedding for when we get a new home. Even though we met less than three months ago, moving in together seems a good idea. He reckons addicts need goals for their recovery.

Frida, Sylvia, and I meet for lunch. I can't believe it's October already. I've been applying for jobs and flat hunting, and they're glad to see I'm getting my life back on track—after all, I've been homeless since May.

I arrive at the union office where I've volunteered to do some work. The evenings are drawing in. It's dark already, and rain patters on the window. Just as I finish some photocopying, my phone rings. It's Ethan.

'Hello? Ethan?'

'I need to meet you ASAP!' There's hysteria in his voice.

'Are you okay?' I ask.

He shouts over blaring music. 'I'm driving to Bristol. Meet me!'

'What?' Because of the drug hot spots, the city is the last place Ethan should drive to with cravings.

'I'm half-way there. There's been a massive row here; someone's pressed my buttons.'

'Calm down! Don't come into Bristol.' I plead with him. 'Let's meet for coffee and talk.'

'Coffee? No thanks!'

'Please. Let's meet. And talk!'

'Bye! Gotta go … I need … to take the edge off! I'll call you in a bit!'

His phone line goes dead.

I have no idea what's got into him. I try to call back. It goes to voicemail. I stand in the rain and try his number. Voicemail again. I drive towards The Arches, a bustling area night and day.

If I can, I'll talk some sense into Ethan. Or maybe I should keep away. He sounded manic on the phone. If left to his own devices, he'll do something stupid. I'd promised when we first got together that I'd stop him picking up another drink.

I look out of my car window and have second thoughts. My instincts tell me I should split. I start my car. A moment later my conscience messes with my instincts. I hold my head in my hands. Suddenly my phone rings.

'Where are you?' Ethan asks. He still sounds manic.

'The Arches. Where are you?'

'Not far from there. Meet me outside the supermarket.'

'But what's happening?' I ask.

'I've just seen my mate. There's a wicked batch of white in town.' It's his first mention of scoring drugs; I know he's referring to cocaine.

'Are you crazy?'

'See you soon!' he says and hangs up.

If I hurry, I can get to him in time before he relapses. I see the Co-op shop lights in the darkness. Ethan's car is parked just outside. I pull into a space next to it, and he jumps out to greet me. He's as high as a kite and stinks of beer. I'm too late. His pupils are pinned. He fumbles with Rizla papers and messes with his hair, then remembers a roll up that's tucked behind his ear. He reaches for it and lights up, then inhales so fast that it smokes away in an instant.

'Quick, follow me,' he says.

He takes my hand and frogmarches me into the Co-op. He doesn't even have to look for the aisle. Feeling powerless, I stand by and watch him while he picks up cans of Red Bull and a twenty-four case of bottled beer. He rushes to the tills and asks the cashier for something else. She reaches up to the spirits behind her and scans a litre bottle of vodka.

He flashes me a smile and winks. 'Quick, this way.' Outside, he points to the passenger seat of his car and says, 'Get in, just for a second!' Once inside, he fumbles around in the glovebox, grabs a CD and a small, folded paper packet, then sprinkles a line of beige powder onto the CD case and chops it with his bankcard. 'Try. Quickly. We're running out of time.'

I shake my head. 'No. Stop this. I don't want it!'

'Just this one bump! We're running out of time!'

'No. Let's get out of here.'

He shrugs. 'Please yourself.' After rolling up a fiver, he hoovers up three lines, then sniffs. He follows that by popping the cap off a beer using the bottom of his lighter and glugging it down. 'That's better! Now follow me in your car!'

He doesn't tell me where we're going, but I tailgate him. After a ten-minute drive, he pulls up outside a large hotel. I park behind him.

He runs over to my car and holds open the door. 'Listen. I'm just having a one-night binge, a blowout. It's not like a proper relapse! Why do you look so scared?'

'I promised not to let you relapse,' I reply.

'It's not your fault; so it doesn't count.' Without asking, he grabs bags from my backseat and proceeds to carry them to the hotel reception. The audacity of him, taking charge of my luggage like this without my permission, is baffling.

'No,' I protest. 'Please don't do that!'

He's not listening. He dashes out, runs towards his car, with me following close behind in a panic, he opens the boot, unzips a large holdall, roughly empties it, dumping the contents in the trunk and like a smuggler, methodically packs the bottles of beer, vodka, and Red Bull. He'd packed so much gear when he left the commune in a temper, it seems he'd made up his mind to relapse.

'Come on, then.' He pulls my arm and leads me into the hotel lobby. It's spacious and brilliantly lit with massive palms growing in huge pots. The reception desk reflects the lights on its polished mahogany surface.

The receptionist looks at us, puzzled.

'Double room, please!' Ethan announces.

The receptionist tells us there's a room available, but it's not cheap at over £100 per night.

'We'll take it!' Ethan says.

I look on, horrified by the state he's in, and the hotel's rates. The receptionist places a key on the polished surface and asks Ethan to enter his pin number to pay.

His card gets declined, so he turns to me. 'She'll pay!'

The receptionist looks at me expectantly.

Ethan leans into my ear. 'Darling, it's just until tomorrow. I'll pay you back! I get paid my welfare tomorrow! I promise! And I'll go back to the commune tomorrow too.' Without batting an eyelid, he grabs the key, loads the bags and holdalls onto a luggage trolley, and with the sound of glass bottles chinking from the pile of luggage, dashes towards the elevator. It's almost like a well-practiced routine, the way he's passed the buck to me by making me pay.

He keeps his finger on the elevator door button until I'm inside, then he presses the button for the fourth floor. He checks his reflection in the elevator mirror, his breath fogging the mirror. Ding! Fourth floor.

Ethan rushes out of the elevator, pushing the luggage trolley. I'm being swept along by a force other than my own two feet.

He opens the room door. The lamps are already switched on, and a huge mirror hangs above a desk. Ethan checks his pinned pupils in it and styles his hair, then he retrieves a fag and lights it.

He grabs two bottles of beer and peeks underneath the desk. Embedded in the wood is a sort of hidden bottle opener. He flips the tops off two beers and plonks one next to me, while he glugs the other, then he flicks on the TV and mutes the sound. The 'No Smoking' sign, he tosses in the bin.

'Get that down you! We're running out of time!' he says.

I frown. 'Why do you keep saying we're running out of time?'

'It's my mate. He's got me some white! I gotta get it before he uses it!' *As if that's an explanation!* He checks his iPhone, then starts calling someone. No answer. 'He's not picking up. C'mon. He lives a short walk from here. Ten minutes max.'

He pulls on his jacket, stuffs the room key into his pocket

and frogmarches me back to the elevator. Again he tries that phone number. No answer. In the mirrored elevator he inspects his eyes. Ding! Ground floor.

We start walking. Ethan takes hold of my hand and inhales deeply. 'It's so good to feel free and be away from the commune!' He's high, and tipsy.

We walk much longer than ten minutes.

'Please can we go back?' I ask.

'Don't be silly!' When we reach a block of flats, he says, 'Now, you wait here!' Then he disappears into the porch. Two minutes later he reappears and grabs my hand. We walk to the end of the street where he stops and pulls out a folded paper packet.

He peeks inside. 'Looks a bit light. He's been at it. But I'm not going back!'

The receptionist gives us a strange look when we return, and her eyes fix on us while we call the elevator.

As soon as he closes the door to our room, Ethan flings off his jacket and throws it on the bed. He grabs a beer, kicks off his shoes and inspects the paper packet, then he arranges lines, directly on the table, chopping, scraping up, and re-chopping. He snorts two lines and drains another bottle of beer.

He turns to me, feeling my stare. 'I told you. It's a one-night blowout, not a real relapse!'

'How could you afford this?'

'The money I made from selling my clothes to that bloke!'

'So you just blew the lot on this stuff?' I'm speechless by the way he's lost five months of sobriety. And, by the looks of it, he's flat broke. He hasn't saved a dime from his welfare benefits in the five months he's been living rent free at the commune. He'd previously mentioned his mum pays the £75 a week to the community purse. Clearly, he's got a problem with spending.

He belches. 'Stop fretting.'

Ethan does more lines. When he speaks, he clicks his dry tongue and gulps more beer. The speed at which he knocks back beer is alarming. The empties rapidly begin to line up on the desk, a stark reminder of how much alcohol he's drinking.

Ethan seems to have forgotten I'm here. I hold half a bottle of warm beer, perplexed. At the back of my mind, I know I'll have to drive Ethan back to the commune in the morning; he's bound to be unfit to drive himself back.

The booze and drugs don't sedate Ethan, not one bit. On the contrary, he can't stop talking.

'I miss my old life, when I was with my Koemi.' He slurs his words. 'She's older than me. We met in a hotel bar. A few days later she invited me to Paris. She paid for my flight and promised me Cristal Champagne for when I arrived! Then she took me on a shopping spree. I got used to living the high life with her.' He only pauses speaking when he swigs beer. It's running low, so he makes a start on the vodka, mixed with Red Bull.

I feel awkward, like I'm an intruder at Ethan's private party and his trip down memory lane. It's like I'm no longer with him. He's gone, as if a body snatcher has abducted him.

I'm sure the vodka will knock him out, but it doesn't. He knocks back one after another while I sit on a narrow windowsill, staring out. Ethan unsteadily climbs out of his trousers and lies down on the bed, getting more bombed. He attempts to stand up, but plops back down again.

'Am I handsome?' he asks.

'Sure, yes,' I reply. 'Why don't you get some sleep?'

'Because I think there's something shitty about the white! It's given me an erectile droop fucking drezfuncktion! I've slept with thousands of women.' He slurs, can't focus and his temperature has shot up; his pale complexion is fiery red.

The more he drinks, the more he rambles. He talks obsessively about Koemi, as if he's wounded from their relationship that ended almost a decade ago or might not have closure. He can't pronounce erectile dysfunction, yet he's fixated on it.

Suddenly, he sits up, bolt upright. 'I love you!' he blurts out, then belches.

He tries to make eye contact, but I'm taken aback. It's not like this is a romantic date; just look at us! He's wasted, sweating buckets and possibly in blackout.

'You do love me back? Don't you?' The dryness of his mouth makes his lips stick to his teeth. He sounds hoarse from so much talking.

'Yes, but stop with the vodka?' I reply.

'Don't leave me alone in this room if I fall asleep.'

'I won't, don't worry.'

I feel shattered. I try to nap, but Ethan keeps waking me up with his yabbering and staggering around the room, hunting for the next beer. He asks me to roll up his cigarettes. His fingers are like jelly, and he can't coordinate his hands.

'What's Koemi doing today? Fucking hell! Erectile's droop fucking drezfuncktion!' he exclaims.

Every time I doze off, Ethan shakes me awake. When dawn seeps through the curtain, I know sleep is off limits. Ethan sits up to light half a fag, then plops down on his pillow. He's out cold with the cigarette smouldering in his hand. I drop the butt end into an empty beer bottle.

We have to check out by ten, otherwise there's a penalty charge. I make coffee in an attempt to sober him up, but he won't wake. I shower, pack our stuff that Ethan's strewn everywhere and charge our phones. At five to ten the telephone rings. I don't pick up; it must be reception. The sound makes Ethan stir.

He grimaces and looks straight under the bed. To my surprise, he retrieves his stash—three beers. He pops the caps and chugs one down.

'Please don't! We have to check out, otherwise there's a penalty charge!'

'What?' He continues to gulp beer.

I start to dress him, lifting his deadweight limbs—socks first, trousers and t-shirt. He stands unsteadily. We're already half an hour late checking out. I dash around, and without his help, tie his laces, open the windows to air out the fume-filled room and assist him to the elevator. He tries to look in the mirrors, sticks out his tongue, blinks, squints. He doesn't like what he sees and turns away.

Ethan steadies himself by grabbing the reception desk counter while I return the key. The receptionist unsmilingly presents me with the chip and pin device, where I proceed to pay the late check-out charge.

My intention is to drive him straight back to the commune because last night was not a real relapse, it was just a one-off blowout.

Chapter Thirteen

I don't know how much Ethan remembers of last night. He's unsteady getting in my car; he's in no fit state to drive, of course.

'Don't move. Take a nap while I move your mum's car,' I say. If I don't move it, the hotel will get it towed away. After a while I find a parking spot, lock the car, and run all the way back to my car.

I'm half expecting Ethan to have wandered off, but as I get closer, I see him still sitting in the passenger seat, snoring.

When I slam the car door shut and start the engine, he stirs.

'We need to get you back to the community today,' I say.

He looks at me with swollen eyes and slowly shakes his head. 'Tomorrow. Leave it until tomorrow. I need to get my head together!'

'What's wrong with today?' I ask.

'I have to sleep this off! *Fuck!* I promise I'll go back tomorrow. Please.' He places his cold hand onto mine.

'All right. But you definitely have to go back tomorrow.'

He nods. 'Okay. Drive to a motel; they're cheap.'

Reluctantly, I agree and punch the nearest motel postcode into my SatNav.

We're almost there, when Ethan asks me to stop by the supermarket. He wants food. The shop's huge, but Ethan knows his way around. I follow him, only to find myself in the booze aisle, Ethan heaves booze from the shelves.

'What are you doing?' I ask.

He shakes his head. 'Nothing. I just need to take the edge off. Don't make a scene.'

I sigh. What else can I do?

When we line up at the kiosk to pay, his card gets declined again. It seems it's not his welfare payday after all.

'She'll pay!' Ethan chimes up.

I'm caught off guard, so I reach into my pocket for my bankcard. I don't understand how he can stomach more booze and not be hung over.

The motel rates are not as cheap as Ethan had led me to believe. After I foot the bill, I try to calculate how much I've blown in the last twenty-four hours, but I reassure myself that Ethan will be fine once he's slept off his binge.

He closes the curtains where the afternoon sun is pouring in, then flops into bed, pops the top off a beer and guzzles until he crashes out. He wakes for a pee and reaches for another beer. By late afternoon he's on the gin and cola. Shit! I don't get it. Why the hell is he sabotaging returning to the commune? Rodney might refer him to an alternative commune for addicts if he'd show some respect. I don't want to sit here, watching him get shitfaced. Why do I feel responsible for him? Why is he so self-centred? He's taking advantage of me and my good nature. Why don't I give him a piece of my mind? This is beyond surreal.

'I'm definitely going to return to the commune tomorrow. I swear I will!' he promises.

Like a replay of the night before, he rambles non-stop all night long, slurring his words and jumping to and from different topics, like Koemi, erectile dysfunction, sex workers, boozy adventures with old flames, regrets, anything apart from what's happening now.

The next morning, Ethan has a beer for breakfast. He sees a missed call from Rodney and plucks up the courage to phone him back. 'Hi, Rodney. I've had a slight relapse … just one bottle of gin,' he says while pouring another. 'Okay. Thanks for being so understanding. Oh, one more thing, please let this be between us two; don't tell my mum I've had a slip!' He listens for a moment. 'Thanks, Rodney! Okay. I'll be back tomorrow, sober. Bye!'

The community rules usually require one week clean and sober. Rodney, by bending the rules in allowing him back with one day sober, is doing him a favour.

The drugs and booze have messed with his brain chemistry; he can't switch off—apart from when he catnaps. He's adamant another night in a motel with booze will help take the edge off.

It's day four of Ethan's relapse. He hasn't got a stop button, and he looks sick. His eyes are red, half closed and swollen. His eye sockets are turning purple. He can only eat a portion of rice from a Chinese takeaway, which isn't enough to soak up the booze.

'I want to show you a beautiful village. I'll get sober and go back to the community tomorrow; just do this one thing for me,' he says while chain-smoking.

So I drive us to a pretty little village. Quaint cottages and mock Tudor houses line the street. I can tell he knows the old village pub well by the way he knows his way around. He orders a pint of ale, a latte for me and walks to a table. We take a seat, and he whips his Macbook from his bag, but the background is noisy, so he carries it to the porch. He nods for me to follow him, then logs into Skype. Phoebe answers the video call.

'Bee! How's it going?' he declares.

'Umm, all right.'

'I'm with my girlfriend!'

'Oh, that's nice. Trina? Isn't it? The one you brought to Aunt Pearl's and introduced us to when you went camping?'

'No! Not Trina! She's crazy! I'm with a different one. Magda.'

I don't think Phoebe remembers me from that day when I'd met her. All the same it's a revelation about Trina meeting his family.

Ethan keeps ducking right, hiding from the camera's view, to gulp mouthfuls of ale. Each time he ducks, the pub entrance behind him comes into view for Phoebe to see.

She twigs. 'I know that pub. So you're drinking?'

'I'm not! I'm sober as a judge!'

Without another word, Phoebe ends the call.

He tries to call her again, twice. 'She's blocked me,' Ethan says.

I don't understand Phoebe's fury, but Ethan shrugs it off and orders another ale, then persuades me to drive to the discount booze store for more. It's like being on a merry-go-round.

After a few more days of Ethan drinking, his father calls. Ethan dupes him by speaking without slurring. His dad wants him to drive over and sign some papers at his home. Ethan doesn't mention me, or that he can't drive himself. Unbeknownst to his father, I'm swept into their arrangement.

Ethan gulps gin throughout the long drive, and by the time we arrive at the cottage, he's plastered. But he reckons he can wing it.

'Don't tell him I've been drinking,' Ethan says conspiratorially as we walk to the front door. He knocks.

His father opens the door, looks directly into Ethan's eyes, and then ushers us in, looking furious. Ethan introduces me. His father shakes my hand and offers to make tea.

Once settled at the table with mugs of tea, he asks, 'Have you been drinking, Ethan?' He turns to me. 'Has he, Magda? Has he been drinking?'

'Errr ... N, No?' I lie.

He slams a mug on the table. 'Magda, please wait in my study. I need to speak to Ethan.' He shows me into a tidy, small room.

Then the yelling starts.

'Not again, Ethan! How many more bloody times! You idiot!' his father shouts.

I hear Ethan protest, or deny. A door slams. More yelling.

A few minutes later the door bursts open. 'Magda, please take him away. And I don't want to see him until his six weeks of rehab is completed. Do not contact me before then!' His father takes a gulp of tea, still glaring at Ethan. He's so incensed that his face turns fiery red.

Ethan tries to embrace him to say goodbye. His father attempts to push him away, but Ethan throws both arms around his dad, like a naughty boy who's trying to make up. 'I love you, Daddy!'

'I love you too, Ethan. But I want you out of my sight and remember what I said!' He shows us out. 'Good luck with rehab!' The door bangs shut the second we're outside.

Ethan's father hadn't explained anything to me, and I'm too embarrassed to ask. My encounters with Ethan's family, so far, are not good.

'Fucking great! He's gonna tell the whole family now!' Ethan says.

The seatbelt hurts his bloated belly, so he decides to undo it and drape it over his shoulder, so it looks like he's wearing one.

'Please wear the seatbelt,' I plead.

'No! Shut up,' he replies.

I sigh.

Ethan tries calling his phone contacts and continues trying

all hours of the day and night. But word is travelled fast; no one will pick up. He insists he'll stop drinking tomorrow.

I agree to just one more night of this. There are no hotel rooms available. It's already dark, and Ethan's sozzled.

'I need to speak to my mate,' he says when I point out that we have nowhere to go. 'We'll go to his house.'

He instructs me to drive for another hour, then yells, 'Stop the car,' when he sees a cash point across the road. I pull up, and he staggers out, opens my door and yanks at my arm until I follow him. 'I get paid tomorrow,' he says. 'You have to get me some cash out, £100.'

'What for this time?' I ask.

'Just hurry.'

I shrug and shake my head.

He watches while I enter my pin number. After I hand over the cash, he asks me to wait in my car. 'I'll be back. Wait here!' he says as he runs off.

Ten minutes later he appears again, walking with a swagger and accompanied by a scruffy, shifty looking bloke. They both jump into my car.

'Drive where we tell you!' Ethan demands.

I frown. 'What's happening?'

'Just drive!' he replies, then asks the scruffy man, 'You can score whisky, bruvva?'

The dealer nods and takes a drag of a cigarette. His fingernails are black with dirt.

'Yeah, we're getting whisky, Magda,' Ethan says. 'You know, whisky! That's crack! Stones! A few fat rocks!' He gulps a small bottle of Lucozade as fast as he can. Not that he's thirsty; it's the empty plastic bottle he wants.

Chapter Fourteen

Ethan tells me to take lefts, rights, drive straight, and park, then he hands a bunch of notes to the dealer, who jumps out of my car.

'Don't bump me, bruvva!' Ethan calls out.

'I wouldn't rip you off!' the man replies as he runs off.

Ethan shakes the empty bottle and roots around for chewing gum, a pin badge, a hairband, a drinking straw, and foil from chocolate. Within minutes he's made a crack pipe. Oh my God … he's just opened Pandora's Box. A crack relapse is a major catalyst, a disaster. He's heading towards the nine circles of Hell, like in Dante's 'Inferno.' And judging by the way he whipped that pipe up from rubbish, so quickly, signals to me that he's made them hundreds of times before. This is when it registers— he's a crack addict.

'I'm not putting up with this,' I blurt out, then make a run for it, sprinting down the dark street with only my car keys! Thinking, *God, where am I going?*

Ethan follows, catches up, grabs hold of my jacket hood and tugs on it. 'Don't make a scene. Dealers get real pissed off when there's a scene. Most of 'em carry knives,' he warns.

I know there's no way I can eject Ethan and his tooled-up dealer from my car. Unless I could manage to call the cops, but wait … what good would that do? What if this dealer is armed? What if the cops project blame onto me for this shit storm?

The dealer returns, wanting his tip. Ethan splits the tiny cling-film-wrapped white balls, picks the smallest and drops it into the grubby hand.

'Can't we smoke some off?' the dealer asks.

'Yo! What d'ya think this is for, bruvva?' Ethan replies, holding up his crack pipe. He carefully unwraps a small stone of crack, breaks off a tiny piece, and drops it onto some cigarette ash on the foil of the pipe. Next, he lights the crumb of crack, inhales, and doesn't exhale for half a minute; when he does, he coughs and splutters.

'That's good,' he says, closing his eyes, then he turns to me. 'You try it; just one. I won't take no for an answer.'

I know how bossy he is, and that he'll nag, so I do what he wants. It smells foul, like chemicals, and it tastes bad. I don't see how it's made him so high. Maybe his brain receptors are damaged after his years of addiction. His highs last only a matter of minutes, so he keeps loading the pipe to smoke more. My small car fills with the horrible smell.

Ethan and the dealer smoke off the remaining stone. Ethan high fives the dealer goodbye and finishes off his remaining crack. The high does not calm him down. He rambles non-stop with an inflated ego, talking of Koemi and the perils of abandonment.

We have to sleep in my car. Ethan insists a bottle will help his come down off the drugs. Holding his iPhone torch, he searches his pockets and the footwell for crumbs of crack. Underneath the passenger seat, he finds crack the size of a breadcrumb and makes another pipe out of an empty Red Bull can. He loads the pipe, lights it with the upside-down flame of his lighter and smokes until he's high and rambling a load of nonsense.

'Guess when I took a hit off my first crack pipe?' he says. 'It was straight after me and Koemi split up. I was at an AA meeting, and I sat next to an older woman, Elsie, a prostitute. She invited me over to her place for a few quick hits; she had top grade rocks. She was my favourite prostitute! She always scored great crack! Whores always score good gear!'

'Oh, that sounds grim,' I say.

'Fuck off!' he replies. 'You don't get it. I was eleven when I first tried drinking. Morning vodka martinis with my granddad. He taught me how to drink. I couldn't believe how good booze made me feel!'

I imagine him as a small boy shaking up martinis. The way he keeps swearing at me, without provocation, is infuriating. It reminds me of my first days of school when the playground bullies kicked and swore at me, even called me names concerning my biracial father and Irish mother. The unprovoked expletives and racial abuse seemed surreal. According to my mother, if danger lurked, a good defence was to be mindful, she'd quote, 'He that spareth his words hath knowledge.' She quoted Proverbs and the Bible a lot. So I shut down by not speaking outside home—I later learned that selective mutism is associated with anxiety.

My father reported my bruised shins to the head-teacher nun. He was shocked when she told him there were special schools for children like me—mute. I did not mention any of this to my elder siblings; a large age gap separates us, and my tense family were not the kind who talked things out. I learned at an early age to mimic my father's passiveness, or maybe I just took after him. He'd remain unruffled when my mother's mental illness spiralled, and her prescription meds escalated. He worked hard, long hours, and remained calm, pragmatic and patient.

And here I am now, blind-sided by Ethan, in this surreal setting, being told to fuck off with my default mutism reactivated, being stoical, because I feel responsible for Ethan, and I want to ensure he gets to rehab. I guess that's why I stay with him.

'I joined AA about twenty years ago, but I'm in and out of it.' He gulps more booze, saying his mouth is really dry.

I had no idea his battle with addiction had been going on for so long.

He paints a blurred picture of an idyllic childhood littered with emotional pain. 'I was packed off to boarding school at the age of five; that's when my parents divorced. Following year, my dad's business goes bust, so I gets yanked out of my nice school and dumped in a shitty state school. How about that! Abandoned! My dad's a nightmare. Anyway, I was selling Special Brew from my locker by the age of thirteen! I used to get tanked on the way to school!'

Ethan continues to guzzle beer, smoke, and ramble. His bladder fills fast when he's drinking, so he hops out of my car, flings the door wide open, then holds onto the outer car roof while peeing up the rear side door. The way he pees, by blocking his body in the open passenger car door, despite the state he's in, seems like a learned technique designed so the driver is unable to drive off and leave him behind. When he's done peeing, he hops back in my car with his splattered urine down his trousers and trainers. The open door has let in the cold, so he nags me to start the car and switch on the heater.

Spilt beer and wine soak the front of his sweatshirt. He accidentally kicks over a bottle of beer he'd left propped up in the footwell. It topples over, and he just watches it glug into a beer puddle.

I reach for a toilet roll that's on the back seat so I can mop up the worst of the spillage. While manoeuvring myself around from my driver's seat, I get my upper body trapped half-way between the front seats. That's when I feel the first ferocious slap to my backside.

'Hey!' I yell. I try to turn my body, but it only makes things worse, and I get myself wedged.

Ethan proceeds to deliver savage clouts, as hard as he can, one after another, all landing on my backside and the backs of my thighs.

'You're hurting me!' I shout. 'Please stop! STOP.' It's no good, he continues with his assault. I kick my legs in an attempt to stop him beating me, while trying to wriggle myself free. Eventually I manage it, but my backside and legs throb with pain.

I plonk back down in my driver's seat, completely shaken. 'Why did you do that?' I ask, incensed at his behaviour.

He smirks. 'When girls say no, they mean yes!'

I press my lips together and look out my window, feeling vulnerable. I can't call the police. I have absolutely no idea of my location. And how crazy would this look to the cops? With the two of us hiding out in the pitch-dark, remote countryside in a Yaris that reeks like a chemistry laboratory of burnt crack and booze? He pops off another cap of beer with the bottom of his lighter and guzzles as if nothing just happened. He's more interested in talking about himself.

'Fuck this!' he shouts. 'Koemi was my favourite, and the richest. I loved her more than Racy and Foxy Doxy—they were all rich as well. Zesty Zora was fun but flat broke.'

It seems his love interests go back twenty and some years. He maintains they were all heavy users.

'My Donna was amazing! We're still friends. She was my best friend's wife. I used to babysit for them. Once we went on holiday together; that's when we started our affair. I really wasn't gonna cheat on my best mate with his missus, but I can never say no. It was meant to be a short holiday romance. Yeah, meant to be!' He brags about his wild, promiscuous past, his virility, probably to impress me, or to put me off. This Ethan is like Jeckyll and Hyde.

I dread to think what I've spent on his booze and hotel rooms during his relapse, but now—with his drinking and using—we're often turned away at reception when hotel staff clock his drunken state. We always seem to attract sniggers and pointed fingers. I'd like to tell those people that he's sick; he's got a disease. I want to explain it to them, to stop them humiliating us.

The next morning, Ethan takes one bite of croissant and chucks the rest out of the car window. 'Take no notice of some things I say when I'm drunk. I'm probably making it up, just for a laugh.' It seems he can recall fragments of his ramblings, but he can't keep up with himself, or the mishmash of truth or lies.

He doesn't look well: his swollen eyes are bloodshot; his eye sockets are shades of purple; his pale face is red, and when he tries to stand, he sways and falls over all the time. He can barely eat; his stomach is bloated, and he can't sleep. He's got a gash on his cheekbone—doesn't even know how he did it. It's day seven of his relapse.

I attempt to talk him into returning to the community. Maybe someone there can talk some sense into him. He agrees to cooperate, and I drive all the way back to the community. We reach the entrance gate after dark, at suppertime. The residents and staff don't know we're outside, and Ethan won't allow me to call them.

'Just let me smoke, then I'll go in, I promise!' He sits, glued to the passenger seat, not even hopping out to pee, and when he's bursting, he pees directly into a Starbucks cup, then haphazardly tosses the cup of steaming piss out of the window. He smokes a roll-up to delay, and an hour later he needs more alcohol. He says he won't swear, shout or hit me again.

He defeats me again.

It's day ten of his relapse. I'm drained, sleep deprived, fatigued, and I haven't eaten a meal or washed for a week. Ethan's continuously wasted. I'll go insane if I can't break this cycle, but there isn't a good time to catch him sober enough to have a serious conversation. However, I manage to get him to agree to me taking him to A&E for a check-up. The waiting time's at least two hours. He keeps popping outside the main entrance of the hospital to swig beer and smoke, while I sit and wait, just in case we miss his name being called. Eventually the nurse calls for him.

Bruises have appeared on his torso. The nurse explains that his blood has thinned from drinking, so this is why he bruises easily. We're led to a curtained-off area, and he lies stretched out on a gurney. A nurse sets up a saline drip to rehydrate him and gives him a vitamin B shot. Another nurse takes blood samples for liver function tests.

'Don't leave me!' Ethan says.

A few hours later, a doctor throws back the curtain and asks Ethan questions. He knows the doctor is the hospital prescriber, so he asks for Valium to help wean himself off the alcohol. The doctor scratches his head thoughtfully, then offers six 10 mg tablets, one to be taken every four hours. Ethan swallows two Valium tablets on the way to the car.

With Valium in his bloodstream, Ethan manages one day sober, so he calls Rodney, who agrees to allow him back. Once again, I drive him back to the community, where he gets a warm welcome.

Apart from Vinnie, the other residents are new. There's a different vibe, a sadness—what with Ethan relapsing and the impending evictions.

We share a pot of tea in the garden room. Ethan's the centre of attention, but he senses that this is where we part, that I'm leaving him here.

'I need to go to A&E again. I need more Valium otherwise I'll have a seizure,' he announces to his audience. 'I can't quit drinking this quickly. I might die!'

A discussion starts between staff, residents, and Ethan. It's decided I should take him to the nearest A&E, an hour's drive away.

We wait for hours in A&E, and finally Ethan procures another strip of Valium. It's the early hours by the time we get back. We sit in his hut, him snuggled into his bed, me on the floor. Before dawn I stand to go.

Ethan's tired, irritable, ungrateful, and full of self-pity. 'I need rest. Go!' he says curtly.

I blame his rudeness on alcohol withdrawal, but it hurts me all the same. I leave quietly, with not so much as a wave goodbye.

Frida and I meet for lunch. I explain the shortened version of what's been going on with Ethan. She's mortified and offers me a few nights on her couch—her housemates are away. I never realised Sylvia and Frida had been worrying about my safety with Ethan's drinking and using.

Before I finish eating my lunch, he calls me. 'Hi, darling! I've told everyone our plan, and they're all happy!'

'What plan?' I ask.

'That I'm leaving this commune today! To be with you! My rehab date is any day now. And I'm sober; I promise I won't drink. This place closes down in a few weeks, so it's not like it matters. Make space in your car for my stuff; I'm packing now.'

'Ethan, you can't just up sticks!' My reply falls on deaf ears.

'By the way,' he adds, 'I said you'd cook the community

supper this evening as a farewell dinner. And they said it's allowed. Buy enough ingredients for dinner for thirteen! I'm sooo happy! I love you!'

In my heart I don't agree with Ethan's impulsive decision. And yet I find myself zooming back to fetch him. He calls me the entire journey. My instinct tells me to hang up and turn around, but I don't.

Ethan's at the entrance gate, waiting for me. He collects all his stuff and hurriedly crams it into my car, then reaches underneath the passenger seat. To my surprise, he pulls out three cans of Guinness. I guess he'd stashed there some days ago. He flings himself into the corner of his hut and guzzles it down.

I shake my head. 'You said you wouldn't drink.'

He just shrugs.

So much for the ground rules!

The booze takes effect immediately; he becomes clownish.

Ethan and I cook the dinner together. Before we've even digested it, Ethan's in a crazy rush to leave. Everyone gathers in a circle in the kitchen for last goodbyes. I feel bewildered, like I'm not part of this scene, but merely an onlooker.

The residents and staff hand Ethan a signed good-luck card and exchange hugs and playful slaps on the back. Ethan approaches Lori, the commune's co-worker, last. All eyes are on them. When Ethan scoops her up, pulls her in close, and proceeds to lift her gently, an embarrassed silence invades the air. Ethan doesn't notice it. Vinnie looks at Ethan suspiciously. He's guessed Ethan's drunk. Lori squeals with delight. It breaks the awkward silence,

'Put me down,' she cries out, none the wiser.

Ethan eventually lowers her to her feet, and we wave our last goodbye.

Chapter Fifteen

We drive to an out-of-town guesthouse where we spend a few nights. At breakfast we are the only guests in the cramped dining room. The Valium's given Ethan an appetite, and he eats quickly, then nags me to eat faster because he wants to smoke outside. He checks his iPhone every few seconds and impatiently pulls out eyebrow hair.

We check out and have to pay for cleaning because Ethan dropped a takeaway on the duvet last night. Once back in the car, I follow his instructions to our next county.

'Stop. I need tobacco,' he says when we're half-way to wherever we're going.

I wait in the car while he goes to the shop. A few minutes later, he re-emerges, jumps into my car, and hauls his backpack onto his lap. He smells of beer.

'Have you just been drinking?' I ask.

'Darling, just the one to take the edge off!'

I grimace and shake my head.

'Just drive!' he says.

I do as he says, following his directions. We stop outside houses that have been converted into flats.

'This is where Tez lives,' he says. 'Wait for me.' A door opens in response to his knock. Ethan chats for a few minutes, then returns. 'Come and meet Tez; he's cool.'

I get out of the car and join him at the door.

'Hi, I'm Tez,' the man says to me. He offers us tea, which we accept.

The two of them start talking like they're the best of mates.

'I've been sober ten months,' Tez tells Ethan.

'Well, I was sober nearly six months!' Ethan replies.

'I smoke weed to take the edge off,' Tez says. 'I'm off to s core some now.'

'Great. We'll come!' Ethan replies.

We all bundle into Tez's van, and he drives until we reach a park green. It's pitch dark, but the rival drug gangs are easy to spot.

Ethan's first to bolt out of the transit and run to a cashpoint. 'Be right back!' he calls out and runs off again.

Tez meets someone behind his transit. He returns a minute later, shoving something in his pocket.

Ethan seems to be taking ages, but eventually he returns, saying he just scored crack. He peeks inside the cling-film balls, and that's exactly what they are—empty balls of cling film. He's been ripped off.

'FUCK! Not again! I'm always getting bumped!' Ethan shouts. He pulls a small bottle of vodka from his pocket and glugs it neat.

'I'm fucked off with this!' Tez says. 'I'm going!' He starts the transit van and drives.

'Pull in!' Ethan yells. 'I gotta check out that geezer!' He leaps out of the car and runs off, leaving his iPhone on the seat. Its battery is dead.

Tez drops me back at my car so I can search for Ethan, who's off his head on vodka. I drive around looking for him, and eventually spot him. I call out to him across the road. He hears me and waves, then holds up one finger—a sign for me to wait. A hooded man walks past Ethan, drops something into his hand and walks off. He's scored.

Ethan runs across the road to me. 'Let's go, go, go!' He looks over his shoulder in a paranoid frenzy.

Ethan frantically searches the footwell to knock up a crack pipe, but he's out of luck; I threw it away. Back at Tez's house, he buzzes us in. He's chilling with a spliff. Ethan raids the kitchen, finds a cola can in the bin and starts making a crack pipe. Moments later he's flying. Ethan stands up and starts warbling a song and dancing, while Tez and I watch on.

'Tez, Tez!' he calls out.

Tez looks up, unimpressed.

'Remember back in the old days we used to share our girls! You remember that?' Ethan asks.

'Yeah, yeah.'

Ethan springs to his feet and rushes over to where I'm sitting on the floor, hugging my knees. He grabs my ankles and drags me around the room.

'Fuck her now,' he says. 'I'll watch. Help me, hold her down!'

Horrified, I kick my legs to get away, but Ethan's grip is too strong.

'Piss off! Get off me!'

'Fucks sake! Let her go!' Tez shouts.

Ethan's grip loosens long enough for me to scramble to the front door. My heart's racing.

'C'mon, Tez; it'll be a laugh!' Ethan says.

I want to leave, but my legs feel like jelly and my chest's so tight I can barely breathe.

'Fuck off, Ethan!' Tez replies.

'Aw, c'mon Tez!' he nags.

In the blink of an eye, Tez lunges at Ethan and overpowers him. He grabs him by the throat with one hand, seizes his arm with the other and shoves his face into Ethan's. 'Ethan! Shut the fuck up or fuck off! Leave her alone! Do you get me, you fucking piece of shit?'

Ethan's face reddens from the lack of air. He tries to fight his way free, but he's no match for Tez. He looks scared to death and nods until Tez releases his grip.

'Fucking hell, man, where d'ya learn to do that?' Ethan asks while gasping for air. He rubs his reddened neck.

Tez lights a cigarette and plops down on the sofa.

Ethan takes the edge off with more booze and crack. I'm tempted to make a run for it, but seeing as Tez has got my back, I figure I can split tomorrow.

Ethan tries to make a sandwich, but before he's buttered the bread, he plops down on the kitchen floor and blacks out for the night.

Tez steps over Ethan, who's still soundo. He groans and retches. His body spasms.

'Should we call an ambulance?' I ask Tez.

'Nah. He's okay. He just needs to sleep this off. You want breakfast?'

'What if he chokes?' I reply.

Tez scoops Ethan off the floor as if he's light as a feather, and then puts him to bed.

Anyone with an addict in their life is meant to know about the four M's: martyrdom, managing, manipulating, and mothering. Apparently addicts run rings around their targets and loved ones by practicing the four M's; sometimes it's utilised vice-versa. But I haven't heard of one M, let alone four. The four M's make up some recipe ingredients that feed a deformed, dysfunctional relationship or partnership with an addict—which seems to be what Ethan and I have.

My cognitive thinking—knowing, remembering, judging, and problem-solving—is shutting down due to chronic sleep deprivation and stress, so my decision making is off kilter. The prefrontal cortex that handles one's planning, judgment calls and complex decision making is severely impaired when chronically sleep deprived.

It has been five years since I last saw my London therapist. Over the years of us doing 'the work'—therapy—she got me to think about, amongst other things, my inner-child—with her stark childhood—as well as neglect and self-neglect, and the fight-or-flight response; I just remembered it. I'm down to work shift with the union later today; it's the perfect excuse to escape from Ethan who's latching onto me like a barnacle. I'll regain my freedom—time to call it a day. I'm confident Ethan will grasp that I need to work. Won't he? The best way forward, I think, is to leave Ethan with Tez, who seems experienced with relapsers. He can sort him out, and surely, he knows what to do. After work, I might ask Rodney if I can deliver Ethan's stuff to the commune, seeing as my car's fully crammed; I'm sure he'll understand.

Tez mentioned how addicts are usually co-dependant; they make a beeline for, or become romantically involved with, other addicts or non-addicted adult children of addicts, because they accept unacceptable behaviour, tolerate it, and are practically accustomed to it. We can only take care of ourselves when we have the courage to change and detach.

When Ethan wakes, he says he needs air. He dashes out of the front door and returns clutching a litre of vodka.

Tez grabs it off him. 'I'll take that!' he says firmly.

Ethan might recall their altercation because he doesn't argue back.

Tez invites Ethan to hang out with him all day, says he'll keep an eye on him. I'm still shaken up, so I need to have a break from Ethan, and work my shift.

He shadows me while I walk away. 'Take me with you!'

I shake my head. 'I can't.'

'I'm going with you,' Ethan replies. 'I'm sorry about yesterday. It won't happen again.' He pulls on my sleeve—and on my heartstrings. Tears smart his eyes. He stands in front of my driver's door to block it.

I sigh. 'Okay, it looks like I haven't got a choice. You better start thinking about getting clean and sober, though.' I can't help feeling Ethan's taken me hostage.

My bankcard gets declined when I go to pay for fuel. *What? Why?* I walk back to where Ethan waits in my car with the window open. I stand and stare at him, hands on my hips. 'Ethan, my money's gone from my bank account.'

'It's only money,' he replies. 'Who cares!'

Me! I do! But I say nothing, just rummage for my credit card that's hidden in the boot. I feel my resentment simmering under the surface.

Both of us living in my car is becoming unbearable.

I start to log Ethan's alcohol units in a notebook. It's increasing by the day. He rambles constantly about the same old things, and takes trips to buy booze, where he uses me to purchase it for him—they can't serve liquor to him in his drunken state.

I can scarcely believe it's only seven weeks since we made our pledge to be a couple, that same week he went camping. I'm just thinking that it feels as if the rehab funding won't ever be approved when his phone rings. He puts the call on speakerphone.

''Allo?' Ethan yells.

'Hi, Ethan! It's Josie, from rehab admissions!'

I pray for good news.

He grins. 'Josie! How are you?'

'I'm good, thanks. How are you?'

'Not so good, Josie. My belly's bloated; it's killing me.'

'Sorry to hear that. I'm calling with news; you've been approved for six weeks of funding. We'll get your phone assessment done, and you'll be admitted for treatment next week! How does that sound?'

To me it sounds fantastic.

Ethan says, 'Next week? Really?'

'Yes, really,' she replies.

'Well, I think I've just fallen madly in love with you!' he says.

She laughs and explains that he'll have a Valium detox in the medical wing. Then she lists what's contraband, such as hand sanitizer and toiletries that contain alcohol, also caffeine, sugary drinks, scissors, and sharp objects. He mustn't have any pending criminal charges; romantic relationships with other clients are forbidden, and eviction is swift if rules are broken. He'll be searched upon his arrival. There's zero tolerance for relapses after admission. Mobile phones aren't allowed, nor are computers or large amounts of cash. (There's no chance of that.) They'll need to see his most recent blood test results. After his detox he'll be allowed to use the payphone in the evenings. He'll be given the rule guidelines booklet after he signs the paperwork.

He names me as his next of kin—it seems odd that he doesn't name his parents.

We're equally thrilled that rehab is on the horizon—maybe me more than him. After all, he's numbed by drugs and booze, whereas I'm soaking up the trauma day by day. I'm not sure if he understands the substantial cost of his treatment—funded with taxpayers' money. However, he does realise that it hasn't been easy to get it approved.

We decide to find a hotel, somewhere we can bide our time in comfort until Ethan's admission. He needs a decent rest to gain strength for his detox. The only hotel that has rooms is in another town. It's expensive for my budget, but provided he doesn't appear pissed at the reception, we'll take it.

I stand with bated breath when the receptionist swipes my bankcard; one beep and my payment clears. I can see why the hotel's rates are steep; it's not the Ritz, but it offers sumptuous comfort.

We take much-needed baths and read the food menu. After judging the prices, we decide on pizza delivery. Ethan relaxes on the bed. I notice that his bloated torso is badly bruised, and he rubs his sore tummy. He dials a number and starts talking:

'Hi, Mum. I thought you'd like to know I got funding. I'll be in rehab next week!' He takes a turn speaking to his stepdad, and they share a few jokes. He randomly turns his speakerphone on and off.

They seem to get along fine. Their conversation is jovial, and the family detachment is clear. They're nonchalant about not offering to help towards funds for the week ahead, and the fact that his family don't want to put him up is swept under the carpet. They say things like, 'By golly, isn't Magda a saint for being a huge support.'

As for me, I miss not having my life or a home. I miss my daughters. I miss Ethan and me the way we were.

A few days before his admission, we go on a day trip, just to do something that normal couples might do. He wants to show me the Cerne Abbas chalk giant, but he can't stop knocking back cans of Guinness during the long drive. He's so blotto by the time we reach the giant that he stumbles and falls head over heels, tumbling all the way to the bottom of a grassy hill. He gets up and laughs, but then notices he's ripped his jacket on barbed wire, and his mood changes. He says that nothing's fun with me; his old flames and conquests were all better than I, all smarter and funnier than me.

It hurts, but I remind myself that it's just the booze talking.

On admission morning Ethan gets up before the alarm. He's in a great mood and wants to make a good impression by shaving and wearing his best clothes. The wine stains in his clothes didn't wash out, though. He hands me his wallet, expecting me to send him money in drips, as he doesn't trust himself with cash. Also, he wants to take a slight detour on the way to rehab to visit Pearl, his aunt. Upon our arrival I get the impression she'd rather not let me in. Regardless, it's just a flying visit. I didn't notice when Ethan stole those bottles from her wine rack, and yet he must have done it right under our noses.

He nervously chain-smokes and gulps wine from the bottle while I navigate the roads to rehab. A wooden sign tells us to bear left into a country lane. It's crowded with autumnal trees. Ethan instructs me to stop, and I park under a tree. He hops out for a pee, taking a bottle with him.

'Don't sabotage this, Ethan! If we're late, they'll turn you away!

'Alright, alright,' he replies, 'but I'm scared! And I love you.'

'I know you're scared,' I reply. 'I love you too. But you need to do this.' And this rehab is meant to be the best in the country.

He drains the last drop from his stolen bottle. He's well hammered now.

I recognise the old mansion and rambling grounds from the website he'd shown me in July when we'd first met. I help him out of my car, guiding his head so he doesn't clonk it on the car door. Inside it's all high ceilings and original features. The smiling staff welcome us, and hellos echo in the reception area as clients in recovery stroll outside for a smoke in the wind. Men and women of all ages walk by; some look healthy, others limp, with jaundiced yellow complexions and toothless smiles. Ethan sways, looking like a lost soul.

A notice board on the wall advertises a Halloween film night in the TV lounge this Saturday. Payphones hang on the walls with chairs sitting next to them. Visiting time is Sunday afternoons.

'Welcome, Ethan. How lovely to meet you,' a smartly dressed woman says as she offers to shake his hand, unaware he's not washed his hands since he peed outside. 'We'll take him from here,' she adds. 'Don't worry about him.'

Two women steady him, taking an arm each. I peck him quickly on the cheek. His reddened face is clammy and sweaty. I touch his freezing hand, but he seems unaware of me. He looks straight through me with glazed, purple eyes.

'Darling, I've just fallen madly in love with you!' he yells to one of the admission staff. 'Will you marry me?'

'My hubby wouldn't like that!' she replies.

I roll my eyes, half wanting to shake him back to this reality.

The woman winks at me and nods to say it's okay. The two women lead him off towards a corridor. A heavy oak door bangs behind them.

Chapter Sixteen

Driving without Ethan beside me is weird. Silent. I'm so used his constant raging and rambling. Frida and I agree to meet this evening; she's helping me move the car that's been parked near that hotel ever since he relapsed almost a month ago. The plan is that I'll drive his mum's car; Frida will tailgate in mine, and I'll park his mum's car somewhere legal, until she's ready to collect it. But more importantly, I'll get to see Frida.

My previously spotless car show signs of Ethan's relapse, a reminder of the trauma. The terrible smell of stale smoke and piss hangs in the air, and the carpet's sticky with spilt booze. It needs a good clean, but there's nothing I can do about the cigarette burns on the interior where he'd dropped his fags and lost them in the dark. Thank goodness that's all in the past.

I've heard the first forty-eight hours are a crucial time for an addict during a detox, so it puts my mind at rest when I call the reception for news of him and am told he's doing just fine.

By day three he's up on his feet. He calls me from the payphone to say how he thought he was going to die, how he sweated buckets in detox, and had double vision and terrible nightmares. He never wants to go through that again and insists that this time he'll beat the battle with the bottle once and for all.

After Ethan's detox, he's transferred from the medical room to a shared dormitory with other male clients. Much to Ethan's chagrin, they snore, sleepwalk, or are night shouters with the detox terrors. He tells me he has befriended a heroin addict who's let him in on a secret; the man is in a secret ménage à trois with two female clients. The secret's short lived, however, when a row breaks out during the Halloween film night. One of the staff detected the vodka the three had smuggled in. All three are chucked out on the spot, escorted into a taxi at 11 pm. Ethan's glad they're gone.

On my arrival for my first visit, I sign the visitors' register. A member of staff runs upstairs to Ethan's dormitory to tell him I'm in reception.

'He won't be long; he's preening himself for you,' the woman jokes.

I hear footsteps running down the stairs. Ethan rushes up to me. He smiles, takes my face in his soap-smelling hands to kiss my nose, then hugs me tightly. He looks completely different to when I dropped him off five days ago. His eyes are focused; he can walk without swaying or tripping over; his face isn't sweaty and red. Even his bloated tummy has gone down enough for him to fasten his trousers. I can smell him, perfume and soap instead of bad breath, stale beer and piss. He's put product in his hair, which was previously matted and greasy. His dark purple eyes are turning to shades of faded lilac.

'Come, let's have tea.' He takes me by the hand and leads me to the main lounge. It has bookcases and comfy sofas, and patio doors allow daylight to flood in. Ethan wants to show me around the rehab and grounds before the family lectures begin, so we take our tea outside where he talks nineteen to the dozen.

He says he's so happy that, for once, he got through a relapse without getting arrested.

His counsellor's great. He's helping Ethan make a start on his Twelve Step workbook. Ethan's dreading writing his life story—he has to read it aloud in group—so I offer to help him write it out before I leave, at least the bits he wants to tell.

It's time for the lecture.

We sit in a crowded room of next-of-kins, wives, husbands, mothers, fathers, sisters, brothers, partners, boyfriends, girlfriends, and adult children of addicts. I listen to the counsellor who is holding the meeting. She uses terminology that's alien to me. She uses phrases like; relapse prevention, powerlessness over alcohol, dry drunk, addiction is a merry-go-round, enabler, tough love, one day at a time, amends and ... rock bottom. There's so much to take in.

After the lecture we go to the quiet chapel, and I start writing his life story, the little I know of it: he was a happy child, but developed anxiety soon after his parent's acrimonious divorce; his father faced financial difficulties, so by the age of eleven he was drinking with his family, and he has a challenging relationship with his stepfather.

At the end of visiting, Ethan walks me to my car. Staff watch the departing visitors like hawks, maybe to detect or deter an exchange of contraband. Ethan envelopes me in a reassuring embrace and kisses my cheek before lighting another fag and waving goodbye.

I drive back to Bristol, feeling more optimistic than before my visit. In the evening Ethan calls me from the payphone to say goodnight. He's had his shower and is planning an early night.

My phone ringing wakes me at 8 am. At first, I'm puzzled to see Ethan's iPhone number displayed; I wonder why he is using his confiscated phone.

'Darling! It's me, Ethan! Thank God you answered! You've got to come and get me. I've been evicted!' he blurts out.

I frown. 'What did you say?'

'I relapsed. Last night. They would've booted me out on the spot, but because I'm homeless they let me stay the night,' he replies.

'You're kidding me? You're telling me you relapsed on your fifth day?' This is surreal.

'I don't know what happened! Last night I was jumping over the hedge, then running to the local pub, like it was someone else, not me. It was last orders, so I bought a pack of beer and ran back to rehab. I must have drunk them on the way back. You'd better hurry; I'm in reception with all my bags, waiting for you.'

'Oh my God!' I reply.

The minute I start my car I wonder if I should leave him to deal with the consequences. On second thoughts, that would be heartless. For the first hour while driving I keep thinking, 'Stop; it's not too late. Turn around. But then I think, 'What are his chances without me?' He has been abandoned by his family, friends, sponsor, and his AA contacts. No one has given him the time of day since he relapsed, and I still can't fathom why.

How could he do this! All the time, effort, energy, support, money, and trauma to get this far! For nothing!

I wonder if the rehab will change their minds or issue a warning instead. I'm led to an office, where Ethan's suitcase and bags are, and a woman matter-of-factly signs his discharge papers.

Ethan walks in, plucks his eyebrow. 'I'm sorry about last night,' he says to her.

'Not everyone succeeds the first time,' she replies without looking up.

78

I pop into the restroom, and when I return to the office, the discharge is done and dusted. The woman escorts us out the side door.

Ethan throws his case and bags into my car, then dithers, rolling a cigarette. I drive two minutes up the lane, and he tells me to bear right. I see it now. A quaint old pub in the middle of lush countryside. So this is where he'd got the beers. The pub's closed because it's early morning.

'Come on, let's get out of here,' Ethan says.

Chapter Seventeen

'What now, Ethan?' I ask.

He lights a cigarette and takes a close look at his reflection in the sun visor mirror. 'Just drive. Anywhere. I don't care where. I promise I won't drink. I really missed you.' He's distant, not affectionate or happy to see me. He seems so casual, whereas I'm desperate.

'We're both homeless, so it's back to living in my car, is it?' I ask.

'No, my mum will understand. I'll tell her what happened; she'll help. I know she will.'

It's strange he thinks this, considering that when the community gave him eviction notice, none of his family offered to accommodate him. Eventually we end up at Portishead motorway services. It's time we stopped for lunch. I use the restroom, after which I look for Ethan, only to find he has wandered off.

I gloomily return to my car. A few minutes later, I spot Ethan sprinting towards me with a huge grin. In full view, he reaches inside his jacket and presents a green magnum-sized bottle. He hands it to me before checking under my car, where he grabs another that he had stolen and stashed beforehand.

'There's no security guards,' he says. 'I'm dashing back for a third!'

I glare at him. 'No, you're not. We're getting out of here!'

He shrugs and hops in the passenger seat, then pops the cork.

I half expect the police to appear while we make our getaway to join the motorway. Ethan guzzles the fizzy booze and burps.

I ask him to stop drinking, but he won't listen. It occurs to me he's an experienced shoplifter, fast and audacious.

Before long he is flat out drunk. I know how quickly he becomes alcohol dependent, and the only thing I can think of is to call Geoff, his key worker at the Turning Point Centre.

'We'll have to apply for funding again, start from scratch,' Geoff says. 'Drop in tomorrow; there's a few walk-in appointments available.'

Ethan's so intoxicated by the time we arrive at the centre for the appointment that we are told to wait outside for a few hours, so he can sober up. When it's time to go in, he asks if I can help him fill in the application form. His answers reveal things I didn't know about him before, like how he'd abused prescription drugs over the years, his co-dependency issues, his penchant for prostitutes, unsafe sex and how many HIV tests he'd had in the last year. I want to shake some sense into him, but I can't.

When we stand up to leave, Geoff says, 'I'll be in touch. Ethan's lucky to have you. But you must get on with your life. Don't be his enabler; you mean well, but it won't help him.'

I'm quite confounded by this advice.

Chapter Eighteen

A bitterly cold week goes by with us living in my car, and not before time, Ethan decides to be up front to his mother about his being discharged from rehab. He places a call on speakerphone, while sitting in the passenger seat smoking and swigging a costly wine he'd got for free by stealing.

'Hello? Ethan? I thought you were in rehab?' his mum says. She seems startled to see his number displayed on her phone.

'Hi, Mum. It didn't work out. That rehab was useless! It's gone downhill! People were relapsing around me, smuggling in vodka. I was getting cravings, so I had to discharge myself. I'm not drinking!'

'Oh! Well, so long as you're sober,' she replies.

'Don't worry, I've been offered a different rehab.' Ethan lies.

'Oh! That's good news! When?'

'Soon.' Ethan lies again.

'Well, that's a relief. Oh, I meant to ask you; I need my car.'

'Oh, I'll hand you over to Magda about that.'

I tell her where her car is parked.

'Thanks,' she says. 'So he's sober now?'

Ethan glares at me.

I grimace, but lie for him anyway, 'Yes, clean and sober.'

'Good. Howard and I are staying with Pearl. I can't worry about Ethan; I need a rest.'

I look at Ethan, but he shakes his head. He's lost his nerve, and the call ends without him asking for help.

'Did you hear that?' he says, his eyes wild. 'Howard this; Howard that! And not poor Ethan! Or any offer of a bed! Oh NO! Ethan gets pushed away!'

I sit quietly and listen to his rage.

Ethan decides to make another call; this time to his cousin, Theo, who has spare bedrooms in his spacious home.

Theo's harder to convince. He seems suspicious, and he ends the call abruptly.

Ethan's family rejection visibly upsets him, so he cheers himself up with another booze shoplifting spree. The buzz of not getting caught pleases him, as if he's achieved something.

By the middle of the night, Ethan's voice is hoarse from talking, smoking, and drinking. I start my car so we can switch the heater on.

Ethan can't sleep; he rambles on and on. 'I don't see why I'm the black sheep of the family. At first it was good when Howard and Mum got together, then it changed after their wedding. He's not judged though. Howard was like my big brother; we had such laughs. When me and Phoebe were young, he used to take us to raves. He used to buy our drugs and booze. You name it—E's, dexies, weed and cocaine. We'd all get wasted together. And when I was sixteen Howard sorted out my first prostitutes; we shared whores! Can you believe that? Our brotherly secret. Not only that; Howard was having affairs. One was with my mum's best friend, for years, straight after their wedding! He's a cheat. And he had loads of affairs! One time I grassed him up. But my mum took him back and pushed me away. Once I fixed him up with one of my ex-girlfriends, and he jumped at the chance. We share our secrets, see?' He guzzles more booze, his head falls back onto the headrest, and he's out cold.

I wonder if there's any truth in his revelations.

Despite this never-ending chaos, the two of us living in my small car, not showering, sleeping, or eating properly, I hold onto hope.

Ethan's cough wakes him. He's unwell, so we return to the hospital just before midnight. The A&E has a long waiting time, and Ethan keeps dashing outside. When I think his name is due to be called, I look outside and see him standing outside the entrance doors, nattering on his iPhone again. He looks at me with rage in his eyes, and I don't know why.

'She's been a good friend to me,' I hear him slur as I walk outside. 'Oh, here she is now.' He pauses. 'Well, I'm calling to let you know she's crazy about you!'

Who in the hell is he talking to?

I try to prise his iPhone from him before he humiliates me further, but he shoves me aside and blathers on. 'Oh, Cedders, I think you'd make a lovely couple, bruvver!'

The penny drops. I can't believe it. He's jabbering a load of lies to Cedric behind my back. It's not the first time Ethan has tried to push me at another man; I think of Tez. I take a step towards Ethan, but he raises his hand and stomps back to my car, bored of waiting for his name to be called.

'Ethan, why did you lie about me to Cedric?' I ask as I get into the driver's seat.

'Shut it. Hand me your phone!' he demands.

My eyes widen. 'My what?'

'Fucking phone! NOW!' he yells.

His anger scares me. I reach into my pocket and take out my crappy phone.

'Good. Now show me all your text messages!'

I find my messages and hand him the phone. I don't know what he's looking for, but I've got nothing to hide.

He scrutinizes my texts. None are recent since I haven't had the time for messages. Ethan squints his eyes and mockingly reads aloud the few old texts Cedric had sent.

'Where's the ones to Cedders lover boy that you deleted? EH?' he yells.

'There's never been any!' I reply.

He throws my phone on the floor, and yells, 'Drive me to get more booze, you cunt!'

I'm scared out of my wits, so I obey.

The next three days follow the same kind of pattern.

I think back to the times when I'd read about women's rights, domestic violence and psychology. If I admit to myself that Ethan is my perpetrator that might mean I have to admit defeat, and that seems wrong. Ethan's coercive controlling behaviour is perplexing. I've never read about coercive control, so I don't know what to make of it. I seem to be adapting to his unacceptable behaviour, and I'm aware there are negative connotations for me—the lurking consequences are deadly. As things are, I'm his enabler, in denial.

Addiction is sometimes referred to as an octopus; it reaches out all its tentacles and drags in everything that's within its reach. This is why I should detach, untangle myself, but the longer I stay, the tighter his grip becomes. Ethan's developed typical addict's traits. He's dishonest and is a trophy winning manipulator. When one's not like that oneself, it's difficult to accept that one can't change an addict's foibles. The key word is 'acceptance.' I need to lose my fear to make way for acceptance. I must accept that I can't change him or cure him. I feel optimistic that rehab will rescue Ethan and then he'll change. After all, it's a well-known fact in AA and Twelve Step groups that relapse is part of recovery.

Ethan proceeds to get wasted again. He scrolls through his contacts and dials numbers. The first contacts won't pick up.

Then he calls Denise. 'Hi, darling! I need a bed for a few nights!'

She makes up an excuse that she's got a migraine.

Donna is next. 'Darling, Donna! It's been ages! How's the kids?' He slurs his words.

'Are you drinking?' she asks.

'No, of course not!'

She hangs up. You'd never guess they were once lovers.

'Can you stop phoning your old flames just to beg for free housing, Ethan?' I ask. 'You're making a fool of yourself.'

'They're not old flames,' he mutters.

My phone rings. The timing's bad, but I catch it before it stops ringing. It's Frida. I try to sound as if I have everything under control—she knows about me camping in my car with Ethan on his relapse. Ethan decides to take charge of my phone, so he snatches the handset off me and starts talking nonsense to Frida. She makes her excuses and says goodbye. He seems to be cutting me off from everyone, even my daughters.

I need to use the restroom in the local superstore. Ethan insists on accompanying me. When I open the door of the ladies, he stands in the toilet doorway.

'Ladies only!' the cleaner calls out while waving her floor mop.

Ethan grins. 'Well, I am a lady!'

The women queuing give him a queer look. Nonetheless, he shadows me, and when I reach the toilet cubicle, he holds out his hand and says, 'Phone and car keys.'

He's drawing unwanted attention to us, so I do as he asks.

Chapter Nineteen

Seeing as Ethan's extended family have blocked his number, he reckons an uninvited visit might be a better strategy. He'll be in a stronger position to gain pity if he's on their doorstep. His cousin, who has a country pad, is on his list. Only problem is, Ethan does not remember his address. He persuades me to drive around the countryside in circles for hours, turning around, getting lost, going back on ourselves, until we finally find his cousin's home at dusk.

'You wait 'til you see the welcome my cousin's gonna give me! I think I'm his favourite cousin. He's gonna be stoked to see me after so many years!' Ethan says between huge gulps of wine.

Dogs bark when I swing my car into the sweeping driveway. A man opens a door to see what's going on. Ethan springs out of my car to give him a hug. The man pats Ethan on the back, getting a waft of booze.

'My favourite cousin!' Ethan says.

His cousin frowns. 'Hello, Ethan. What a shame you've relapsed!'

'No, I'm not drinking!'

His cousin flinches at the lie. 'Good luck with rehab. One

day, when you're better, we'll do lunch.' He retreats into the house and closes the door, not even waving when we drive off.

'Wait,' Ethan says, 'I just thought of another relation. They're not far from here. Let's go.'

The secluded mansion's lights are on. A portly man opens the door and greets us. Despite the shock of us turning up out of the blue, he offers us tea. 'So what's been happening? What brings you to this neck of the woods?'

'I haven't seen you in so long,' Ethan replies in his Bertie accent. 'I happened to be passing and I thought I'd pop by.'

The portly man makes a pot of tea and offers a slice of homemade cake. He listens, while Ethan tells his sorry tale, then he shows us the way out.

Ethan grumbles about all the empty spare rooms they have and how they prefer to keep them that way; empty. I think there's more to this than meets the eye; they must have a reason why they want to keep their distance.

We're almost out of fuel again, so I pull into a petrol station. Ethan sits in my car beside the fuel pump, rolling a cigarette. As I approach my car after paying, I see him nattering away on his iPhone and flicking his lighter up to his cigarette, unaware he's next to the fuel pump with the No Mobiles and No Smoking signs stuck all around. I break into a run to stop a potential explosion.

Our next road trip is to Ethan's doctor, whose surgery is some distance away. It's the repeated charade of me going into the doctor's surgery with him to beg for Valium. This time the doctor agrees to prescribe five days' worth of Valium.

I fire up the engine and switch the heater on full blast.

Ethan sits, inspecting the precious blister pack of Valium. 'Five days' worth! Do you know what that means?'

'No, unless you mean you can detox yourself,' I reply.

'Correct! But I need to ask my mum something.' He calls and she answers—for a change. She's probably heard how he's doing the rounds asking the relatives for bed and board.

'Hi, Mum! How are you?'

'I'm fine. I hear you've been visiting our relations.'

'Oh! Well, that's why I'm calling. I'm sick of waiting for funding; I've got Valium, enough to detox myself, but I need shelter, I haven't seen Aunty Myrtle in years! So I'm going to visit her. I haven't got her address or number, though, so can you text it to me?' He doesn't explain to her what it's like to detox, with all the jitters, sweating and stuff.

'I'm not sure, Ethan. It's short notice for Myrtle. Don't go to her until I call you back.'

Ethan translates this as a green light. 'Quick! We're leaving now, this second. Let's go!'

'You were just told to wait, though,' I protest.

'No. Do exactly what I tell you!'

I sigh. 'So where does Myrtle live?'

'Scotland. She'll be happy to see me.'

'Scotland?' I ask.

'Yes. We're wasting time!'

I shake my head but tap Aberdeen into my SatNav.

'My mum's only got time for Howard. Myrtle will look after me until I'm well,' he says. 'She lives miles away from anywhere, so I won't be near alcohol or drugs. I can't get clean and sober when they're everywhere I go. It's down to you to help me get into recovery.'

I promise myself that this is the last long journey I get roped into doing. He seems so sure this is his only option to get clean and sober. Maybe he's right; he'll be far away from temptation. My SatNav tells me it is a nine-hour journey, over five hundred miles.

Ethan chatters animatedly, saying he can't wait to get there. He slurs about what a perfect place Myrtle has for recovery, while he chain-smokes, swigs from a bottle, and pops another pill. He jumps from one topic to the next, with rants about his family in-between. Concentrating on driving isn't easy.

Two hundred miles later, we reach Staffordshire. I spot a motorway services and pull in. I could use a pit stop. 'Ethan, I have no idea if we're going in the right direction. Has your mum sent a text with the address?' I ask.

He checks both our phones since he always takes charge of my phone now and keeps both in his pocket. He squints to read the new text; his vision must be blurred because he hands my phone to me. The text says: *Phone me. Urgent. It's about Scotland. Thanks. Vicky.*

I look at him dismayed. Right on cue, my phone rings. It's Theo; I put him on speakerphone.

'Hi, how are you?' Theo asks.

'I'm okay. Ethan has me on a road trip,' I reply.

'Yes. You'll have to turn around. We've had a family discussion. It's not agreeable that Ethan goes to visit Myrtle. He needs to sort his own life out.'

'What a cunt! Fucking interfering cunt!' Ethan shouts. He rummages around the glovebox in a temper, searching for his Valium, and throws the contents straight out the passenger window while cussing. I watch as my A-Z maps, papers, and even my box of locking wheel nuts fly out of the window. He finds his Valium, proceeds to eat the entire blister pack in one go and washes them down with gulps of red wine. I try to soothe him, while he pops out one tablet after another. When that doesn't work, I try to grab the tablets from his cold hands, but it's like fighting the tide.

I jump out of my car in the drizzling rain and dark to retrieve what's now strewn around the car park. The box of locking wheel nuts has burst open; the wheel nuts have gone their separate ways. Ethan remains in the passenger seat, hastily popping the Valium. He scoffs the lot, crunching them until they resemble sherbet before washing them down. On my hands and knees, I search frantically for the wheel nuts. It doesn't help that I haven't got a torch. Somehow, I find them, scattered far from where he threw them, then I return to Ethan.

He flings open the passenger door and falls out of the car. Trying to stand fails; he just falls in a heap on the concrete and lies still, out cold. I think he's OD'd, so I dial 999, stammering to the emergency operator that I need an ambulance.

I manage to get him into recovery position on the concrete. Waiting for the ambulance feels like eternity, but at last I see the blue flashing lights and stand to wave. Two paramedics get out of the ambulance and approach Ethan, who is still out cold. They start with asking: What's his name? What's he taken? What's he … but before the paramedic finishes that question, Ethan jumps up and lunges towards him.

'Who the fuck are you? Fuck off!'

The paramedics step backwards into the ambulance and lock themselves in. A moment later, to my surprise, the vehicle starts, drives towards the exit and parks. I don't know what's going on.

Ethan staggers back to my car. 'What you waiting for? Get in and drive!'

I do so, but I have to pass the ambulance. I stop beside it and unwind the passenger window to apologise.

The driver half opens the ambulance window and calls out to me, 'The police are on their way. We've requested police assistance.' Then he closes the window.

'He's not well! He hasn't done anything wrong!' I reply, even though he had.

I'm so scared of the police showing up to arrest Ethan that I drive away and join the motorway. I'm sure the police have my car registration number now. They'll be looking for him, or both of us.

When we're far away, I find a suburb where we can park for the night. Ethan's already snoring his head off.

When he wakes up in the morning, he doesn't mention the incident, just suggests we get breakfast. He's stranded, penniless, relapsed and has only me to lean on, so he sweet-talks me, cooing, 'You see how I've only got you!'

I'm in fast-flowing traffic on a dual carriageway heavy with traffic when without a word of warning, Ethan opens the passenger door, throws himself out of my car and hurtles towards the grass verge. I gasp in horror and slow immediately. If I wasn't driving in the inside lane there's a good chance he would've been run down. Cars and lorries beep their horns. I can't do an emergency stop without causing a pile-up. The passenger door isn't shut properly and rattles, but all I can do is drive on. Further along I indicate and pull in where I shouldn't. The car behind me witnessed the whole thing. They've probably taken my registration number and reported it to the police.

I jump out of my car and see Ethan dodging the traffic, crossing to the opposite side of the dual carriageway.

'Ethan! What are you doing?' I call out. 'Come back!'

He can't hear me, not with the roar of traffic and all the lorries beeping at him. He makes it to the other side of the carriageway, removes his trainers and throws them in a tantrum at a beeping lorry. Then he runs shouting, pointing, and swearing in a rage of fury. I can't work out what he's shouting. Retreat is my only option. When I return to my car, I spot his iPhone in the footwell. I'll have to leave him stranded. I drive a few miles until I reach a retail park, then with shaking hands, I call Theo.

'Theo, what shall I do?' I ask. I want him to say he'll take over from here, that he'll rescue Ethan.

'Sod him. Tough love! You're not responsible for him, neither am I,' Theo replies. 'Let him get on with it. I've got my life and you're entitled to yours!'

To me, it seems so harsh.

Seeing as his iPhone is in the car, Ethan can't be contacted, and after throwing his shoes at the lorries, he's not even wearing footwear in the freezing weather. Abandon him or find him? I want to be sure I make the right decision. At dusk, I've made up my mind to abandon him, when my phone starts to ring. I don't recognise the number.

'Hello! This is accident and emergency,' a woman says. 'We've got Ethan here with us. He's just been discharged and needs to be collected. He can't find his wallet or phone, and he told us you're his next of kin! Hold on, he'd like a quick word.'

'Sweetie,' Ethan says, 'I'm so happy you answered your phone. Please come and get me. I'm stranded. But I'm sober. I promise I won't drink. I promise!' He sounds so sincere, so desperate, that I can't drive to the hospital fast enough.

Upon my arrival I find Ethan anxiously watching the entrance doors. He sees me and shuffles towards me, wearing a pair of white, backless hospital slippers. Apparently, a lorry driver called an ambulance when Ethan was dodging traffic. I hand him a bag with his spare pair of trainers in it, and he hugs me.

'Nothing comes between us, not even my addiction,' Ethan says.

But I'm not certain he won't flip in a second.

The duty A&E doctor has prescribed more Valium, so Ethan feels compelled to pop another benzo within minutes of the last. He fixates on polishing them off, which in a blink of an eye, he does.

Chapter Twenty

Despite Ethan's dishevelled, drunken appearance, his booze shoplifting, or choring as he calls it, is still bountiful. He can spot a decent vino from a mile off, and lucky for him, security stickers on booze are few and far between.

His choring takes a matter of minutes, during which I'm allowed to wait in my car. It is the only time I'm permitted to be alone, although he confiscates my car keys and phone so I can't skedaddle.

Before midnight I suggest we cross the Bristol Suspension Bridge to park for the night near Pill village. I stop at the barrier to search for coins and realise I forgot about change to pay the toll. Ethan's temper erupts; he shouts while I frantically search for coins, and I'm relieved when I find some. I pay the toll, the barrier lifts, with still Ethan hollering. While driving along the bridge, he leans across, and, to my horror, grabs the steering wheel and tugs it, veering to the left. Sure we're going to crash, I fight for control of my car, my heart pounding.

'Let go!' I shout at the top of my voice.

He abruptly lets go but doesn't register what he's done. I cross the bridge and find a lay-by to pull into for the night, by which time he's conked out.

The smell of urine wakes me before daybreak. His trousers stink really bad.

'We need to go to the launderette,' I say.

'Yes, let's get our clothes washed!' Ethan agrees.

Though a homeless alkie, he likes to wear clean clothes. A local drug centre offers shower facilities for registered alcoholics and addicts; I might bring him there. Otherwise, some superstores have disabled toilets.

Ethan unearths his washbag and towel. I walk with him to the supermarket's disabled toilet. He's so wobbly on his legs, I have to help him balance and go into the loo with him, like an unpaid carer—I guess in a way I am. Ethan wants to be thorough and have a strip-down wash, a hair wash and a shave, but he's uncoordinated, so I do it for him. Water goes everywhere. He finishes off with squirts of perfume and a huge handful of my face cream.

'Good as new!' he says.

Next, we go to the launderette. While our laundry is tumbling in the driers, we step outside. Ethan spots a hair salon next door. He decides he wants a trim and bursts into the salon. It's empty apart from an old lady sporting a new purple rinse.

'Can I help you?' the hairdresser calls out to Ethan.

'Darling, I would love one of those,' Ethan exclaims, pointing to the bemused woman with the mauve, bouffant hair.

'Thank you, dearie!' the old lady rasps, grateful for the compliment.

'Have you been drinking, my love?' the hairdresser asks.

'I'm sober as a judge,' he replies.

She shakes her head. 'Come back when you are.'

But he's adamant about getting a trim. He turns to me and says, 'You'll have to do it. I've got split ends; use your craft cutter.'

I make a start with the razor-sharp blade. We stand in the middle of the street where I lop off his locks in front of passers-by, 'More! Shorter!' Ethan says.

I busily chop away. Clumps of hair blow down the windy street.

He checks his reflection in a shop window and grins. 'That's the best hair cut I've ever had!'

We both laugh at the absurdity of it. It's been so long since we laughed together.

Friday's rush-hour traffic has started, but we head off to Ethan's doctor, who is in the next county. Ethan staggers into the consultation room and beckons me to follow. He has a notion that he stands a better chance of getting a script if I accompany him. His doctor asks what's been going on, and why hasn't he been for a check-up lately.

Ethan justifies relapsing: he was upset, evicted by the community, ended up homeless; his sponsor's no good.

The doctor nods and rubs his chin. 'Taking Valium with alcohol is dangerous. It could do more harm than good.' We find he won't budge on this.

Outside it's already dark. In desperation Ethan pulls his iPhone from his pocket and calls some contacts, without success. He tries his mum's number. She picks up, and he puts the call on speakerphone.

'Mum, I need to see you,' Ethan begs, 'just for the weekend.'

There's a pause. I hold my breath, hoping she'll say yes and offer help. I feel isolated in this chaos.

'Please, Mum!'

'How much have you drunk today?' she asks.

'Nothing today! I … I'm sober.' He lies.

She can probably hear the despair in his voice, but I think she suspects he's not sober. 'All right. But I don't want any trouble. I'll cook some dinner. This is just for the weekend.'

'We're on our way,' Ethan replies.

I brace myself for our drive.

He repeatedly tops up the paper cup with red wine. Red stains the white cup, and it's soggy around the brim.

'You have to slow down drinking,' I plead. 'Stop topping up!' But he won't listen.

'Fucking Howard! You'll meet him. The fuck. He's not the black sheep. I am!' Ethan bemoans. 'He can't be trusted. I've never done anything wrong, apart from ...' He trails off.

'There's no point in this journey,' I say, 'not if you're going to shout and drink. Let's forget it. I'll turn around.'

'Fuck off! I'll shut up!' He pours another.

We're ten minutes away and Ethan's wasted. I pull into a lay-by and stop. 'Stop drinking or I'll turn back!' I warn.

Enraged, he winds the car window down and launches a full cup of wine out the window. Red wine splatters all over the upholstery and splashes up his arm, on the seat and even the interior roof. 'Fucking satisfied?' he shouts.

I glare at him and continue driving.

Howard must hear my car because he comes to greet us. Ethan's mood changes. He can't wait to jump out to hug Howard. In response, Howard smiles awkwardly, prises the bottle from Ethan's hand and discreetly hides it in a rose bush. I heave our overnight bags from the backseat and follow Howard.

Ethan's mother stands in the doorway of the kitchen/diner. She looks shaken to see that Ethan is worse for wear but leads us through to the smaller dining room. 'Hello, I'm Vicky,' she says to me, 'and you've met Howard. It's nice to meet you. It's a pity it's under these circumstances.'

'It's nice to meet you too,' I reply.

She pulls out a dining chair and asks us to sit. The small round table is set for four, and the smell of dinner wafts from the stove. She gives a weary smile and says, 'I've cooked sausages, with potatoes and runner beans.'

'Thank you; that's very kind,' I reply.

'Pour wine,' Ethan interjects, 'with dinner. Pour wine!'

'Would you sit down, please, Ethan. I'll pour wine,' Howard says. He pops the cork and pours out three glasses and half a glass for Ethan.

Ethan smiles. 'Good!'

Vicky plates up and seats herself. 'Do sit, Ethan.'

Ethan sways and plonks himself down.

Howard makes small talk, asking questions like how I met Ethan.

All of a sudden, Ethan falls off his chair. Howard manages to grab the table just in time before Ethan upends it. Vicky puts down her fork and pushes her meal away. I don't know where to look.

'Leave him; just eat,' Howard says.

I take small bites of potato and sips of wine. It's dismal. This is the first time his mother and I have met, and Ethan's in this state.

'Fucking hell! What just happened?' Ethan yells. He belches and struggles to get up but falls flat on his back and waves his legs in the air.

I look at Vicky and Howard, uncertain if they'll throw us out. Howard continues eating, ignoring what's going on. Vicky puts her hands up to her face and lets out a wail like a wounded animal, then starts to weep her heart out.

'Ethan, sit at the table,' I say.

He gets on all fours, rests his chin on the table next to his plate, then opens his mouth wide, chases a potato and wolfs it down. He pokes out his tongue to show us the contents of his mouth.

'I thought he might be bad, but I didn't think he'd be *this* bad,' Vicky says. She blows her nose. Her shoulders shake with her heavy sobs. Howard doesn't try to console her; he seems to have detached himself from the drama.

Vicky prepares black coffee to sober Ethan up.

'Fucking coffee!' Ethan plops down on the sofa.

'Do stop swearing,' Vicky says.

'Do fuck off,' Ethan retorts.

'Stop! You know how I can't bear swearing.'

'Cunts!' Ethan retorts.

Without another word Vicky pulls out her phone and starts filming him. 'What do you think then, Magda? About all this? Eh?'

I don't answer.

Ethan stands up to make a speech. 'Do you know the problem with me? I'm too kind.'

In unison Vicky and Howard say, 'Oh, do come off it!'

Ethan sees red. 'Fuck off! Who are you anyway? You married that cheating cunt who fucked your best friend. And others! You know it. I'm telling it the way it is!' Ethan snatches a screwdriver from the kitchen worktop and lunges at Howard with it.

Howard wrestles Ethan to the floor, forces him onto his stomach, straddles Ethan's back and snatches the weapon out of his hand. He holds Ethan's right arm behind his back and when he starts kicking to free himself, Vicky helps to hold Ethan down. When he stops kicking, Howard remains sitting on him, and Vicky warns Howard she's calling the cops. She dials 999 and asks for them to attend, then she makes another call to a friend and asks if she can help calm down the drama.

The police arrive, but Vicky dithers when asked if she wants Ethan arrested. They take Ethan away and drop him off in town where he can sober up.

The friend arrives. 'Hi, I'm Denise,' she says.

It's bizarre that I know all about Ethan having had drunken flings with her a few decades ago.

'A night on the streets might shock him into getting sober,' she says.

Everyone goes to bed. Moments later someone knocks nonstop at the front door.

It's Ethan, of course. 'Oi! Open the door!' he shouts from outside.

The lights go on and everyone charges downstairs to see what's happening. The patio door slides open and in walks Ethan.

When he sees Denise, he can't believe his eyes and charges towards her to give her a big bear hug, while Howard pays the taxi driver for Ethan's fare.

The minute Howard walks back in the room, Ethan starts swearing, hurling the most offensive, obscene abuse I've ever heard him dish out.

I feel so embarrassed.

The way this has got out of control is utterly incomprehensible to me, because I naïvely thought he'd taper the booze, or at least behave himself, if only for his mother's sake. I thought she'd be his awakening—the key for him to stop. It's mad to think an addict can quit their addiction for someone else's sake; they can't. That's the nature of the disease. It has to be for them; I ought to know this. The drama is so upsetting. I can barely speak.

Vicky sighs. 'That's enough. Let's get you to bed, Ethan.'

I rummage around in our overnight bags for toothbrushes while Ethan kicks off his trainers and flops on the bed. A knock sounds on the bedroom door. It opens, and to my amazement, two cops walk in. Vicky must have called them again.

They question each of us separately downstairs. Vicky implores me to cooperate by giving a statement that incriminates

Ethan, but I won't. I don't see how it would help him. Ethan looks dumbstruck. I can see him trying to figure out why the cops have been called out a second time after he'd calmed down.

The police continue questioning me: Has Ethan been violent to you in the past? Assaulted you? All to which I lie by saying, 'No'.

Just when I think I've got Ethan off the hook, I see him being handcuffed and arrested. Howard grabs Ethan's parka. No one knows where his socks and trainers are, so Vicky grabs the first thing to hand for Ethan's feet. I watch helplessly as Ethan shuffles out of the door with a policeman holding onto his arm. I look down at his feet and notice he is wearing a pair of Vicky's baby pink mule slippers with orange sequins and feathers; they're three sizes too small. The police bundle him into their van and speed off.

There's a shocked silence.

Vicky ambles over to me. 'We had him arrested so he can get a detox. The police or the courts can arrange rehab fast. It's for the best,' she says. 'And for the record, all he said was true, about Howard's affairs. Everything. It's ancient history now, so he should drop it.'

She lowers her voice and continues, 'We've been through hell with Ethan's addiction. His crack addiction started around the same time as his prostitute problem. In the past we've arranged free housing for him to live with our relatives, found him private flat rentals and paid his deposits and rent. We've paid off his debts too. I even moved to get away from him. I can't cope with him anymore! Neither can any of us. He sabotages his recovery every time. And his violence is another worry. He assaulted his dad in the past. We have to be cruel to be kind. Hopefully, he'll get sent to jail and get help there.' She looks at me as if she expects a response, or maybe it's her attempt to clear some of the fog for my own good.

'Try to get some sleep. We'll talk tomorrow,' she adds.

I return to the guest wing and plop down on the bed. Something bulky lies under the duvet. I pull back the covers and discover umpteen bottles of wine hidden there. After returning them to Vicky, I finally snuggle into bed. I'm worried sick about Ethan.

Chapter TWEnty-One

I'm shaken awake. Denise's face is inches away from mine.

'Wake up! You have to leave. Now!' she says. 'The police are on their way here to take witness statements, and if Ethan returns and sees your car outside, there'll be trouble. And have you seen his phone? The police said he's lost his phone! Quickly. Go!'

Without delay I dress, scoop up our bags and load my car. I can't find Ethan's iPhone, and the battery must be flat because it goes to voicemail each time I call it. I spot Ethan's socks and trainers under a set of drawers and imagine him clippity clopping around the police cell in Vicky's fluffy mules.

I give his trainers to Howard so he can send them via the police to Ethan. Without so much as a wash or a coffee, I pack my car and fire up the engine.

Before I speed off, Howard meanders towards my car to waffle apologies about Vicky being too tired to say goodbye, then he shoos me away. 'Go. Before the police arrive.'

I drive aimlessly for a few hours, then stop at an old coaching inn to rest. The last few days replay in my mind. My hopes of Vicky working with me to get Ethan straightened out have been blown away. She wants him jailed and out of her hair. The trauma he has caused me doesn't register with his family; they can't acknowledge it. Their coping mechanism is tough love. I don't get it.

My phone rings, number unknown.

'It's me. Ethan! I'm sober. I'm at the police station. I'm allowed this one call. I've been interviewed. Police told me you wouldn't back up the allegations!'

'I didn't,' I reply. 'I didn't say anything. That's harsh, getting you arrested. I can't work them out.'

'I know. I told you what Howard was like. Anyway, I told my police station solicitor about how Denise seduced me in the past, so I should get off. Can you meet me later when I'm released?'

'Yes, and I found your phone.'

'Thanks. And thanks for not grassing. I'll call you later.'

The first thing I notice when I see Ethan is that he's wearing his own shoes. He doesn't seem surprised by my running back to him. I'm beginning to resemble his boomerang. He looks much better than the other night. He's pleased no further action will be taken due to lack of evidence.

'Did they slag me off?' Ethan asks.

'Well, they were upset. Your mum thought that by getting you arrested you'd get offered a free rehab and detoxed. She said that's why she did it.'

'It doesn't work like that.' He checks my phone to be sure I haven't been in contact with Vicky.

'We should get out of here,' I say.

I don't know how Ethan can escape this cycle of addiction without support, and I don't think tough love is the answer. I'm optimistic Ethan can beat this. When he does, we'll be happy together.

Chapter Twenty-two

Theo phones to see how Ethan's feeling. He's decided to take over as the family point of contact, and he gives Ethan pep talks in an attempt to talk him into getting sober. Theo knows the family resentments are sky high.

It's dark, pouring with rain. Ethan says I should drive to the mall where there are public toilets so he can freshen up. He's pissed but insists on having a wash. The disabled toilets are closed, so I tell him I'll wait for him by the main doors while he goes to the men's restroom. He confiscates my car keys but allows me to keep my phone, just in case we get separated. I wait by the doors and after half an hour, I wonder what's taking so long. I call him, but there's no answer.

Only two stores stock booze. I check them both but find he's not at either. Perhaps the information desk can make a public announcement over the public address system. They agree to call out his name. Moments later I can't believe my ears when I hear Ethan yelling. Looking terrified, he runs towards me as fast as he can with a security guard hot on his heels. He runs straight into me, almost knocking me over, throws his arms around me and hugs me tightly.

'This man is drunk,' the security guard says. 'We don't allow inebriated people in the mall. He has to leave at once!'

'Where was he?' I ask.

'Tucked up in bed, fast asleep in one of our display beds in John Lewis home furnishings. Take him away before I call the police.'

The drive-thru is close by, so I pull in to buy food—junk food is better than nothing to soak up his booze. He eats half and chucks the rest out of the window.

'When are you taking me to the mall?' he asks, rubbing his bloated belly.

'We've been. Remember? You took a nap in John Lewis.'

'What nap?'

'Never mind.'

Ethan spends the next few days getting checked by medics, choring booze and drinking. Having him as my passenger is such a burden. I'll get the rap should he cause an accident by jumping out of my moving car.

Rain continues to pelt down on the metal roof. Ethan stares out at the rain, smokes, picks his nose, and swigs beer. He can't face breakfast. His phone rings,

'Hi, Ethan! It's Tia from the alcohol and drugs centre. Your name is next on our list. We can book you in for an assessment for a non-residential detox. Would you come in to see us tomorrow morning?'

'Tomorrow? Really. Yes, so you'll detox me tomorrow?' Ethan replies.

'No, tomorrow's your assessment. Your detox date will be the following week.'

'Oh, I see. Yes, I'll be there!' Ethan replies.

The out-patient detoxification treatment programme will get him off the booze, provided someone supervises Ethan's detox. Also, for safety reasons, he has to detox at a residential address and must attend the clinic every morning for the ten-day treatment.

Ethan gets straight on the phone to Theo.

'That's a stroke of luck, Ethan. After your detox you'll need recovery somewhere comfortable and safe. I'll call a Christian community charity on your behalf.'

Ethan thanks him, although he'd rather be offered his spare bedroom, but he's burnt his bridges.

The next morning, keen to give a good impression at his assessment, Ethan wants to wash and shave. It's down to me to drive somewhere he can freshen up.

I miss sober conversations with Ethan. I miss Frida and Sylvia even more; I miss my life. I'm determined to get it all back, with Ethan by my side, clean and sober. We'll pick up where we left off. He's too out of it to be aware of our predicament, and by the time we reach the clinic, he's smashed.

On our way to reception, he shoves handfuls of mints into his mouth to mask the stench of booze. Ethan sits next to a depressed-looking man and strikes up a conversation.

'You here for detox?'

'Yeah, this is day five. I'm rattling like a mofo,' the man replies.

Ethan's quite taken with him and gives him a hug, followed by a vigorous rubbing of the man's shaved head. 'A rub for luck!' Ethan calls out before planting sloppy kisses on his head. He keels over on the floor, laughing hysterically. Tears of drunken joy roll down his cheeks while he clutches his bloated belly.

The man is called into the treatment room. Tia punches the door security code and opens it, but she doesn't walk into the waiting area; a serious looking key worker enters instead.

He walks over to where Ethan is on the floor, still waving his legs in the air. 'Sorry to keep you. It's bad news. Your detox assessment can't proceed. I've been watching you through that glass window. You can't even stand. Let alone be assessed. Make an appointment with Tia for next week. And don't turn up here in this kind of state again, otherwise we'll postpone,' he says.

Ethan looks flabbergasted. 'Yeah! B ... but!'

'But nothing,' the man snaps before marching off.

My heart sinks.

Chapter Twenty-three

Tia comes over with a breathalyser in her hand. 'This is the way out, Ethan. Try again next week. You have to blow below ninety.'

Ethan storms towards the door, grabs me by my sleeve and roughly drags me out of the clinic. The tirade begins.

'This! All THIS is your fault, you fucking cunt!' His shouts reverberate around the small clinic's car park where I'd parked.

'Don't make a scene!' I plead.

He lunges towards me and shoves me over. I try to get up, but he gives me another push, and I'm back on the ground with him shouting and swearing in my face. He grips my arm to pull me up. While still tightly gripping my arm, he marches me to my car, walking so fast I can't keep up. The scene plays out under the watchful eye of a security camera.

Ethan hasn't seen a medic in a few days, and he's a dreadful hypochondriac, so he insists on visiting A&E. In reception he clowns around and catches the eye of a weirdo who whispers in his ear. They dash to the loo together and re-emerge five minutes later.

Ethan meanders over to me and says, 'Quick, you gotta pay

this dude a tenner! I just scored a bump of coke from him!' Ethan's so thirsty that he goes to a vending machine, leaving his jacket behind.

I've had enough. As soon as he's out of sight, I reach into his pocket to retrieve my car keys, then flee towards the basement car park.

Just as I start my car Ethan appears out of nowhere and dives in front of it, forcing me to stop. He throws himself on the bonnet. 'Darling, I'm sorry! I won't let you down again. I'm sick. I'm an addict. If I had cancer everyone would feel sorry for me. But no one gets it. Only you. Help me,' he pleads.

I feel trapped. On the other hand, I can see he's in the grips of this disease. He alleges that his brain receptors require booze to come down off the cocaine, to prevent him giving a seizure.

The open-all-hours shop sells booze that's well over-priced. Before the transaction for his vodka has gone through, Ethan grabs the bottle from the shop counter and dashes outside, eager to swig it straight. I hear a smash, and he walks back into the shop looking dumbfounded.

'I need another!' he yells.

The cashier looks daggers at him.

'All right! I'm sorry about the mess,' Ethan says. 'All right? Just wine, instead. Please?'

My book where I log Ethan's alcohol consumption is filling up fast.

'You and that logbook,' he scoffs. 'One thing I hate about you is you're so boring. Addicts interest me.'

I don't react; I know he's being provocative.

For once, Ethan makes an effort to slow down his all-night drinking for his next assessment. We arrive at the clinic at 9 am. Ethan can stand at the reception desk without swaying. He's tipsy, but sober enough to know where he's at.

Tia looks closely, but her steady gaze doesn't give anything away.

After ten minutes of anxious waiting, she calls Ethan. The door buzzes us through, and Tia shows us into a small office where a nurse asks the same old questions. He blows over ninety on the breathalyser. He has another go, breathes in deeply through his nose—like a diver without their aqualung—and steadily blows for so long we can't believe our eyes, considering he's a chain-smoker. He keeps blowing until he's red in the face.

The nurse nods while she scribbles notes, then looks up and says, 'So, Ethan. All done. Bravo, you did it. We'll go ahead with your detox. It'll be a ten-day out-patient detox. We'll administer diazepam every morning, under supervision, and taper you down daily. On your first day, try not to drink too much before you arrive. We'll see you on Monday. Make an appointment at the front desk.'

Ethan looks stunned, but nods and heads towards the front desk. Before I can follow him, Tia lets the door slam shut behind him. Ethan looks for me through the door's window. He tries but can't open it without the code.

'Magda, step in here a moment.' Tia points towards a small office.

I follow her and take a seat.

She offers me a leaflet. 'Take this; you need it. Call them; they're for people like you who are struggling with an alcoholic or addict. We saw what happened last week, the altercation in the car park, and we had to file a report about what he did to you for our case workers in the upstairs offices.'

'Oh. But ... I—'

She interrupts me: 'It's been filed. We'll see you on Monday for his detox appointment.'

Ethan would never allow me to call the organisation, but it's strange that I matter enough to be offered a helpline.

By Friday we're counting down the days to his detox. Ethan's belly hurts like mad, whether he drinks wine or beer, he gets acid reflux, and antacid tablets do nothing for it. He wants me to drive to an out-of-town A&E, one where he isn't known. We sit in the waiting area until his name is called, then we follow a nurse to a consultation room.

She checks his blood pressure, asks him the usual questions and decides he needs a liver-function blood test, a saline drip for dehydration and a vitamin B injection.

Eventually a doctor peeps behind the curtain. I reiterate how he has relapsed and starts his detox on Monday. The doctor has a serious expression; he can see Ethan's already going into withdrawal because he hasn't had booze in a few hours. The doctor dashes off and returns after a few minutes. He walks to where Ethan's lying on the gurney and informs him that the hospital has a bed available on the men's general ward. He can be admitted for a few nights and start a Valium detox straight away.

A porter wheels him to the ward, and a nurse gives Ethan hospital pyjamas. I sit in the armchair at his bedside. A moment later Ethan shits his PJ's. I approach a nurse to ask for help with clean stuff.

'You can stay on the ward,' she says. 'Don't worry about the visiting hours. Sleep in the armchair if you like. Tell us what you want from the menu, and just ask if you'd like tea or coffee.'

I smile. 'Thanks.'

She turns to Ethan and says, 'Ethan, aren't you lucky to have someone who supports you?'

'Oh. Yes, I suppose I am,' Ethan feebly agrees.

During the night Ethan starts to sweat profusely. The toxins seep from his pores, and he feels too ill to eat, drink water, or even chain-smoke. Since his hospital admission, he's been as nice as pie to me.

Ethan laps up the attention from the medical staff, enjoying being cared for as a sick patient whose illness isn't self-inflicted. Nothing can be done to change the stigma attached to addiction.

The only time I leave Ethan's hospital bedside is when I go to the loo or the vending machine, even then I leave my phone and car keys on his table where he can see them.

By Sunday Ethan feels well enough for me to leave him resting in bed while I race to a superstore for essentials and fuel.

Before Ethan's discharge, a doctor pulls the curtain around Ethan's bed and examines his bloated tummy. 'Your liver is slightly enlarged,' he says. 'It'll take time to go down, and it can only recover if you stop drinking.'

Ethan's eyes widen. 'My liver! Enlarged? Am I going to die?'

The doctor shakes his head and smiles. 'You won't die today. But you'll die of an alcohol-related disease, if you carry on like this.' He signs Ethan's discharge notes.

Theo's booked a chalet at a trailer park for us. I collect the keys from reception while Ethan waits in my car. Our chalet is one of dozens crammed in a grassy field. The weather's bad, so it's good to have shelter.

Ethan chain-smokes and runs a bath, but as soon as he's out of it, he gets the sweats. I notice the bruises on his arms from the drips and blood tests. He can't shake off his cravings, so he steadies his nerves with double doses of Valium from the hospital pharmacy. When he soaks the bed, I change the soggy sheets.

By 10 pm he has popped all his Valium, and the increased dose knocks him out. I lie beside him and doze off.

Ethan shakes me awake. He looks scared. 'I woke up, opened my eyes, but I couldn't move,' he says in a panic. 'It was like I was paralysed or something. I tried to wake you up, but my arms wouldn't move! I could only blink!'

He calls an ambulance so a medic can check his heart. We're hard to find—the chalets all look the same in the dark—but the paramedic eventually locates us. She asks the same questions as usual, checks his pupils, blood pressure and heart. According to her he'll be fine.

Thank God it's Monday. Ethan's tried to taper his booze intake all morning. A woman in the clinic waiting room catches my attention. Her partner, sitting beside her, can't keep awake. In slow motion he slumps sideways, sliding into her lap.

She angrily tries to shake him awake. 'He's just relapsed again,' she fumes.

Looking remorseful, he tries to open his glazed eyes. When he reaches out to try and touch her ringed left hand, she snatches it away and fiddles with the ring.

'It's a challenge!' I say to her.

'I've had it up to here!' she retorts, touching her temple with two fingers like she's holding a pistol to her head.

Ethan's name is called.

Tia's pleased to see Ethan's in better shape. She leads us to the medical room where a woman takes Ethan's blood pressure. Her trainee colleague does his weight, height and asks the usual questions.

After he has swallowed his first dose of diazepam, the woman asks Ethan to open his mouth. She has a good look inside to make sure he has swallowed the pill, asking him to lift his tongue and move it side to side, left, right, up, down, then say 'Ahhh.' She then reminds Ethan that it's vitally important that he not consume alcohol. When she suggests he has another vitamin B injection, he readily agrees. In the rush to have the jab, he yanks his trousers down, exposes his bare backside and bends over. The nurse stifles a giggle.

We make an appointment for the next morning for his next Valium dose.

The chalet is about an hour's drive from the clinic, depending on traffic; we stop en route to shop for Ethan's snacks. I've got more errands to run—bedding laundry, preparing dinner. He relaxes while I work like a trojan. At the end of the day, when I have a bath, I have to keep the bathroom door open, as Ethan's paranoid I'll contact someone. He flops on the bed to relax and opens his computer to check his emails.

'Oh, wonderful!' he calls out with a grin like the cat who's got the cream.

'What is?' I hope it's someone offering to lend a hand.

'I checked my mails, and my Koemi has messaged me. And there's one from Trina.'

'Gee. That's wonderful,' I say with just a touch of sarcasm. If they knew the full story, they'd avoid him like the plague. I'm scared that a disagreement between us will set him off, though, so I let it slide. His insolence and duplicity are well and truly getting on my nerves.

He knows my help with his detox appointments is essential, so he's secretive about replying to his emails.

Late in the night, he gets spooked by nightmares and wakes me by squeezing onto me so tightly that I can't breathe. I reassure him that sleep disturbances are to be expected while he's detoxing. Four days into detox, he's already looking better, and by day five the clinic agree that Ethan can complete his detox under the supervision of the Christian Brothers. Tia's colleague hands me his meds—Valium and vitamin B tablets—with instructions.

Theo arranges for Ethan to stay with the Christian Brothers' farmstead community, where he'll be charged a nominal sum from his welfare benefits towards his bed and board. It's an ideal place where he can recuperate during early recovery. Ethan's keen as mustard to get settled.

Brother Matthew from the community calls to ask what time we'll arrive. 'We're all looking forward to welcoming Ethan. We think he might be anxious, so we'd like to invite you to stay for the first three days in the guest block. It'll help him settle. This is a difficult time for him. We have a waiting list of people, including addicts in recovery, who want to join us, but we've held a meeting and decided to accommodate Ethan straight away.'

'That's kind of you. Thank you!' I reply.

Our no-smoking chalet stinks where Ethan's been chain-smoking, so he squirts his perfume around. For the first time in ages, he manages to fasten his trousers—only just—where his belly is not as bloated. The journey to the Christian Brothers' farmstead is a few hours' drive away.

Chapter Twenty-four

The closer we get to the farmstead, the more uneasy Ethan becomes. He chain-smokes and plucks at his patchy eyebrows. The winding roads become narrower. Rows of pretty cottages become fewer, until there are none, just mile after mile of countryside.

'I'm having second thoughts. I don't wanna go! Turn around!' Ethan blurts out.

'We're nearly there,' I reply. 'You must give it a try.'

'No, I've got a gut feeling. I'm not gonna fit in. I've changed my mind.'

'You're just nervous,' I say. I'm used to Ethan chopping and changing his muddled mind.

He shrugs. 'Maybe.'

The Jacobean farmstead is more remote than I'd imagined, but we finally reach it. A handful of vehicles park in front of a barn, so I pull in beside them. We walk towards the large white, ancient manor house, past refurbished outbuildings and rows of horse loose boxes that have been converted into living quarters. No one answers the door, so we push it open and an indoor bell tinkles. Inside is gloomy. The ceilings are high; the stone hallway floor is muddy where wellington boots are lined up in rows and wax coats hang on coat hooks. A rotund woman emerges.

She smiles and greets us. 'You found us, then. And you're just in time for tea. Brother Matthew's in the diner. Come follow me.' She leads us into the adjacent dining room. Large, long wooden tables with benches and chairs that would easily seat thirty dominate the room. It feels like going back in time.

Apart from a water urn for hot water that's used for tea and coffee, I see no modern gadgets. Ethan's eyes scan the room. He fiddles in his pocket to check his iPhone and finds he has no signal, not one bar.

A black-clad brother with a large cross dangling around his neck sits at one of the tables with a stack paperwork. He stands when he sees us. 'Hello, hello. Welcome. I'm Brother Matthew. We meet at last,' he says cheerfully.

I recognise his voice from our phone calls, but he's older than I'd imagined. He seems genuinely happy to see us, as if he's greeting long-lost friends, which is something, seeing as Ethan's been ostracized by almost everyone he knows.

'Let me show you both around. Ethan, you'll be spending your first week in the converted loose boxes near the courtyard, and when you've done your week's probation, you'll be allocated a private room in the outbuilding quarters. Magda, you'll be staying in the guest block.'

We follow him while he strides outside towards a small maze with a fifteenth century brick chapel in the centre. He leads us to a horse loose box and opens the top half of the door. Inside looks cosy, but it's very basic, just a single bed, a small heater, a light and a basin. My room is in a brick block, one of six super-warm rooms with new en-suite bathrooms. Compared to where Ethan's staying, it's swanky.

Brother Matthew hands us an itinerary print-out with the

details of mealtimes and ground rules. 'Ask if you have any questions or need anything. I'll see you both at supper.'

We walk back to my car to fetch Ethan's luggage.

'I'm not sure about this place,' he says.

I sigh. 'We've just got here.'

'I don't like it!'

'You'll feel better once you've eaten.'

It's not until supper time, when everyone gathers together, that I see how many inmates reside here. The dining room's full of various types of people, all sitting in rows at the tables. Despite the dining room being full to capacity, it's quiet. One of the brothers leads grace before eating, then gradually conversations quietly get underway that break the silence. Ovenware of hot potatoes, vegetables and fish are placed on each table.

A man who looks around thirty sits opposite Ethan and strikes up a conversation. 'Hi! My name's Hugo.'

'Hi, I'm Ethan,'

'Hi, Ethan. Welcome. You look worried. What's up?'

'Oh, do I … I'm sorry; it's not you!' Ethan replies.

Hugo laughs. 'I was the same when I first got here ten months ago.'

'Ten months! That's ages! Why are you here?' Ethan asks.

'Addiction. Cocaine. I had to leave London and be in the countryside. Rehab didn't work out for me. I'm ten months clean now. You get used to it, takes a few months. My partner phones me every day.'

Ethan nods. 'I'm an addict, an alcoholic. I'm almost a week clean and sober. How do you get a phone signal? Mine's not working.'

'Oh yeah, it's only Vodaphone that gets a good signal here,' Hugo replies.

'Thanks; I'll have to get a new sim card.' Ethan's fretting

about his signal. His iPhone did happen to catch a bar outside the chapel.

After supper a team of inmates clear the table and the inmates on the rota for washing-up make a start on the mountain of dishes.

Coffee and biscuits are served in the lounge, not that Ethan's interested; he wants to go to the chapel to try and call Theo. As soon as Ethan gets through to Theo, he lets off steam by saying how much he dislikes the farmstead.

Theo tries to reason with him. 'Where else can you go?' I hear him say. 'You need to be away from old triggers and temptations. Get some clean time. Who else will give you accommodation that's this cheap, after all the times you've messed up? Keep your eyes on the prize.'

The prize being sobriety. It's not what Ethan wants to hear.

At bedtime we go to our separate accommodation, but within minutes I hear tapping on my door. I instinctively know it's Ethan, which is against the rules. He creeps inside and closes my door without making a sound.

'You can't leave me here,' he whispers. 'I can't hack it. Inmates aren't even allowed cars. Look at the restrictions. Look at how remote this place is. I won't even be able to get to AA meetings or find a new sponsor!'

'What are your options?' I reply.

He shrugs. 'I dunno.' Instead of returning to his room, he continues to talk until the early hours.

The December weather's biting. It feels colder in the desolate countryside than the city. Howling wind, endless rain and gloomy clouds create an eerie atmosphere. We've spoken to a few residents. Some sit in silence like medicated zombies in a world of their own. The old manor house is full of addicts in recovery, drifters, tent dwellers, the unwanted, the unknown, nomads and wanderers—one of whom told us that he'd walked ten miles to get here, because he's so desperate for a weekend of shelter, a hot meal, warmth and company.

Apart from house chores, there is not a lot to do to pass the time. There's not so much as a corner shop for miles, and there's no TV. The slow shared WiFi can only be used for an allocated amount of time to check emails or place online orders, and someone inspects each delivered package to ensure it contains nothing contraband. Residents are expected to integrate, not leave the site without permission, and must comply with the rota duties, including milking cows before the early communal breakfast. Once a week a supervised trip into town is allowed when the minibus is used, which is when attending the weekly AA meeting is possible. The farmstead is strictly dry and random breathalyser tests take place. Residents must abide by the ground rules or face eviction. Away days or weekends away are forbidden. The rules are stringent, more so than the relaxed community that suited Ethan before. The rigid rules help retain order in the large number of residents.

In addition, Brother Matthew tells Ethan he can't have visitors for his first three months of residency, including Christmas, which is just a matter of weeks away.

'I can't believe my life is so shit!' Ethan whinges. 'And to think I was living the high life once, with Koemi. Now look at me!'

His mention of Koemi jogs my memory. 'What did you do about that email she sent?'

'Umm. Just a teeny reply, while you had your back turned, darling. Only to tell her I was grateful she messaged me.'

'Oh. I see. And Trina, the camper? What about that email?'

'Umm. Okay. I admit, behind your back I secretly wrote her a teeny reply as well, only to say how lovely it was to hear from her!' He won't even make eye contact with me.

'Oh. That's charming, Ethan! Charming, secretive, and ungrateful! You're stringing people along. You don't want me speaking to my daughters, or anyone else for that matter, and here you are, reconnecting with old flames on the quiet, while you make me work like your unpaid slave.'

He winces. 'I promise I won't be secretive again.'

'Where is everyone since you relapsed?' I ask. I'm genuinely curious.

He fidgets, plucks an eyebrow and rolls a cigarette without answering.

Ethan's actions, his secrecy, lies, and shadiness are an insult. I wonder if my role in all this is nothing more than his selfish requirement for an unpaid skivvy. A chauffeur. A full-time carer, and an unpaid one to boot, as well as a financial source—an all-round drudge.

I feel bewildered. Ethan's hidden a lot of his addiction history from me. It's a mystery why the pieces don't fit together. I don't know what to say or do. Because I'm so hurt, I'd like to have some space from him, or get some sleep, but Ethan won't allow that to happen. He rambles his resentments for the entire night until he returns to his loose box.

The farmstead bell rings at 7 am for breakfast, my last one here. Ethan's already pacing in the courtyard when I see him. Brother Matthew flings open the main door and calls out.

'Morning, Ethan! Guess what? Your mother's just called to say she's dropping by today for a quick visit.'

It transpires that Theo has spoken to Vicky informing her that Ethan is at the farmstead. We haven't seen her since the night he was arrested less than a month ago. Ethan's surprised she's driving all the way here. The prospect of seeing her makes him edgy at the breakfast table, so he tries to make himself useful to distract himself. Before long, we hear the sound of a car approaching.

Vicky parks outside the farmhouse and greets Ethan by giving him a hug. 'You look so much better than the last time I saw you!'

'Oh, umm … thanks. Do I? … Look I'm sorry about that night. I really am!' he says in his best Bertie accent, one he hasn't used in ages.

'It was a terrible night, but let's not go into it,' Vicky replies.

'Yeah, right,' Ethan replies. 'How about I make you tea? And show you around?'

We walk together towards the farmhouse. Vicky scans the converted outbuildings where the full-time residents live. She admires the courtyard and beyond, where the hills are visible through a patchy mist. Her eyes grow wide in awe and her face lights up at the unspoiled farmstead. 'Ethan, you're so lucky to be offered this place for your recovery. It's perfect! You have to surrender to recovery and embrace this opportunity.'

'Yes, Mum. Surrender,' he replies.

Vicky and I go shopping together in the nearest town, a half-hour's drive away. I spot a Quaker building; perhaps that's where the AA meetings are held. We find a phone shop where she buys Ethan a cheap handset and a Vodaphone sim, so he won't feel so cut off, plus some small gifts for Christmas. On the drive back, accelerating along the miles of windy, country lanes, she becomes serious.

'I'm desperate for this to work out,' she says. 'I think it's his last chance. Howard doesn't want me to have anything to do with Ethan again. But I told him, how can I not? He's my son! But my worry is, he's now obsessed with you.'

I'm so alarmed by what she's said, my heart skips a beat. Howard's grudge is raw, but I've had worse treatment from

Ethan that I've cast aside. Also, she thinks the answer to Ethan's sobriety is to embrace the farmstead without support. But his needs are complex. It's like she doesn't know him. She says Ethan's obsessed with me, but she doesn't know that he's too sneaky to be trusted, and that he's even been emailing his ex-sweethearts while I slave for him. That's not him being obsessed with me; that's more like co-dependency.

Ethan goes quiet when she leaves, as if he senses matriarchal abandonment, reminding him, a grown man, of his rejection in childhood. I collect my overnight bag and prepare to leave.

'Did she mention Howard?' Ethan asks.

I want to give a truthful answer, one that's not too painful for him to hear. 'This is between you and me if I tell you.'

'I promise it'll always be between you and me; I wouldn't break a promise,' he replies.

'Okay. She said Howard wants her to have nothing to do with you, but she won't agree to that. She forgives you and wants to see you get better.'

'See? I told you Howard wants me out of the way!'

I hope Ethan will keep in mind that his mum's desperate for him to find recovery, and I trust he won't let me down by his blabbermouth.

Brother Matthew reminds Ethan that it is lunchtime. I feel rushed to say goodbye and hop into my car. Ethan walks alongside my car, puffing on a cigarette while I pull away. He waves with a forced smile.

Chapter Twenty-five

Two miles up the dirt track road, I pull into a lay-by to take deep breaths and reflect. Just thinking about what we've been through makes my heart pound; and here we are, on the path to recovery. It's been a rocky start for us, and I can't visit him until March.

I have a mixed bag of feelings, sadness with optimism. Ultimately this is a lifeline. He has shelter with kind people. He won't have financial worries—his welfare money won't be affected. He's away from triggers, and he's out of his family's hair. I'm relieved he's safe, warm and literally dry.

Driving is peaceful without Ethan by my side.

I hope to spend a week with Sylvia and another with Frida. Up until Ethan derailed me, I've strived to give all the affection and protection to my daughters that my mother had been unable to give me. I'll keep conversation simple, so not to cause upset by going into detail about all that's gone on with Ethan. I hadn't even been aware Frida's job has caused RSI; she might have to quit her job over it.

Ethan hasn't called all evening. It's not a good sign; something's probably up. I send him a text to see how he's feeling. He waits ten minutes to send a reply to make me feel guilty: *I've run out of gummy bears. Nearest shop is a hundred miles away.*

Over the next few days, Ethan's phone calls become more frequent. He's dying to leave. Whilst driving to do an errand, my phone rings. I pull over to answer; it's Ethan. My phone battery's almost dead, so I plug it into the car lighter to charge. For the first few minutes he sounds lonely, then without warning his mood turns sour.

'Have you talked to any of my people? Theo? My mum? Eh? How about Cedric?' he snaps.

'I haven't spoken to anyone. I've only received texts wishing you luck,' I reply.

'Is that a fact? Because I don't buy that!'

For the next two hours, I make the mistake of defending myself. When he's finished his tirade, I shakily start my car, but find it's dead. I realise my phone's been charging with the engine switched off throughout my admonishment. I stand in the darkness and rain while I attempt to flag down motorists for a jump-start. On the verge of tears, stranded and soaked, I'm mystified by Ethan's abuse and controlling behaviour. Eventually a motorist stops to help me.

Within the hour, Ethan calls again. I fear the repercussions if I don't pick up.

'I phoned to say sorry!' he coos. 'Don't hang up!'

'Thanks for apologising, but I can't speak; I'm drained.'

'No, you're not drained. Listen to me. I have to leave here. I can't take it. The last five days have been murder. It's boring, too restrictive. If you don't pick me up by tomorrow, I'm gonna walk to the nearest pub and relapse. And it will be ALL your fault.'

I sigh. Someone has to help him. And there's only me.

While driving all the way back to the farmstead, where I'd left him only six days previously, I'm filled with trepidation. So much for spending two weeks with my daughters. Ethan's forced me to postpone that.

It's pitch dark with no lights in the eerie country lanes. My SatNav gets me lost. Try as I might to call Ethan to ask him for directions, his line is busy. At last, I find my bearings. When I pull into the farmstead, I see Ethan outside the manor house. All his bags are packed, stacked and waiting to be loaded back into my car. His phone's glued to his ear, and while continuing to speak to whoever it is, he starts loading up without so much as looking up or saying hello.

We say goodbye to the Christian brothers.

'Good luck, Ethan. Remember, don't ever pick up a drink!' Brother Matthew warns.

'I know; never again,' he replies.

Ethan jumps into my passenger seat. Despite the countless sugar-coated text messages he'd sent beforehand, reminding me how we belong together because our love is one of a kind, he moodily taps a postcode into my SatNav and instructs me to drive. An hour later we arrive at the destination he's chosen, a shabby B&B.

His mood is hostile, and he isn't done with making demands. He starts with my phone, checking my texts and call history, then confiscating it. Next, he rummages through my backpack, searches my pockets, then checks my computer's browser history, my Facebook account and my emails. I don't dare object; I'm as obedient as a well-trained dog. It's just like old times.

Chapter TWenty-six

We climb the flights of stairs to our room, and as soon as we're inside, Ethan flings open the window to smoke. The view below shows the backyard where the bins are kept. He's chosen the gloomy room, so doesn't blame me for the booking; if anything, his mood has improved now that he's quit the farmstead. I know his niceness is fleeting; he's prone to mood swings. He searches online for a better hotel, which means more reckless spending, but he says his comfort is essential; otherwise he'll relapse. Our next hotel, a Georgian building, has a coastal view.

At breakfast Vicky calls unexpectedly. Ethan places his phone on the table.

'Hi, Ethan, can you talk?' she asks.

'Hi, Mum. Yes, I can, I was about to call you.'

'Good, I wanted to ask if you need me to send you anything to the farmstead.'

'Oh! About that. Yes, I mean, no. I left; I'm not there anymore.' There's a pause while Vicky takes that in. 'Mum, it was weird there, and nobody liked me. Not just that, I couldn't get to AA meetings.'

'That's a pity,' Vicky says. 'I had high hopes you'd stay there. So long as you stay sober, you'll be fine. Perhaps we could meet for lunch at Claudia's café tomorrow?'

The little village café is an hour's drive from our hotel, and we have a mad rush to get there. When we arrive Phoebe and Vicky are already seated at a table. They stand to greet us.

While we're studying the menu, Ethan asks, 'Is Howard all right?'

'Yes, he's still cooling off,' Vicky replies.

'Good, I'm sorry about all that. I'll make it up to you and Howard. And I've already made plans to get my life sorted. I'm looking for work, and housing, everything's under control,' he lies.

Vicky believes him. 'Well done! Oh. I think you must send Howard a written apology.'

Ethan pretends to be okay with the suggestion that he must grovel for Howard's forgiveness.

When Vicky pays for lunch without having mentioned or considered Ethan's recovery, I realise that his family have passed the buck to me.

'Ethan, it's not the right time for a family Christmas,' she says, 'maybe next year, if you're well. And I'm going abroad after New Year.'

Ethan understands she wants to spend the festive season with Howard, Phoebe, the family, and definitely not with him. He's deeply hurt but doesn't show it; that is until our drive back to our hotel when he makes his feelings known. The chip on his shoulder just got bigger.

The following morning we prepare to check out of the hotel. I foot the bill at the reception desk, after which Ethan allows me to visit the ladies loo. I leave him with my jacket and our bags. A few minutes later, when I return, I can't see him; he's moved from the lobby. I look for him down the corridor and spot him sitting on a sofa inspecting his phone. On the table beside him sit two pints of Guinness, both half drunk. My heart sinks.

He looks up at me and smiles. 'It's just the one, to take the edge off, darling! I even ordered one for you. I found some cash in your jacket pocket.'

Later he regrets relapsing within days and wants Valium to help him come off the booze, which mean another mad goose chase to A&E.

Self-pity eats away at him. He tries calling Loday, a family friend, who he has known since he was a teenager. A Tibetan Buddhist monk, he's based in Newcastle, a student with the Pathgate Institute of Buddhist Studies.

'Hi, Loday, I'm really sick,' Ethan tells him.

'I'm sorry to hear that. So it didn't it work out for you at the farm community?'

'No. It closed down. I left that place months ago.' He passes his iPhone to me so I can translate his slurring to English.

I update Loday with the way things are.

'Magda, I can't do much to help,' Loday says in response. 'If he gets sober, he can visit us and spend Christmas here at Pathgate; there's room in the sangha. Other than that, I'm always here for moral support by phone.'

Ethan can't wait to speak to Theo, to ask him if he'll book a flight to Newcastle. Theo refuses. He reminds Ethan that since he's intoxicated an airline won't allow him to board a plane; besides, the sangha is dry, and they have a strict ban on alcohol and drugs, so it's not an option.

The last thing we need is the flu. Regardless, Ethan catches it, then me. Ethan's thing of washing himself in germ-ridden puddles doesn't help; it's a wonder we're not sicker. When he sneezes, he doesn't cover his mouth, and I have to hold a tissue to his snotty nose when he blows. He's too pissed to hold a hanky, and his chain-smoking makes his chesty cough worse. When he catnaps, I have to stifle my coughs and sneezes for fear of waking him, because if I do, he'll have me haring around the booze aisles, come what may. We desperately need warmth to recover.

It's possible Vicky feels bad about vetoing Ethan from the family Christmas. She still has no idea he relapsed soon after that lunch at Claudia's Café. She calls me to ask if I'd agree to drive Ethan to Wales for a short break, she's found an isolated place in the Welsh countryside, she's even offered to pay for the guesthouse. She thinks he might benefit from fresh air and be distracted for Christmas. In addition, we'll get a chance to recover from our flu. I comply with Ethan's instruction to not mention his relapse to Vicky. Somewhere within he must know he has to get sober, before he's full-blown, alcohol dependent again. Maybe if he sees how much support I provide, he won't feel as neglected by his family. I'm still sure we can get back to the way we were.

I agree to stand by Ethan again. Surely, I'll get him sober. Vicky's probably relieved I'm around to take the heat off the family. Christmas is less than a week away, so I buy Frida and Sylvia gifts that I wrap and deliver. We snatch a few minutes together while Ethan catnaps in my car.

Our drive to the Welsh accommodation is long. Despite poor signage we find the isolated house, a family home with a cosy guest annex that has a small kitchen and bathroom adjacent to the bedroom. The owners of the annex meet us, and I manage to hide Ethan away before he blurts out something drunk stupid that might sabotage our booking. Ethan gets a bee in his bonnet about going grocery shopping in the nearby village before we unpack.

We park in the retail car park, and I try to keep up with him while he races towards the huge supermarket. He checks his bank account at the ATM, sees his welfare money's been paid early due to the Christmas holiday and withdraws a wad of cash. Then he grabs a large trolley, and his walk turns to a run towards the booze aisle. I can barely keep up. He speedily crams it full of cases or beer, bottles of wine, cola, and a bottle of Jack Daniels.

'What do you think you're doing?' I ask in amazement.

'It's Christmas. I just need a Christmas blowout. Everyone will be having a Christmas booze-up. I'll stop drinking on Boxing Day.'

'No. Put it back!' I plead.

He refuses to listen. 'We'll buy some food. Steak? Or fish?' He tosses a few food items on top of the booze. At the checkout Ethan hastily pays, using all the cash he withdrew. We don't even make it back to where my car is parked before he frantically unearths the beer and breaks open a case.

I don't know what to do with him.

Chapter Twenty-seven

Once again, I'm stranded in the remote countryside with Ethan blotto and a phone signal that barely catches one bar. I want to tell Vicky that Ethan's relapsed, and I need her help. But curiously, I'm afraid the news would spoil her Christmas preparations. I'm at my wits' end.

Outside is freezing cold, dark and there's a downpour. Maybe I should count my blessings; we have warmth, shelter for a week, and we can get better, mentally and physically.

Ethan's hungry for dinner. I prepare fish, potatoes, and vegetables while Ethan gulps his beer and warbles a tune. When dinner smells done, he follows me into the kitchen to get himself more beer. At least he's looking forward to us having a meal. I retrieve our dinner from the oven, then turn my back on Ethan to hang the oven gloves on a wall hook. Suddenly BAM! Fists hit the back of my head, nearly knocking me over with the force. 'Smells great!' he says as if nothing just happened.

Tears of pain sting my eyes. I turn to face him. 'What did you do that for?'

He doesn't answer, just gives me a glazed look. I'm not sure if he's in blackout, but either way my instinct tells me I'd better retreat. He walks unsteadily into the bathroom and bangs the door shut—a chance for me to escape until he cools off. I dash out of the kitchen, grab my trainers and jacket, and the car keys from a table near the patio door, then rush out the patio door and run to my car. My socks get wet and muddy because I haven't had time to put shoes on; I'm still holding them. While running I point my keys and unlock my car. I throw myself into the driver's seat, put my foot down and speed away.

I realise I left my SatNav behind—it's in the annex—so I can't drive far for fear of getting lost. I drive for two miles and then pull into a lay-by. There's no street lighting; all around me is black countryside. It's spooky. I check for a phone signal and call Frida. I don't want to alarm her, but just in case something untoward should happen, I admit that Ethan's relapsed and say where we're staying.

Frida and I talk for over an hour while rain pelts on my car roof. She tells me not to worry about her. She's left her job but says she's okay. I know she's not. I don't feel safe out here, but without a SatNav to show me the way, I have no other option than to return to the annex, which doesn't feel much safer.

Upon my return I quietly open the patio door. The lights are on. I peep inside. The double bed is bulky and messy. He's in it, snoring. I noiselessly close the door behind me and return to the scene of the crime, the kitchen. Dirty plates and squashed beer cans cover the worktop. I open a cupboard, looking for a hiding place to stash the kitchen knives, and find a floor mop and metal bucket inside. After wrapping the knives in tea-towels, I place them inside the bucket, then start clearing away. The foil-covered leftover dinner is empty apart from one bite-sized potato. Ethan's wolfed down both our dinners. I make myself a bed on the floor with a pillow and an itchy blanket and doze off to sleep, exhausted.

Ethan prods me awake. 'What are you doing down there?'

I'm not sure exactly how long I've slept, maybe three hours. He goes to the bathroom, keeping the door open, and on the way back grabs another beer from the fridge. His rambling starts—grudges, regrets, and tales of wonderful Christmases past. He talks himself hoarse, chain-smokes and drinks until he keels over and passes out.

Ethan knows his excessive drinking will go on without intervention, so on Christmas Eve he agrees we should call his key worker. He'll have to be detoxed. Again. His key worker is sympathetic and offers an appointment, but due to the Christmas holiday, the next one isn't available for another week. She says if he can taper his alcohol, she'll bend the rules by securing housing for him at a half-way house where he'll get further support. It is a massive relief that help is a week away.

I'm on my guard while preparing dinner, taking care to not turn my back on him. He even helps out by laying the table, but everywhere I look I see alcohol—cans in the fridge, bottles in the wine rack, and a bottle of Jack Daniels on the counter.

He drains his merlot in the blink of an eye; then pours a triple JD. 'Try one. Just one. I won't stop nagging!' He bolts one down.

Something feels wrong drinking with Ethan because alcohol is his poison. It's odd the way he nags me to be his drinking companion, as if it excuses or normalises it.

He's in a bad way mixing his drinks.

'Oh! Where you been?' he calls out.

'You know where, washing up.'

'Oh. Great. Thing is this. I feel so sorry for you!' He laughs.

'Why's that?' I respond.

'Because this is going to hurt!' He waves the empty whiskey bottle around, 'Yeah, I feel sorry for you because it's gonna hurt when I ram this bottle up your fucking jacksy. See? And it's square! So that'll really hurt!'

I freeze for a split second, then reply, 'I feel sorry for you too.'
'Huh? Why?'
'Because I might have to call the police. Do you want to spend Christmas day in the cells?'

'Woah! What?' He backs up and drops the bottle to the floor, not wanting to spend Christmas rattling in a police cell without booze.

When I wake on Christmas morning, I see Ethan with a glass in one hand, rubbing his bloated belly with the other. I remind myself that this nightmare will be over in one week's time when Ethan has his appointment.

Vicky sends a Happy Christmas text message, and I call Frida and Sylvia with a weak signal I managed to get by the patio door. I keep my voice steady, feigning Christmas joy.

The next morning dawns wet again. Ethan fixates on his family neglecting him, so I offer to drive us for some sea air, to distract him, when Vicky calls unexpectedly.

'Hi, Mum,' he says, 'it's just as well you phoned. Things aren't going well between me and Magda. It's not working out. It's not me. It's her. Poor me. You'll have to do something!'

My blood boils. He's winding Vicky up, and hasn't admitted he's relapsed. Fresh air is off the cards. He walks out of earshot to whinge some more. Finally, the call ends.

Vicky calls me straight back, clearly suspecting that something's up.

'So. What's going on?' she asks.

'There's no easy way to say this, but I'm afraid he's relapsed again,' I reply.

'Oh. I knew it!' She sounds exasperated.

I go on to tell her he's alcohol dependent again, but not to worry, I'll ferry him to his upcoming appointment. It'll work out this time. We end the call with hope in our hearts.

With Ethan's secret of relapsing out of the bag, he is in a foul mood. Without warning he grabs his computer and throws it with great force across the room. It smashes against the wall, leaving a hole the size of a cricket ball in the middle of the wall. The owners of the annex will be furious.

I try to keep out of his way while he berates, smokes and drinks. While I'm lying on my stomach on the floor colouring pages of Ethan's 'get rid of stress' colouring book, he walks up beside me and kicks me hard in my side. Shocked, winded, and hurt, I instinctively curl into foetal position. Ethan delivers more kicks, then nonchalantly whistles and toddles off to the fridge.

I hide behind a floor-length curtain, making myself as small as possible by curling into ball. Though I try to be stoic, hot tears run down my cheeks. I wait for him to eventually pass out.

Only when he's flat out on the bed snoring loudly do I dare move. I crawl towards the kitchen and pull myself up to stand. I throb with pain and my hands shake. I remind myself that in a matter of days Ethan will have his next appointment, then he'll be clean and sober, and this hell will be over. We can get back to the way we were.

When he wakes up, he doesn't know what day it is or how long he's been out cold—it's only been a few hours—but he agrees we have to drive to a DIY store. The hole he made in the wall has to be fixed to save Vicky getting sent a repair bill. I pay for plaster, sandpaper, paint, paintbrushes, and a trowel.

My phone rings on our drive back through the dark of night. Ethan's slow to get it out of his pocket, so it stops calling. He sees it's Cedric's number.

'Pull the fuck over! Now! Call him back, you cunt!' Ethan yells.

Too terrified to disobey, I pull into a lay-by. He signs for me to turn on the speakerphone.

I call back and try to sound as if all's well and under control, but Cedric's suspicious.

'Did you guys have a good Christmas?' he asks.

Ethan, his face like thunder, sways and leans in so as not to miss a word.

I stare out at the rain. 'Umm. Sure. Ethan and I are in Wales.'

'Oh, nice. What's that like?'

'It hasn't stopped raining since we got here; it's wet and cold. That's Wales for you.' I'm unable to force a conversation.

Ethan snatches my phone and slurs on about what a diabolical place the farmstead was and how he was treated so badly.

Cedric, twigging that Ethan's hammered, ends the call.

'You're a cunt,' Ethan sneers. 'Let's play I Spy. I spy a C for cunt!'

I'm sure that sometimes he pretends he's in blackout to excuse his behaviour. I ignore his vulgarity and keep driving.

When we return to the annex, I prepare the plaster. Ethan pops the caps off more beer. I'm not sure if he feels bad about causing the wall damage, but he offers to help me and even takes over. A few hours later it looks as good as new, which is incredible seeing as he's sloshed. For once, something has been accomplished.

Chapter Twenty-eight

We check out tomorrow. To save myself time in the morning I start packing, tidying, and recycling the ton of booze empties. Ethan's almost run out of booze. Just as I'm about to get ready for bed, he throws my jacket at me, 'Shop shuts soon; get a move on.'

While we zoom along the dual carriageway with windscreen wipers racing, Ethan flicks fag ash out of the window. I concentrate on the road, exasperated to be dragged out this late and by his refusal to wear a seatbelt. He shifts his feet, and in a split second, he springs straight out of the passenger window. Again! In my exhausted state, I forgot to child lock the windows and doors. I brake hard and pull over to look for him. I see him on all fours on the verge, so I go to help him.

He looks at me with rage and lunges towards me. 'I'm gonna kill you!'

I sprint back to my car and speed off without hesitation, leaving him shouting and flailing his arms around. A few miles later I stop and fumble around to find his phone. I can't find it, but I spot my phone in the footwell and call Frida. Thank goodness she picks up. The sound of her voice reminds me that my life is still waiting for me; my daughters are waiting for me. I want my life back.

After a while of talking, I wonder if he's cooled off. My hands are still shaking. I call his number; it goes to voicemail. I start driving to retrace my route, but I can't see him walking along the dual carriageway where I'd left him, and it's too dark to see where it's not well lit. After a while, my phone rings; it's a Welsh policeman.

'We found Ethan wandering along the dual carriageway,' he tells me. 'He's fine and we've brought him back to the annex.'

It's a wonder he's not injured. In a way it's a shame they didn't arrest him for being drunk and disorderly, but the mere sight of cops always subdues him. I don't know how on earth he remembered the address to the annex. When I arrive, I see an ambulance but no police squad car. Unsure what's going on, I stay in my car.

A paramedic steps out of the ambulance and walks over to me. 'Are you Magda?'

I nod.

'Don't worry. Ethan called us out. He's in the back of the ambulance having a check-up. He's begging for Valium, but we don't prescribe, we don't carry medicines.'

I wonder if Ethan called the ambulance as a decoy to get rid of the police—a nifty trick he's used in the past to get rid of cops.

The paramedic returns to the ambulance and closes the door.

I can't think what to do. I need help.

Eventually the door of the ambulance opens, and Ethan jumps out. He stomps straight towards me while the emergency services drive off; he may have sent them away. Ethan pulls open my door. Fear grips me, and I worry in case the couple who own the annex hear the commotion. I'm so scared I need to pee with nerves, but I manage to hang on and not wet myself with terror.

Ethan sways at my driver's door in a rage. 'I fucking hate your guts, you fucking cunt! Where's your phone? Delete all my people's numbers. My mum's number, my friends, my cousins, my key workers. Everyone's. I want everyone to stop discussing me. Got it. We are over. You make me sick!' He shouts it all at the top of his lungs.

I nod, but instead of deleting numbers, I switch off my phone and push it under my car seat. He doesn't notice.

He might be drunk, but not too drunk to scam. He wants to cause confusion and play everyone off one another—this trick of his has financial benefits. He's already muddied the waters by lying to Vicky about me.

While Ethan has his liquid breakfast of Leffe beer, I dash around packing our things away and cleaning. We have to check out by 10 am and drive back to England. He lolls around drinking and chain-smoking, not lifting a finger to help.

I vacuum throughout, clean the bathroom, wash-up, clean up, dust, strip the bed, load the washing machine with bedding and towels and wash the floors. I put the knives back where they belong and ask Ethan to smoke outside so I can air the room. I fling the doors wide open to rid the annex of the stench of booze and tobacco. He unsteadily wobbles outside to smoke, only to march back inside to take a pee leaving his muddy footprints on the floors I just cleaned.

'I'll load the car, just sit in the car and wait for me,' I say.

He stumbles outside, feebly waving his tobacco pouch, a sign for me to roll him a cigarette because of his jelly fingers. I roll him one that he tries to light, but he drops his lighter in the footwell. I dash back for our bags.

Before leaving, I scan the annex for a last look; it's as good as new.

When I knock on the door of the owner's house to return their key, the wife opens the front door. She doesn't look too pleased. 'Oh. Thank you. Nice stay?' she asks with a strong Welsh accent.

'Yes, it's been lovely!' I lie.

'Really? The police woke us up last night. Everything okay? Is it? It's just that Ethan knocked late last night asking us for alcohol. That's very rude.'

'Umm. Oh! I'm really sorry about that; he hasn't been well lately.' After all my efforts to contain this chaos, I realise I haven't. It's too complicated to explain to the woman that Ethan's a relapsed alcoholic, so I don't.

Ethan's slumped in the passenger seat, snoring, the cigarette between his fingers soggy with wine. He half clasps the wine in his other hand—it's almost gone. I gently extract the bottle from his hold, replace the cap and hide it behind my car seat.

I set my SatNav and set off for the long drive ahead. Within minutes of driving down the country road, the SatNav directions disturbs Ethan's sleep. I had hoped to get some mileage done before he woke up.

'What the fuck is going on!' Ethan sits bolt upright with his purple eyes wide open. 'Stop the fucking car!'

'I'll pull in; hang on a second, please,' I say in a reassuring voice.

'Stop! Now!' he shouts.

I'm not sure where the next lay-by is, so I stop at an emergency stop. At that moment, my hidden phone starts ringing. I answer, it's Theo.

'Hi, Magda, I got quite a few missed calls from Ethan a short while ago. Everything okay?'

Ethan must have called Theo when I was checking out.

'Errr ... No ... Not exactly,' I reply.

'Theo. Fuck off.' Ethan wrestles my phone out of my hand,

shouting at the top of his voice. 'I'm with this fucking cunt, Theo! And I'm fucking off now!' He throws my phone at me, flings open the passenger door, jumps out and opens the rear car door, then drags his luggage out and throws it all into the middle of the road.

I put my phone to my ear. Theo's still on the line; he can hear everything.

'Magda, you have to get away. I want you to get as far away from him as possible for your own safety. Do it now and call me soon as you can.' Theo says firmly.

Ethan stands in the road swearing and shouting with his case and bags strewn around him. He slams the car doors shut with such force it hurts my ears. I get my foot down and roar away, my heart racing. After driving for a while, I reach a small village and stop. I drop my head on the steering wheel for a few minutes, then Theo calls again.

'Are you okay? Are you safe?' he asks.

'Sort of, I mean … Yes, I'm safe.' I can barely form a sentence.

'Good. He just called me. His phone's almost out of battery. He's completely out of his head. Blotto. He said he's stranded in the countryside in the pouring rain, with his luggage and no money. He demanded that I drive all the way to Wales to pick him up. For about one minute I actually almost agreed, but then I thought better of it. This is my day off so … no. I'm putting myself first. I want to be with my wife and kids, not spend all day bloody rescuing him from Wales. Let him get on with it. It's called tough love. And I'm not going to transfer any of my money for his train fare into his bank account either. It'll go on booze. He's had enough out of me and the family over the years!'

'So how will he get back to England for his appointment? With no lift and no money?' I reply.

'I don't care. Let him hitchhike,' Theo says.

'No one will pick up a drunk, especially with all that luggage,' I point out.

'Don't worry about it. You've done enough. He'll have to throw his luggage into a ditch and try to hitch. Leave him, return to your daughters and back to your own life. No one will judge you. Let him hit rock bottom. Let him go to hell.' Our call ends.

Part of me wants to listen to Theo and be as tough as he is. The other part feels empathy, knowing Ethan's sick. He's vulnerable; he might get arrested, and the thought of him sleeping rough in a ditch in the Welsh countryside in the pouring rain fills me with despair.

It's a long shot, but I drive back to the annex to see if Ethan's walked back there. He hasn't. Maybe he somehow found his way to the large superstore. I drive all the way there to look, but there's no sign of him. I try his phone number numerous times. It goes straight to voicemail, probably because his phone's out of battery. I drive in circles looking for him, even park my car and run around on foot to anywhere that sells booze. After six hours of searching, I still can't find him, and it's getting dark. I try the local hospital.

The receptionist says, 'Oh, Ethan. Yes, he was here briefly this morning. He arrived by ambulance and was meant to wait and see a doctor, but he disappeared!'

Ethan must have called an ambulance from the remote roadside where he threw his temper tantrum and just used it as transport.

Thinking that maybe he's been arrested, I phone the Welsh police. A woman takes my details and tells me they'll run a search to see if he's in the system or if he's being held at any local police stations. When the operator comes back on the line, she tells me that he's not on the police system, so I report him as a missing person. She asks me to wait and places me on hold again.

'We have a police officer near the A&E. Can you wait for him by the main doors, and he'll speak to you?' she asks when she returns.

A police officer arrives after a short wait, and we stand outside in the cold while he gathers information and jots details down in his small notepad. The pouring rain is now a gentle drizzle. He asks Ethan's full name, address, date of birth, height, weight, hair and eye colour, and if I have a recent a photo of him. After that he's listed as a missing person, and the Welsh police force start looking for him.

It's freezing cold. I'm exhausted, hungry, dehydrated. My head hurts and my body aches. I can't take much more. I wish this wasn't happening. His appointment is so close. When he gets sober, we can put this nightmare behind us.

It pours with rain for hours while I sit like a lemon in the car park. All of a sudden, my phone rings. I jump at the sound. To my amazement it's Aunt Pearl.

'Hello. It's me, Pearl,' she says.

'Pearl. Have you heard from Ethan? I'm so worried! I've got the Welsh police out looking for him,' I blurt out in a panic. 'I've reported him as a missing person.'

'Oh, don't worry. He's fine. He's just charged his phone and called me. Try his number; if you can't get through, call me back!'

I call Ethan's number. Sure enough, he picks up. 'Where are you? You're reported as a missing person!' I exclaim.

'Am I? No, I'm not missing. I'm in a building next to the hospital,' he replies, all chipper.

I can't believe it; he's a five-minute walk from where I'm parked. I arrange to meet him at the entrance door of the building he has described. I hadn't noticed it before because it's set back and has a footpath that runs through a courtyard. He stands waving at the entrance door and lets me in through double doors. He's wide eyed with excitement.

'Look, follow me! I want to show you.' He has a spring in his step.

The inside of the building is well lit, modern, and warm. He leads me up a long corridor lined with closed doors and casually opens one in the middle of the passageway. Inside is a spotless room. It has a comfortable-looking armchair, a single bed, a TV, a table, and an en-suite bathroom. His case, bags and backpack are stacked against a radiator. It transpires that the building is the private-health hospital wing for patients who are not NHS. I realise that's why it is so clinical looking. He's snuck in early this morning and been posing as a private patient all day. He has shoplifted alcohol at some point and has spent the whole day quaffing alcohol in bed, watching TV, relaxing in the warm. He's even had hot meals brought to him by catering staff who were the only staff to have spotted him. He'd been crafty enough not to raise the alarm by smoking indoors. I can't believe my eyes. I imagined he was comatose in a ditch somewhere.

Without warning, a nurse and a porter appear at the doorway, glaring at us.

'Who are you? What are you doing here?' the nurse asks. She looks astonished by the state of Ethan and the messy bed.

'Errr … it's me, sweetie. I'm Ethan.' He smiles as he says it, hoping he'll pull off being a private patient a bit longer and eek out his stay.

She purses her lips, then says, 'Well, Ethan, I think you had better leave before I call security!'

'I'm leaving! I was waiting for someone. Don't call security. I'm going now.'

The perplexed nurse and porter escort us out of the building.

'It was lovely in there,' Ethan says while we load his stuff back into my car. 'Aren't you proud of me, that I managed not to lose any of my bags?'

I nod. 'Yes, I don't know how you managed it.'

He checks his phone. The screen is smashed. He wants to tell Aunt Pearl I found him.

I phone the Welsh police to call off the missing person search. I can't wait for his appointment. I don't think he has a clue what kind of impact he's having on my well-being. I drive us to a near-by drive-thru to buy hot drinks and a take-away.

Ethan shouts his orders through the speaker, 'I want eight quarter pounders, eight extra-large fries, ten chicken burgers and twenty banana milkshakes!'

I quickly rectify the order and change it to two cheeseburgers and two cups of coffee, then I park in a space while our food is prepared.

Ethan digs around his pocket for his phone and proceeds to call Theo. 'Hi, Theo. I've been found. She didn't leave me stranded. We're having food. Everything's great!'

There's a pause. I feel bad I went against Theo's advice, but if I'd taken his suggestion, I don't see how it'd have helped Ethan.

'Ethan, you must behave yourself and not hurt Magda,' Theo says. 'She's looking out for you, so be grateful!' He proceeds to give Ethan a long pep talk about the importance to get clean and sober, and that he'll have to face the consequences if he doesn't.

When the call ends, I brace myself for the drive back to England. I need to buy mineral water and replace my fuel that was wasted in my search for him. We make a pit stop at a familiar-looking garage where Ethan replenishes his booze supply while I foot the bill. When I finally drive across the Severn Bridge into England, I feel relieved to be back on home turf. I think that when he's sober, he'll be thankful by how I've stood by him. On the other hand, he might not give a damn.

Chapter Twenty-nine

The superstore closes at 10 pm. The car park is near empty. Ethan holds out his hand for my car keys and pockets them. Inside only a handful of shoppers wander the aisles. One minute Ethan's with me, browsing, the next he's gone. I guess he's dashed to the booze aisle. Only when I go looking for him, I can't see him anywhere.

I nip outside to see if he's waiting in my car. He's not, so it's back to the superstore to ask around. No one knows of him. So I check the car park again and this time see a police van pull away. I rush back to customer services. Two bottles of wine sit on the counter.

'Sorry, I've lost someone. Do you know if he's here? His name's Ethan.'

'Ah, you just missed him. He's been arrested; the police have taken him away.'

'Arrested? What police station?'

'Dunno,' the cashier replies.

I walk dejectedly back to my car. Then I remember. Oh no. I'm locked out of my car; Ethan's got my car keys. But I think I've got a spare key hidden in the boot for emergencies. Luckily for me, Ethan forgot to confiscate my phone. Unluckily it only has two percent of battery left.

I walk some distance to the nearest pub to see if I can borrow a phone. A bartender offers the use of his one so I can call the RAC breakdown recovery. The operator offers to send a mechanic over to me within two hours—a long time to wait, alone and in the howling wind and rain. I call Frida to let her know I'm in another tight spot.

I'm so mad at Ethan. Then again, I wonder how he's faring in the police cell. At long last the lights of the RAC recovery vehicle are in sight. The mechanic uses a window tool and unlocks my car with one click. What a relief when, after a search, I find the spare car key.

Sylvia, who'd got the head's up from Frida, makes a cup of tea when I arrive at her place. I change out of my rain-soaked clothes and start phoning around local police stations until I finally track Ethan down. I can't help thinking how scared he must be, but at least he's got warmth and shelter for the night.

Around mid-morning we meet outside the police station. They've released him on bail. His appointment with his key worker is this morning, but before he plonks himself into the passenger seat, he chores a bottle of Pinot and glugs it down. Within minutes he's out cold.

When we arrive for the appointment, he groans something about toilet and looks down at where he's pissed himself in my car seat.

A key worker who's smoking outside the building spots us and walks over. 'Oh, hi Ethan. I see you're a bit worse for wear.' She looks at me. 'He won't be seen today, not in this state. Make another appointment for next week.'

Theo gets word about Ethan's latest arrest and calls me to see what's happening.

'Try dropping him off at a hostel for addicts,' he says. 'I've found one that's local. It may not seem right, but it's for the best. He needs to stop relying on you.'

The hostel's not easy to find, and it's a dingy, noisy place, full to the rafters with addicts.

Ethan looks over his shoulder, takes off his beloved watch and fastens it on my wrist. 'Look after this for me, and don't lose it,' he says in a hoarse whisper, then promptly pretends to faint.

A first aider throws a blanket over him, and we wait for the medics. They only stay with Ethan for ten minutes. They want Ethan to keep his alcohol levels topped up, otherwise he's in danger of having a seizure.

Ethan tries to shadow me when I back away to split, but he gets distracted.

Just for tonight, I want the night off, to get my head together, so I leave alone. While driving down the street, past the hostel, I glance to my right and see Ethan squatting in the gutter with his pants down, shitting. It's heart breaking to see him in this condition. I want to stop and rescue him, but instinct tells me, 'No.' Ethan's hitting rock bottom is his only way up.

An hour later I call Ethan to explain this, but it seems he's blocked my number.

Chapter Thirty

Frida makes a light breakfast and a pot of coffee; I don't go into detail about how much distress Ethan has caused. The police, I learn, have made a few visits to her address because my car's registered there, so she knows there's been drama. It appears various police forces want to question me, probably regarding reported motoring incidents.

Not being with Ethan feels weird; not hearing his berating, blathering, and rambling is bliss. On the other hand, I'm worried about him. Despite the distraction it brings, my hands tremble as I sort through his stuff to do his laundry. My car smells of piss, fags, and booze.

I phone the addiction services to find out the time of Ethan's next appointment. No one knows, and they've not sent me an email. Since he's incapable of dealing with anything, I check his computer for new mail, but there are none from them. However, he does have an unread message sent over a week ago from Trina.

She writes: *Hello Ethan. The way things started and ended so suddenly between us has wounded me deeply. I'm broken physically, mentally, spiritually and emotionally, even though you had to finish what we had together. Thank you for inviting me to the community in the summer; you gave me a special day. Good luck with your AA Steps. Love from Trina.*

I realise I've uncovered another one of Ethan's lies. The message is enlightening. Learning about his romance with Trina doesn't affect me, since I'd suspected as much. Even the fact he'd given Trina a special day in the very place where we'd met and made our first plans together seem oddly heartless, and unromantic seeing as he was sober at that time. Now he's drinking himself to death.

In the early evening I'm taken by surprise when Loday phones me. He speaks calmly and wants to know how I'm feeling.

'Hi, Loday, it's nice to hear from you,' I say.

'Hello, Magda, I'm calling with news about Ethan. He's staying with someone called Trina. I don't know her, but apparently, she's a Buddhist, so he must be safe. I've just been speaking to her. She's already taken him to a doctor today to get Valium. She said she's got two weeks off work, so she's offered to cure him in that time. She thinks she can get him clean and sober without a detox or rehab in two weeks. Now don't you worry about his next rehab. Trina's cancelled her New Year's Eve plans, and from now on, she's tending to him.'

'Oh. Okay. Thanks for letting me know. He needs rehab, though; he needs professional help.'

'We'll see. Trina's sure she knows best. She's got everything under control. I'll call you tomorrow,' Loday adds cheerfully.

Ethan has the ability to reel people in for favours and hang onto them, even after he betrays them, although Trina might not know she has been betrayed. Ethan's given me hell with his jealousy by accusing me of carrying on with Cedric, but I don't harbour bad feelings about how he's thrown himself at Trina. I'm ready to surrender, to let go. I think maybe it's for the best that I bury my hopes of Ethan and I ever being the way we were. Besides, the sadness I feel tells me 'the way we were' never existed in the first place, because of Ethan's colossal deceit.

Regardless of Trina's naivety, deep down she must care for Ethan. It's not abnormal for a relapsed alkie to sweet-talk their way back into the lives of old flames to wangle free housing and favours. He's at the top of his game when it comes to manipulating people.

Sylvia's invited Frida and me over to her place for New Year's Eve. We'll spend a quiet night in and watch TV. Safe, calm, and cosy. My shaky hands aren't trembling nearly as much. I'm already starting to feel less stressed with the help of having Sylvia and Frida back in my life.

On New Year's morning, we have breakfast together—boiled eggs with toast—but my stomach is still delicate with stress. My heart sinks when my phone rings. It's Loday.

'Hi, Magda, how are you?'

'I'm doing all right. What's wrong?'

'Oh. I wanted to warn you. Trina decided she couldn't cope with Ethan, so she's just kicked him out. He wouldn't taper his drinking. She was fed up with him guzzling the vodka she bought to taper his drinking. And she became frightened of him. He kept bullying and shouting at her and snatching her phone when she answered her calls. When Trina went to the corner shop, he got paranoid that we were talking about him, which we were. Oh, and she got upset when I told her about you and all you've done for him since it all started—you know, his detoxes and rehabs and all that. He hadn't even mentioned any of it, including you. She was shocked. She's taken it badly; she's not in a good way,' Loday says. 'Anyhow, after Trina kicked him out, he went straight over to Theo's house to be rescued, but he turned Ethan away at the front door. Theo was firm with Ethan. So I need to warn you that Ethan might contact you for a rescue.'

It's an eye-opener hearing that Trina's dumped Ethan so hastily, especially after all her hopes and promises to work a miracle with him. And by what Loday's said, I'm not sure if Theo's being too harsh. Theo seems a friendly sort of chap, but at the same time, he's dead shrewd.

'Thanks for letting me know,' I say. 'I've got my worries with Frida; her RSI is so painful she's resigned from her job.'

'Well, if there's anything I can do to help. Wait. I just thought of something; Frida sounds like she needs to rest somewhere away from stress, what with her RSI symptoms. We have space here at the sangha if she'd like to stay for a bit. We can meet her at Newcastle airport. It'd do her the world of good. I can confirm this once I get it authorized, but I'm sure it won't be a problem.'

'Thanks, Loday. That does sound like exactly what she needs. I'll speak to her and maybe we can work something out.'

Although rehab is up in the air, at least Loday's offering to help Frida. After I check my email, I find there's still no news from any of the addiction centres. However, a new email has arrived from Vicky. She includes a link in her message that leads me to a website about tough love and how not to allow an addict to destroy your life. She mentions that she's been ill in bed and she believes Ethan's addiction is ruining her health. Ethan's drug and alcohol addiction over the decades must be driving her mad; it's little wonder she's so detached.

Chapter Thirty-one

I have thirty missed calls from Ethan this morning, and I know there isn't anything I can do to stop his drinking. I pick up his thirty-first call.

'I think I'm dying,' he says. 'Please, please meet me just for one cup of coffee!'

'I can't today. Another day,' I reply, but he nags, asks, and sobs until I agree to one cup of coffee. I promise myself it will be just that, one coffee.

When I see him on the other side of the main road, he jumps and waves, delighted to see me, then races across the road and hugs me tightly. Without wasting a moment, he takes me by the arm and leads me to the supermarket's booze aisle. I try to shake him off, but he hangs onto me even as he lifts wine from the shop shelf.

A security guard rushes over to us. 'Leave this store! Take him away! Otherwise, I'm calling the police. He just got barred because he was trying to shoplift.'

I feel embarrassed being told off by security.

The chaos has already started.

'Oh, Magda, poor me, I was with an old friend who threw

me out for no reason,' Ethan whinges.

'Who was this friend who would do such a thing?' I ask, knowing it was Trina.

He shrugs. 'I can't remember.'

'Oh, that's terrible,' I say.

Ethan pulls his phone from his pocket and hastily calls an old mate. 'Heyyy, it's me; guess what? My Magda's come out to rescue me. Everything's fine.' he says cheerily.

I can't believe it; that's not the arrangement we'd made, but I hold my anger and offer to buy Ethan lunch from Waitrose. Just as the cashier's about to serve me, Ethan sneaks up behind, and when she turns her back, he reaches over, grabs a special-offer bottle of rum and bolts outside. The cashier faces me again, none the wiser. I pay for lunch and scarper.

When I leave the store, I can't see him at first, then I find him sitting on some steps. He's talking on his phone again, his speech incoherent. The bottle of rum's half gone, yet he still swigs it neat and coughs. He hands his phone to me to translate. I recognise her voice; it's Marlene from the community.

'Magda, what's happening?'

'He's not in a good way,' I reply. 'Today he's upset because Trina didn't want him to stay at her flat, so she kicked him out onto the street.'

'Oh, I see. Wait, I know Trina. Yes, we met her back in the summer. Ethan invited her to the community, and we had a lovely day together. They were such a happy couple.'

My stomach lurches at the reminder. His betrayal and first infidelity repulse me, not that I let on. Within seconds Ethan throws himself on his back. He's either playing dead or out cold again.

'Marlene, I better call an ambulance!' I say.

The familiar sight of flashing, blue lights come closer. The paramedics wheel out a stretcher, but Ethan won't come around. They check his heart, wrist and breathing. All seem to be okay.

'Tell her I'm dying!' Ethan whispers as the medics strap him to the stretcher before zooming to A&E.

I phone Theo to tell him what hospital Ethan's been taken to, not that he's surprised or even interested.

A few days later, I get a call from Ethan's father. 'I've decided to help Ethan. Again. His mother's worried sick, so I've arranged to pick him up. He slept in a shop doorway last night. I've told him that he's not allowed to drink at my house, so he'll have to get himself sober. He says you've got his washbag and things, so I'll meet you to collect them, that's if I find him. He's lost his iPhone again. That makes about twenty of the damn things!'

His father arrives with Ethan in the backseat, looking like death warmed up. His dad clips the seatbelt around Ethan, as if he's strapping in a toddler, then child-locks the doors, like his dad's done this a thousand times before. Without so much as a wave, his father roars off and they're gone.

At bedtime I feel better for knowing Ethan's safe, with his dad providing support.

On a positive note, we hear good news from Loday. Frida has been told she's welcome to visit Pathgate for a few weeks of respite. She eagerly packs her backpack, ready to leave tomorrow. We drink tea and enjoy a peaceful day together. After speaking numerous times to Loday, I've got to know and trust him, so it's wonderful to know that Frida will be in a secure environment. The absence of Ethan allows my body to slowly recover. Although I'm not back to normal, I feel better.

After a fairly good night's sleep, I prepare to give Frida a lift to the bus station, where she'll take the shuttle bus to the airport. Once again, my phone rings. It's Ethan.

'Honey, darling, it's me, Ethan. And I'm sober. I've got my

replacement sim, and I'm using a cheapo handset,' he says.

'You're sober? That's good news,' I reply.

'And more great news. I'm in A&E waiting for a detox. I can't believe it, but I need a small favour. I need my driver's licence for photo ID. You've got it somewhere. Please can you drop it off at the hospital?'

It's out of my way, but I agree to do a detour to deliver his ID before going onto the airport shuttle bus stop.

At the hospital Frida waits in my car while I walk to the hospital entrance, where I see Ethan sitting on the ground with another man who's talking to him. Ethan's glugging a bottle of Leffe.

'Hello, you must be Magda,' the man says. 'I've heard a lot about you. My name's Ralph. I'm an alcohol and drugs counsellor here at the hospital.'

'Hi, Ralph. What's happening? When's Ethan going to be admitted for his detox?' I ask.

He frowns. 'Detox? Admission? I don't know what you're talking about. Ethan turned up at A&E and requested Valium. His dad dropped him off. I hear he's chucked Ethan out.'

The penny drops; Ethan's duped me.

'Ethan said you were on your way to take care of him. Isn't he such a gentle drunk?' Ralph says.

I look at Ethan. His eyes well up with tears. The thought of him sleeping in a shop doorway in his state is too much to bear. Reluctantly, I agree to stand by him, for one more night.

'Frida, how lovely to see you,' Ethan says when he sees her waiting in my car.

'Oh, I thought you were being admitted for a detox,' Frida says.

'It's a long story.'

I check the time. I have to hurry so that Frida can catch her bus. Ethan hops back into my car, glad I've not abandoned him.

'Frida's off to meet Loday; she's flying to Newcastle shortly,' I say to Ethan while he lights a cigarette.

'Oh really. That's wonderful,' Ethan says. 'You are going to love it there. The Buddhists will treat you very well. Me and Loday are like brothers. You'll be under his wing and in the inner circle. It's one of the very best places in the world. Rinpoche's a very special guru of the highest order. He's a high lama, one of the highest in the world. I love it there. I've been for Buddhist retreats there. I'm so happy you're going.'

Frida hangs onto every word. She can't wait to get to Pathgate and meet this Rinpoche, where she'll enjoy respite in the safe haven with the Buddhists. We leave the hospital car park and eventually arrive at the bus station. I stop outside where I hug Frida goodbye. She races to catch the airport shuttle bus.

Chapter Thirty-two

Another night of car camping with Ethan lies ahead. At least Frida's arrived in Newcastle. She tells me that her accommodation is in one of the four Buddhist sangha community properties. One is the home of the Rinpoche. The second, where Loday and four other monks live, doubles up as the Buddhist retreat centre. The third house is where male students (both visiting and permanent students) and three older nuns live. The fourth property, where Frida's staying, is home to female visiting students, plus a permanent, devoted female student and the three youngest nuns. Each property has a room that's been converted into a shrine.

Knowing Frida's safe, I have one less thing to worry about. Now I have to focus my attention to Ethan's next detox. I doze off and on through the night, but sleep is impossible. The morning is gloomy and raining. I make an early start to ferry Ethan to another drugs-outreach organisation—another long drive. I let Ethan's father know there's hope and that Ethan's booked for another appointment.

Ethan's state isn't too bad when we arrive at the outreach reception desk. Half- way through the paperwork, someone hands a note to the key worker; she reads it and asks for me to step into another room. To my surprise I find Ethan's father there, sitting in a chair.

'Ethan mustn't know I'm here,' he says. 'I can't manage him. It's all down to you, now. Take this envelope; it'll help towards your expenses. Bless you for your help; I'm done with him! I can't take any more.' He nods and leaves before we can discuss anything.

Inside the envelope is a little money to help towards Ethan's booze, food, tobacco and my fuel for a few days, plus enough for a one-night stay in a motel for us to grab some sleep. Ethan's booze and chain-smoking costs around £50 per day. I have no idea how much debt he's got me in so far. I return to the room where Ethan is charming the staff with jokes. He has no concept of how his life hangs in the balance.

When the appointment ends, Loday calls, and I update him on the latest.

'Sorry I can't do much to help,' he says. 'But if you like I'll search online for a motel. You both need a rest.'

Premier Inn, the motel he's chosen is quite comfortable. Ethan has actually agreed to not confiscate my car keys from now on, due to the last fiasco when I was locked out and had to call the RAC. Visibility is limited this time of night in the motel car park, and when Ethan can't find a particular pair of trousers from his luggage, he starts shouting and throwing all the bags out of my car. He empties them all, throwing the clean clothing everywhere while swearing and shouting at the top of his voice. A car cruises slowly past us.

I gather everything up off the road in a panic and squeeze the clothing back into our bags, while he gulps wine from the bottle. He stops suddenly and dumps the bottle of wine into a hedge when the flashing, blue lights of a police car stop in front of us. Two cops get out of the squad car and approach us.

'There's been a report of a disturbance,' the taller cop says. He looks at Ethan. 'What did you just dump in that bush?'

'Nothing,' Ethan lies.

The other cop walks over to the hedge, unscrews the cap of the wine bottle and pours the remaining wine away.

The tall cop quietly asks me, 'Are you alright? Do you feel in danger?'

'I'm fine!' I lie. He jots notes and goes on to ask further questions: Name? Address? DOB? Ethan's name? Relationship? And so forth. When the questioning is over, they leave. I'm surprised by how Ethan could switch from aggressive to charming in the blink of an eye at the sight of the blue, flashing police car.

We return to our motel room where Ethan watches TV with wine in hand until early evening. I take advantage of a quiet moment and wash my hair. When I return to the main room, I hear Ethan laughing on his phone. He's speaking to Loday. He holds out the phone for me to talk.

'Hello, Ethan sounds a bit brighter,' Loday says.

'Umm. He has his ups and downs,' I reply. 'Did you call with news?'

'Oh, no. I didn't call. Ethan rang me.'

It dawns on me that Ethan, who didn't have Loday's number in this cheap replacement for his lost iPhone, hacked my phone as soon as my back was turned and managed to read and add Loday's number into his contacts, quickly, slyly and efficiently, in spite of being half legless. In the past he'd demanded control of my phone, now he just hacks it. I let the incident slide. I don't like the feeling that Ethan might start drunk dialling Frida or Sylvia.

Loday reminds Ethan to be nice and cooperate.

'Of course, I'll be nice. I promise.'

162

The call ends peacefully. Ethan pours a drink, then from out of nowhere he starts swearing and shouting, and I can't quieten him down. I'm afraid complaints will be made by the people in the next room. I try to take his head in my hands to soothe him, but he pushes me away. His gaze darts across the room to see what he can throw, and they rest on the TV screwed to the wall.

In a panic I phone his father. 'I need help! Ethan's losing it! Can you drive here and help me calm him down?'

'I'm too far away,' he says. 'It'll take me ages. But leave it to me; I'll phone the manager!' The line goes dead.

'Ethan, the manager's on his way. Why don't you get your trainers on so we can tell him we're okay?' What I'm really trying to do is prevent him from smashing up the room. If I can get him outside, just for an hour, he might calm down. He cooperates, for a change, and forces his feet into his trainers. I'm relieved as I shut the door to our room behind us and we walk down the corridor. Halfway down the passageway, however, police intercept us. His father called the cops because he was so worried for my safety.

Two policemen take Ethan somewhere to question him, while a female police officer asks me the same questions as always. I lie to protect him, telling her he hasn't hurt me, then I return to the stillness of our room.

A while later one of the police officers knocks at the door. 'He's calmed down and says he's sorry. He wants to come back to the room and go to sleep. But it's up to you.'

I'm too scared over what he might do next to let him waltz back into our room. I don't trust him. 'I'd rather he doesn't sleep here tonight.'

The police officer nods. 'Okay. We'll phone you later to see that you're all right.'

Once again, my heart pounds and my hands shake.

The officer phones me a while later with an update. 'We've given Ethan a talking to. He hasn't been arrested, and we've released him.'

The TV picture on the wall flickers. I remember how Ethan had eyed it up as if to throw something at it. My mind can't focus, not even on watching a programme, then there's a knock at the door. This time it's the motel porter.

'Hello, my manager sent me,' he says. 'Don't be alarmed, but the police just left. We had to call them. They've just arrested Ethan because we saw him on our cameras running up and down the motel corridors. He got back in the motel by slipping in with other guests. The police will hold him overnight, so don't worry.'

'What was he arrested for?' I ask.

'Trespassing, I think.'

With the assurance there will be no further incidents tonight, I huddle into a ball in bed.

Chapter Thirty-three

Waking up in a quiet room after six hours' sleep feels odd. I've forgotten what normal feels like. After a bath, I make myself a cup of breakfast tea and absentmindedly make two cups, one for Ethan.

There's different staff on reception when I go to check out; this saves me the embarrassment of having to apologise for Ethan's behaviour. I scan the car park, thinking he might be lurking to jump out, but I don't see him. For a while I sit in my car, fretting about him, wondering why everything I've tried so far to get him clean and sober has failed.

My mind plays flashbacks, and my conscience tells me to not judge him, because he's suffering with addiction. Mind over matter. Matter over mind. Merry-go-round. My phone sounds a new text message. From Ethan: *If you can bear to speak to me, please call me. I don't blame you if you never want to speak to me again. I'm sorry.*

I look blankly at the message. He calls five times, but I don't pick up for fear he's lulling me into a false sense of security. I start my car to leave town. I never want to go back there.

My resignation has dealt with some of my fears. Perhaps

that's why I answer Ethan's next phone call. Straight off I can tell he's had a skinful.

'Oi! You! Whore! Gimme back my stuff! Where's my watch? Eh? I'm gonna phone the police and report this as theft. What'd'ya say to that? Eh? I'm telling Theo you're a thief.'

I hang up.

Theo remains his calm self when I inform him of the threat, and I arrange with him to deliver all Ethan's property, watch and all, in person. Theo's trustworthy; Ethan regards him like a brother.

Once again, I run around on Ethan's behalf and deliver his property to Theo. It's a relief to no longer be responsible for his stuff. I don't expect to hear from him for a while, but a week later, he calls me again. All I can hear is his sobbing.

'Thanks for answering your phone. Please, let me say sorry face-to-face. Before I die. I was horrible to you last week,' he says.

I'm not good at handling his emotional blackmail, but I feel strong enough to clear the air face-to-face, so I agree to meet.

When he sees me, Ethan raises his right arm and waves, even though I couldn't miss him. He pulls open the passenger door and hops in.

'What's happened to you?' I ask. He's physically deteriorated and looks terrible.

'You see how I need you,' he replies. 'I've been homeless! Well, almost homeless. I mean, I've been living with junkies in a squat. A woman runs it; she found me on the pavement, so she's taken me in.'

So a do-gooder's taken him in—a bizarre story.

'Don't judge me, but I need a quick sip,' he says while digging into his pocket for what's left of a quart of vodka. The neat alcohol goes straight to his head, and every few seconds, his body jolts. 'I don't feel too good!' he whines.

I fear he might be having some kind of seizure but have no idea if this is a 999 emergency or if he's acting, so I drive him to A&E.

When I arrive at the hospital, a porter sees my distress and helps me ease Ethan into a wheelchair, then I wheel him into A&E. A nurse rushes over to check his breathing and pulse. She doesn't seem alarmed and asks if I can wheel him through the double doors and wait for a doctor. After all the usual questions, a saline drip is fitted to Ethan's arm to rehydrate him and he starts to come around. When he realises where he is, the first thing he wants is Valium.

After an hour of waiting, he starts hollering and swearing about how unjust it is that alcoholics get treated like lepers by the NHS—which isn't true, although stigma around addiction abounds elsewhere. Ethan winces when a nurse takes blood for tests, and within the hour, he discharges himself without being seen by a doctor.

I ferry him to his new home, the squat. From the outside it doesn't look much different from the other shabby Victorian houses on the main road. Inside, however, the wallpaper's peeling off the walls; the carpets are threadbare; the bathroom's grim, and the kitchen's full of dirty pots, pans, dishes, and trash. The lights flicker in the dinginess of the place, and a rank smell permeates the air. On the plus side, the central heating is on full blast, and the house is warm and dry. Ethan proudly shows me into his new room, complete with a roommate.

'Hello, are you Magda?' the man asks.

'Hi. Yes,' I reply.

'My name's Misbah.'

I learn that Misbah is not an alcoholic or addict, but he's been hit by hard times.

'Misbah's my personal chef,' Ethan says. 'He's from Delhi. He was street homeless, but I found him in the subway and brought him back here.'

Misbah nods. It seems he's useful to Ethan; maybe they've rescued each other.

'I protect Ethan from them,' Misbah whispers and points to the ceiling, to upstairs where the junkies squat. Not only does Misbah keep the junkies at bay, he also helps Ethan dress, wash and shave. He listens to Ethan's ranting and massages his head and bloated belly. Ethan has landed on his feet by securing free housing and a free carer.

The double-sized bedroom they share is on the first floor. A dirty window looks out onto the main road where buses and traffic roar past, and by the window is a two-seater corner sofa with its stuffing bursting out. Alongside a wall, empty wine bottles stand in a line, and next to the empties, a single-sized mattress lies on the floor with pillows and blankets. Ethan and Misbah share this bed by topping and tailing.

Apart from Ethan's washbag, Theo's still got the rest of Ethan's stuff, including his passport and bankcard—to prevent him from blowing his entire welfare benefit payment on his payday, like he's done in the past, for a binge. Theo drip-feeds Ethan money daily to make it last, but he remains adamant he won't coddle Ethan. The allowance nowhere near covers Ethan's drinking, chain-smoking and food, so Ethan does 'grafting,' that's begging, on the street. He spins sob stories to unsuspecting strangers to boost his income and feed his addiction.

The elderly woman who runs the squat appears at the bedroom doorway. She's fragile looking, dressed in grey, and around her neck a cross dangles on frayed string. 'I'm so glad you called in to see us,' the old dear says. 'Ethan said he's got a date for rehab soon?' she adds.

'Rehab?' I shake my head. 'No. I've just taken him to the hospital. No one knows anything about rehab.'

'He told me it's all sorted. He can't stay here much longer. He was jumping on my bed last night. With me in it and asking for Valium! I need my sleep. You better let me know when you hear anything,' she says.

Clearly, Ethan's ability to find free carers is one thing; hanging onto them is the tricky part.

'What day is it? What's the time?' Ethan suddenly blurts out.

'It's Tuesday evening, six o'clock,' I reply.

Ethan jumps onto his feet. 'Let's go!'

I frown. 'Where to?'

'To an AA meeting.'

'But you're not sober.'

'I'm powerless over alcohol. But by the time we get there, I won't have drunk for one hour.'

This seems to be a step in the right direction, so I ferry him across town to the AA meeting.

Construction works are in progress at the church hall, so we have to negotiate fencing to get to the entrance door. The meeting has just started.

The chairman recognises Ethan, and though he likely knows Ethan's relapsed again, he looks at him without judgment. 'Hi, you must be Magda,' he says. He is softly spoken, smartly dressed, and looks the picture of health. You'd never guess that ten years ago he was a park-bench-drunk crack-head. 'My name's Jason; come and sit down.'

Six other recovering alcoholics sit in a circle. Jason brings us cups of tea and opens the meeting. A fellow starts to share his story, to celebrate his two years of sobriety.

In the middle of his share, Ethan stands up, whoops and starts applauding. He reaches into his pocket, draws out a can of Guinness that he's smuggled into the meeting and pulls the ring. Brown liquid sprays the astonished group before Ethan gulps huge mouthfuls from the foaming can. 'Cheers! Here's to being sober!' he says.

Jason eases the can of Guinness from his grasp and dashes to the kitchen sink, where he tips what's left of it away, then he beckons Ethan outside the room. 'You're welcome to join us, but without booze. You know that.' He gives Ethan a brotherly pep talk, urging him to find his HP—his higher power.

Then he turns to me. 'Listen, Magda, call me if you need to talk. He's got to hit rock bottom. You mustn't enable. Step back. Let go.'

I don't know where Ethan's rock bottom might be, but it must be somewhere.

'Ethan, she can't cope with you. If you want her support, you must help yourself!' Jason says.

We follow the construction fence back the way we came and head back to my car before the meeting resumes.

Ethan's mad he got thrown out. 'AA is shit,' he says. 'There's something cultish about it. I thought Jason was my friend.'

My first impression of the AA meeting is how the fellowship didn't judge Ethan, and in the few minutes I was there, I saw Jason's kindness.

Deep down, I'm sure Ethan wants to get clean and sober.

A week later, Ethan's outreach worker still has no updates about his funding, and the old dear from the squat wants a word.

'Isn't there news yet, about rehab?' she asks as soon as she opens the rickety front door.

'Not a word; sorry,' I reply.

She's pouring us a cup of tea, when someone hammers on the front door.

'Give all this to him. I can't stand it anymore!' It's Theo's voice.

'I'll withdraw Ethan's welfare money myself and leave a tenner a day under my dustbin.' He dumps all Ethan's belongings—except his bankcard, ID and watch—in the hallway and stomps off.

Apparently, Ethan had been nagging for the return of his stuff, so Theo obliged. Misbah says he'll collect the daily tenner and buy Ethan's booze, to prevent any shoplifting. We carry the bags upstairs and stash them in the bedroom.

In desperation, I leave the squat and call Loday with the lowdown on how crazy this situation has become.

'Let me think about this. I'll ring you back!' Loday says. Later when he calls back, he says, 'Magda, I've decided to arrange a private rehab for Ethan. I've already spoken with the rehab. I'll fund it myself, but I'll need my guru teacher's permission to spend money. He's away for a few days, but it'll be fine. The rehab I've chosen are going to call you later for a telephone assessment. Be ready for when they call; within the next few days, he'll be in the detox wing.'

I can't believe this stroke of luck.

Ethan's face lights up when he hears the good news. The rehab calls for the telephone assessment; I answer their questions on Ethan's behalf, and it all goes like clockwork. Ethan ends the call by telling the rehab staff he's fallen in love with her. She chuckles at his silliness. The final word is with Loday's guru teacher, that high Rinpoche, but it's just a matter of days, and all will be well.

Chapter Thirty-four

The days have dragged waiting for the lama's consent, but eventually Loday calls. I switch on loudspeaker so Ethan can hear.

'Hello. Here I am. Bit of a hitch; my guru teacher has said no to helping Ethan. I'm not allowed to fund his rehab. I'm sorry about that,' he says.

I'm blown away by the shock. Ethan's a student of the guru—be it a wayward one. He took refuge with the lama a few years ago, so to be dismissed like this is a blow, especially because Ethan claims that he and Loday have been like brothers ever since he was a young teenager. He looks crestfallen, no, devastated. I've seen Ethan sad, sob and cry, but never so demoralized. He's speechless, for once.

'Oh, never mind,' I reply, trying to sound upbeat. Now I have to break the bad news to Theo.

The news gradually sinks in. February's approaching, and I've more running around to do. The police need to meet with Ethan. If he doesn't show up, he'll be re-arrested, and he's terrified of being locked up, but due to Ethan's drunken state, he can't travel on public transport, or cabs, nor will bus drivers allow him on board. So I ferry him to the other side of town for the meeting with the police. They've composed a letter of apology to the superstore where Ethan was caught shoplifting on the night I was locked out of my car. All he has to do is sign the apology and promise it won't happen again. He eagerly signs and goes home. Case closed.

Now, for some peace and quiet, I hope. But within minutes my phone rings. I pull over to answer; it's the old dear.

'Can you come back? It's urgent.'

I do a u-turn to drive back. I have to park a mile away and walk the rest.

'Come upstairs, please,' the old dear says when she opens the rickety front door. 'I've evicted Ethan. He has to go. The police are on their way to get rid of him. I can't take any more!' She leads the way to Ethan and Misbah's room.

Misbah looks upset, and the junkies loiter, looking bemused. Ethan's all worked up.

It takes the biscuit for someone to be evicted from a squat. I don't know how he's managed it. How can a squatter evict their own squatter?

A loud knocking sounds on the door, and a moment later, the police march up the staircase and stomp into the squalid bedroom to listen to the wails of the old dear. My phone rings, so I step outside the room and leave the police to do their talking.

'Ethan asked me to call you,' a man says. 'I'm his ex-sponsor from years back. He wants a rescue, says he's getting evicted from the squat tonight.'

'Yes, but do you know how much I've done to help him?' I reply.

'Hear me out. You have to detach with love. You're powerless. Just look at his family! They're detached. Step back. He'll make it if he wants it. Call me if you need to talk.'

The police have restored order in the bedroom. They've asked Ethan to leave and not return. The old dear wants him arrested for anti-social behaviour.

Ethan butts in, 'You can't arrest me! I haven't done nothing. I need an ambulance. I'm gonna have a seizure!'

The police mutter to each other.

'Come on!' one of the cops say. 'On your feet! We won't arrest you; we'll drive you to A&E instead. But there'll be trouble if you come back here.'

This placates Ethan. He holds his arms out while Misbah helps with his jacket. I drop his handset and cigarettes into his pocket. The cops escort him out of the squat and into the squad car.

The old dear plops down on the edge of the sofa with the stuffing bursting out. 'I can't put up with any more stress!'

Misbah peers out the mucky window, watching the squad car as it pulls away. The junkies, who have been lapping up the drama, grin while they eye up Ethan's belongings.

'Ethan promised to give us some of his stuff. We'll take what's ours,' one junky says.

I stare at her, knowing she's lying. 'Well, he's not in any condition for giveaways today, so if you don't mind, I've got work to do.'

They sidle back to their room.

I don't know where to start, then I remember how far away I've parked my car, so I call a cab for ten minutes time. Misbah helps me pack Ethan's stuff. He's also my look-out man, standing on the landing while I run up and down the staircase with Ethan's numerous belongings. My cab arrives in a torrential downpour.

'Wow, that's a lot of gear! You moving house at this hour?' The taxi driver jokes.

'It's a long story!'

I'm relieved when the doors of my car close with everything loaded inside. I can't believe Ethan's belongings, apart from what Theo's kept, are back in my car.

Overnight the rain makes puddles so huge they form little lakes in the roadside and pavements. My phone ringing wakes me.

'Can you believe the old dear booted me out!' Ethan rages. 'Them fucker junkies are still there!'

In one way I understand his bitterness, and yet he's been numbed or in blackout throughout, so he hasn't felt the full impact of the distress he's caused, not in the same way I have. Ethan has no concept of how hard I've tried to help him get clean and sober. I've placed my life on hold. My life is on a downward spiral because of him.

'I've lost all my shit. I bet those fucker junkies have robbed me!' he fumes. 'But listen, I got my own back! After I discharged myself from A&E last night, I snuck back into the squat and slept in the kitchen. No one saw me; I left before sunrise.'

'You're lucky the old dear didn't find you. Anyhow, Misbah helped me get your stuff out. It's in my car.'

'Really? You're kidding!'

'Yes, really. Now you'll have to help me. I can't take any more of this. We need to focus on getting rehab funding. I'll buy you breakfast, and we'll have a talk.'

'Wonderful. Thanks, I'm starving,' he says.

We arrange to meet for a McDonald's breakfast. Also, I call Misbah to give him the update, along with an invite to join us. When I cross the busy road opposite McDonald's, I spot Ethan crouching over one of the mini-lake puddles. He scoops up the dirty water in his hands, washes his face, then cups more puddle water and chucks it over his hair.

'Just freshening up,' he says, as I approach him. He dries his hands on his trousers, wipes his face with his sleeve and retrieves a bent cigarette from his pocket. 'Misbah!' he cries out when he spots him walking towards us. He runs towards him and gives him a great, big hug.

'Okay. Let's eat.' I say. We sit down with our trays. It's like a reunion breakfast. I root around for my hand sanitizer, and Misbah cleans Ethan's puddle hands with the gel. Breakfast is on me, and Misbah makes a sign of thanks with his hands. Ethan bitches about the old dear and junkies, and Misbah nods in agreement, as if to say it's not easy to be a squatter, but it's better than the subway.

'When I get clean and sober, you'll live with us, Misbah. Won't he Magda?' Ethan says. 'We'll get you out of there. I promise.'

'Thank you. Yes please!' Misbah says.

We know it's an empty promise, at least I do.

Ethan tries to answer my ringing phone, but I beat him to it.

It's his dad. 'Have you spoken to Ethan today?'

Ethan bursts into song.

'Ah, I see you have!' his dad retorts.

Ethan yanks my phone out of my hand. 'Dad! I'm dying! I need rehab! Theo's got my watch. Please sell it if you have to. Help me get into rehab.' He hands me back my phone and blows his freezing hands.

'As I was trying to say,' his dad continues, 'we, Ethan's mum and I, have decided to fund rehab between us. We have to borrow money to fund it. We can only afford four weeks; that'll cost ten grand. I've arranged a phone assessment with the rehab, and they'll be calling you later. If he gets arrested again, rehab won't take him.'

I'm surprised his parents have come together to fund Ethan's

176

rehab, despite their differences.

Ethan, jumping for joy, says, 'I've got rehab, Misbah!'

We kill time sitting in my car. A few hours later, the rehab admin phones us to carry out his assessment. As before, I answer all the questions on Ethan's behalf.

'Misbah, I've got a plan; if you'll agree?' I ask.

He nods. I drive back to the squat. Misbah goes in alone to collect what I've suggested, which is his warm coat, thick socks, woolly hat and gloves. Minutes later he reappears and hops into my car's overloaded rear seat.

'Thanks, Misbah. You're amazing,' I say.

'It's nothing. You're welcome,' he replies.

It's more than nothing to me. Misbah has agreed to watch over Ethan with me for the next three freezing February days and nights until rehab admission morning. All three of us will have to live and sleep in my car. We fear Ethan will sabotage rehab again by getting arrested or going missing, so we have the burden to take care of him until his admission. In addition, should Ethan get violent, Misbah has the role of my bodyguard. Ethan's family and friends have their peace and safety from afar; Misbah and I are his guardian angels ensuring he gets to rehab.

Chapter Thirty-five

Tomorrow's rehab admission day. Misbah waits with Ethan while I go and buy us breakfast of warm croissants and coffees. I spot a shop and purchase a surprise present for Ethan. We pack his rehab bag. He'll need all his tops, because of the detox sweats. Ethan's father calls to see if he's prepared.

'I'll meet you and Ethan tomorrow morning, and we'll go to rehab in my car. By the way, can you find any official paperwork or the original box for Ethan's watch? It's quite valuable and worth even more with the box and papers,' he says.

I agree to look, and our short conversation ends abruptly. The twenty-four- hour countdown to rehab has begun.

I've got more than enough to contend with, but I ask Ethan, and I'm surprised when he remembers exactly where the watch papers are. I was half expecting not to find anything.

It's not often a day passes quickly, but today flies by. In the darkness the light of Misbah's iPad illuminates his face as he sits quietly watching his favourite comedy. Every time Ethan uses foul language or lashes out at me or starts shouting, Misbah prays to Allah.

Ethan asks me 'how long to rehab' at frequent intervals

until he zonks out. During the night he wakes and asks again, 'How long?'

'Seven hours.' I yawn.

Next time he shakes me awake. 'How long?'

'Only three hours!'

'Really? Three hours?' He whoops.

We have time for a panini breakfast and coffees. Depending on traffic, the rehab is just over an hour's drive away, and Ethan's dad is on his way to meet us. Ethan chain-smokes, and finishes the last of his booze. He gets super excited when he sees his dad's car.

He parks behind us and calls out, 'Are we ready?'

Ethan gives his dad a hug for a few seconds.

Ethan's dad loads Ethan's belongings, and I hand him the watch papers in an envelope. Then I reach into my car and uncover the present I bought for Ethan.

'Surprise, Ethan! This is for you,' I hold it out.

He looks stunned as he takes the bag and opens it. 'Trainers!' Tears of joy well up in his swollen, purple eyes. 'I don't know what to say,' he adds while kicking off his piss-covered, muddy trainers that need binning. 'How did you know? They fit perfect!'

His father straps Ethan in the backseat, with plastic bags in case he vomits and the child locks on. We drop Misbah back outside the squat and Ethan hugs him goodbye. When Ethan's father stops for petrol, Ethan wangles a bottle of garage red wine; one for the road. Finally, we're on our way to rehab.

Chapter Thirty-six

'I love you, Daddy!' Ethan declares while sitting restrained in the backseat, quaffing his bottle of red to pacify him. He shakes his pouch of tobacco like it's a rattle, gagging for a smoke in the no smoking car.

I sit next to Ethan, behind his sombre father.

'Daddy! I said I love you. Tell me back.'

'I love you,' his father replies.

'I'm going to marry Magda,' Ethan adds with intoxicated seriousness.

His frivolity makes me uneasy.

'Maybe one day, Ethan,' his dad replies. 'But right now, you can't. Your month at rehab is costing us ten grand. That's a lot of money. It looks like I'll have to sell my car to pay for it. I'm retirement age. You're meant to be looking after me! Phoebe said she won't talk to you until you've been sober at least two years.'

I don't know if this is an empty threat.

'And you need to know this rehab has to work. You're a mess: homeless, unemployed, penniless and an addict. You can't get married until you get clean and sober and stand on your own two feet. That means finding a job and growing up. It also means no more bloody women!'

Ethan blows a raspberry while he suppresses a chuckle. He's shitfaced, so he won't remember the dressing down, but hearing it shocks me a little. Ethan told me he'd been in a few steady relationships and was dependable, but the way his father talks is as if Ethan's unbalanced, addicted to women, sex or some kind of freeloader. Come to think of it, Vicky had said something similar that awful night. On the other hand, Ethan let slip in several pissed outbursts that he has no idea of how many flings, affairs, or relationships he's procured and lost, but then he'd recanted. At the last count, I'm not sure what he wanted me to believe, nor wanted to believe himself.

Ethan's father changes the subject and lightens up. 'We're here,' he says, at last.

The rehab, an old, detached house, sits high on a hill. My first impression is how Hitchcock-esque it is.

Ethan's father parks his car and hops out. 'Won't be a minute. No smoking.' He slams the car door shut.

Ethan tries to open it to smoke. He has been fiddling with the same fag the whole drive, but we're locked in because of child locks. He drains the last of his wine, digs into his pocket and says, 'Look after this for me. If I have it on me, I'll relapse!' He hands me his wallet with his bankcard.

At least he's thinking about relapse prevention, despite being pissed.

His father returns a few minutes later. 'Ethan, they're ready for you.'

A member of staff takes Ethan's arm to assist him.

Admission is swift. His father can't wait to leave. Ethan looks confused when two members of staff take over and link their arms with his. I kiss his cheek to say goodbye. He doesn't notice. His face is cold and clammy.

'Will you marry me?' he asks the female member of staff who's holding him up.

'I don't think my husband would like that!' she replies.

He swivels his head around. 'Anyone got a beer?'

'Dear me, Ethan, no! You'll be detoxing soon,' the woman says.

'He'll be right as rain. Don't worry; we'll take good care of him!' she calls out as she takes him away.

All the women I've met who work in addiction facilities talk to him like he's a toddler. It's odd, this regression therapy or whatever it is.

'I'll drop you back to your car. We'll stop off for lunch on the way,' Ethan's dad says. He makes small talk while driving. We soon reach a village and find a small restaurant.

After placing our orders, his dad frowns and says, 'This rehab has to work. I don't know what he's told you, but we've struggled with his addiction for well over two decades. He's never been able to hold down a job because of it. In the past he's been offered jobs, but he gets fired within a week because of his drinking. We've bailed him out many times with helping with housing and paying off thousands of pounds of his debts. He's hocked expensive bicycles, a car, his computers, iPhones, designer clothing, televisions, and even the contents of his last flat—all to drug dealers for next to nothing. In fact, anything he can get his hands on, he's traded for drugs. He's tried relocating several times, but always finds his way back to addiction. Things got worse when he started using crack.' He touches his fingertips together.

'Almost a decade ago, he got clean and sober for a bit, that's the only time though. He's a serial relapser. When he got clean that time, he started working, eating healthily. He even quit smoking and cycled everywhere, but it wasn't to last. This is his last chance; we can't afford to fund more rehabs. He needs to recover by focusing for the next four to six months, without being distracted with having you around. His mum and I are arranging special housing for Ethan for when he gets out of rehab. It's for people like him. He'll have professional support in the accommodation, like a half-way house for his rehabilitation. I can't have him live with me, and the family can't either—it's never worked out. So do you agree? You and Ethan take a break for at least four months? It'll do you good too.'

'I understand; of course, I agree.'

I'm willing to respect Ethan's family's wishes, because I want him to get well. I try to process all the new information but try as I might to piece together Ethan's complex life in addiction, it still baffles me. Some revelations tally with what Ethan's already mentioned, but he has kept a lot under wraps. I don't know the real Ethan. Yes, I do. Actually, my head feels like a fog.

'I'm glad we agree,' his dad says.

Loday invites me to Newcastle, says he'd like me to attend a scheduled two-day spiritual retreat. The lama will give teachings on Buddhism to his students and attendees. It sounds interesting, and I'll get to see Frida, who has been there over a month. I book myself a train ticket and Frida meets me at Newcastle station. She looks happy and wears new burgundy clothing the lama gifted her when she first arrived. A bowl of soup is served the minute I walk through the door of the female sangha house, and as we eat, I listen to Frida recount her news. She can't wait to show me around.

The female student house looks like an average terrace house from the outside, but inside it is spotless and so quiet you could hear a pin drop. It has four bedrooms, two are average-sized bedrooms: one on the ground floor (a converted dining room) and the other on the first floor. Both have bunk-beds. The smallest bedroom sleeps a permanent student, and the middle-sized bedroom sleeps three Buddhist nuns.

The curtains and carpets are deep burgundy, as are the rugs, throws, duvets, towels, face flannels, even coasters. The predominant colour theme in the sangha is burgundy with smatterings of reds, yellows, purple and white that emerge from silk Buddhist wall hangings and an abundance of freshly cut flowers in vases. The shower room is at the top of the staircase, and the loft has been converted into a shrine room. A newly fitted, spotless kitchen contains all mod-cons, a top-notch kitchen range and a vast amount of cooking equipment. The lounge is burgundy with gold touches, and the huge sofas, curtains, carpet, and light shades are also burgundy with cushions to match. An enormous portrait of the lama wearing robes hangs above the fireplace, alongside portraits of His Holiness Penor Rinpoche, Buddha, and a young boy in lama attire. Vases of freshly cut flowers sit in front of the fireplace and on the shelves. After all the hideous chaos and trauma spent with Ethan, this place feels tranquil.

The Buddhist centre/monks' house is a ten-minute walk away. Frida and I hurry there, the wind almost blowing us off our feet. It has a different front door than the female sangha house—black instead of white—but inside is the same burgundy. I slip off my shoes and place them with a pile of other pairs—footwear must not be worn inside any of the holy houses. I stand at the bottom of the stairs sensing someone looking down at me. I look up. I've never seen a photo, but I know it's Loday. He smiles and descends the staircase to greet me, hitching his flowing skirt as he does so. He wears monk's robes in burgundy and gold. His shaved head has a few days' worth of stubble.

'Hi, there you are,' I exclaim. We don't exchange hugs or handshakes, because monks, and their robes, are not to be touched by the likes of me. Even when loaded into a washing machine, only the ordained may touch robes belonging to a monk or nun, except in an emergency.

'Nice to see you,' Loday replies.

After months of talking to him on the phone, we meet at last. He's been the only person to not snub me, and he listened to my anguished days and nights during Ethan's relapse. I feel grateful that I can rely on Loday to support Frida, what with Ethan taking up all my time and energy. I regard him as trustworthy, since most of Ethan's contacts and fair-weather friends jumped ship long ago. We chat a little before Frida and I head back to the female house for evening prayers.

For the first time in months, I drift off to sleep contentedly, with the knowledge I shan't be shaken awake by Ethan throwing another alkie temper tantrum.

The day starts early. We rise at 5.30 am for morning prayer practice followed by breakfast and showers. The queue for the shower room trails all the way down the staircase. After we make our beds, we race to the Buddhist centre for the lama's opening of the retreat.

Numerous times Loday and Ethan have sung the lama's praises; they say the lama has special superpowers that were bestowed upon him at the time of his birth in this life. Also, they say that he can see into the past and future, read minds, has healing powers, is a martial arts expert, has a photographic memory, knows everything, and is highly regarded and loved. By rule of thumb, not everyone has the honour of having an invite to attend the lama retreats, so I am one of the blessed and fortunate indeed.

There is a frisson of excitement in the air when the lama starts his teaching. Everyone attending—about thirty retreat attendees, mostly overseas students—stand and sing him in, while he walks slowly into the shrine room, scattering rice. What was once an average lounge in the monks' terrace house is now the shrine room. The Buddhist centre and office headquarters are upstairs, and the loft has been converted into the monks' sleeping quarters.

The lama's burgundy and gold robes hide his build, but his flabby arms indicate he is hefty. He saunters in the room with his bare feet apart, and moseys forwards with a confident, cowboy swagger. He takes his elevated lama seat, sits crossed legged and opens his teaching with Tibetan texts.

Typically, a teaching lasts around seven hours with a one-hour lunch break. At the start of lunch, all students and attendees gift monetary offerings in white, sealed envelopes, which are piled neatly upon his low table. In addition, prayer and chanting practices are scheduled before and after teaching, so it's a sixteen-hour day altogether.

The students and attendees sit cross-legged on the floor, listening attentively to every holy, compelling word, but I find the long day makes it difficult to concentrate. Whether it's fatigue or me, a lot of the teachings are not easy to understand, but everyone has to make notes of the wise lama's spiritual speeches. Frida seems to have a better grasp of the verbal expressions. My knowledge of Tibetan Buddhism is minimal, apart from what I've read in books by the Dalai Lama. I have a lot to learn.

On the last day of the weekend retreat, Frida is offered the chance to seek refuge with the lama. Ethan had taken refuge two summers before, despite him being an addict and in Buddhism getting intoxicated is forbidden. He feels connected to the sangha (even though the offer of funding his rehab was retracted) and a sense of belonging, what with being friends with Loday for decades.

I'm not entirely sure how seeking refuge works or what it entails. For the ritual of seeking refuge, Frida kneels before the lama in the presence of all the cross-legged, burgundy clad students, including monks, nuns, novices, and attendees, and has a few strands of hair cut off by the lama, then he gives her a Buddhist name, a blessing, a metal pendant with Buddha on it, three Buddha photos and one of himself, and in return she agrees to honour and obey student vows. The lama and Buddhists are friendly, something I've found lacking in the majority of the Catholics and Christians I've met.

The retreat ends joyfully. The revered lama is sung out with an ancient Tibetan song, and we're all one-step closer to enlightenment.

On my last day, Frida shows me around Newcastle city, as Loday has given her permission to take a few hours off dharma duty.

Our first port of call is a cute café where they serve every kind of herbal tea. We visit the art gallery, the quay, and the mall. She talks about how she likes the sangha, how they've offered to help her get back on her feet. She is adjusting to the tough routine. Her first week was relaxed, but since then, errands fill her days. We return to the sangha and discover that a restaurant meal with the lama has been planned for four of us.

My weekend has been enjoyable, but tiring, and now we get ready for the meal. I'm expecting the lama to be dressed in robes, but instead he's wearing a casual outfit—black jeans, and a black leather jacket. One of the lama's favourite students is his personal chauffeur. She's around Frida's age, and although pretty, she's unsmiling and aloof.

The restaurant is top notch, and the waiters seem to know the lama well, but the menu prices are eye-watering expensive. When our food is placed before us, Lama says a mealtime prayer. I've heard that sometimes lama likes to feed diners at his table from his own fork—no matter how full they may feel—and the food offering is a gesture that isn't to be refused. This mealtime we are spared his feeding ritual.

The charming lama talks enthusiastically. He doesn't mention Ethan, his wayward student without whom Frida and I wouldn't be here. Possibly with his superpowers he already knows about Ethan's detox.

We are mindful to pay attention to lama, but my mind wanders with fatigue. He talks about Bruce Lee, and we listen. A constant tension that comes from the fear of making a faux pas in his presence hovers around us. When our meal is finished, lama asks for the bill. He hands the unsmiling student a wad of cash to settle it.

Lama is first to be driven back to his apartment. It's customary for students and his guests to get out of the car and bow heads with palms together in prayer until he reaches the door of his home. Just before he walks away, he drapes a white, satin kata around my neck. It's the done thing when a student or guest leave the sangha.

We return to the female house to collect my backpack. A young nun, Loday, and Frida accompany me to the station, and we have time for coffee before my departure.

The café Loday suggests is bustling, but we find a table and take a seat while Loday orders our lattes. When he returns, he surprises me with snacks for my long journey. Kindness is almost alien to me, and I'm so speechless by his gesture that I briskly hug him. Everyone smiles at my reaction.

At the station, I hug Frida goodbye. She looks happy. I can hardly believe how she has settled and how much she has to look forward to.

During my journey back to the South all I can think about is how we're on the up: Frida has stability, which makes Sylvia less anxious; I'm optimistic, and Ethan is on the road to recovery. In my head I make a gratitude list for all the good things.

My stress-related body aches persist, however. Painkillers don't touch the leg and backache from all the crossed-legged sitting during the retreat. Apart from that, everything's coming up roses.

Chapter Thirty-seven

Five days after Ethan's rehab admission, he's over the worse of his detox. When rehab calls, I think it's with an encouraging update.

'Hello? This is Ethan's counsellor,' the man says, 'can you talk to Ethan? He's decided to discharge himself.'

My jaw drops. 'You're kidding?'

'Hang on; I'll put him on!'

'Hello? I'm packing,' Ethan says. I'm out of here. You'll have to bust me out. Right?'

'No. That's a bad idea. You need this to stay alive. Your family will be angry if you jack it in. They won't forgive you if you walk, and they won't get a refund. So please stay?' The Librium detox he had is a rapid one, rather than a slow taper, so this might be why his thinking is all over the map.

He sighs. 'Okay, I'll stay. But my dad told rehab I mustn't see you again. I'll only stay if you speak to me on the payphone every evening.'

'All right, that's a deal.' He may have emotionally blackmailed me, but at least he's agreed to stay put.

From my previous experience, and Ethan's unpredictable

behaviour, I can't be sure he'll cooperate, but I know I've done my best to ferry him to another rehab, and I've asked him to go the distance.

I call Sylvia, but she doesn't pick up. February cold weather is upon us, the time of year when she struggles most with asthma, so I drive to her home to check on her. I've just caught her at home. She's talking to emergency services, and they want her to attend A&E immediately. Apparently, the tablets she took haven't been digested yet, so she's still lucid. On our rushed journey to A&E, I push thoughts of possible damage to the back of my mind. All this time, while neglecting her, I was thinking Sylvia had been coping just fine, but her anxiety has manifested into something more serious than I'd envisaged. Mental health problems, as well as addiction, do not discriminate.

A nurse takes blood from Sylvia's tiny wrists for tests. I wait with trepidation for the results while Sylvia remains expressionless. Mercifully, there is no damage done, and physically she is okay. A psychiatric assessment is to be carried out for a referral for counselling.

I have a bitter feeling of self-reproach for being missing since getting dragged under with Ethan's addiction. My role as a mother has always been my priority, but now I'm forced to accept how addiction can demolish family relationships. Given Ethan's objections to rehab and all his 'I wants,' not to mention how things are 'up in the air' between us, I decide I must set boundaries.

Try as I might to get my life back on track, however, what Ethan wants is of greater importance. To appease him, I do all I can to make him happy. Two weeks into his treatment, he receives a two-weeks-sober AA chip. At last, he is starting to like rehab. For someone who usually babbles, he rarely mentions what rehab is like; he'll just say it's quite good. For Valentine's

I post him an arty card and write inspirational quotes. He even remembers it's Valentine's Day. This might be a sign his short-term memory is improving. Ethan's co-dependency keeps cropping up in his therapy sessions. He always calls me late in the evening from the payphone that eats coins in the lobby.

Tonight, he calls at his usual time.

'You have to drop whatever you're doing, whenever I say, otherwise I'll relapse!' he says as soon as I answer his call. 'My dad's upset me. He told me he's selling my watch to help pay for my rehab!'

'Okay; alright. Just calm down,' I reply.

'Alright. If I get stressed, I'll drink. You must send me more inspirational cards. No one's ever written to me before, and I don't want to be the only person here who doesn't get any post!'

'Okay, don't worry, I will.'

Within the hour I'm on my way to the post box to send him another card. As I signal right and yield to traffic, the glare of an on-coming car's headlights dazzles me, so I remain stationary. Then SMASH; it crashes into me. The noise of impact is like a mini explosion. I get out of my car to inspect the damage and shake my head in disbelief. I reckon my car's a write-off, not even drivable.

I go through the hoo-ha of contacting my motor insurance company for a courtesy car. It strikes me how Ethan's controlling behaviour, even while he's in rehab, still causes significant problems. I guess I must be scared of him.

Ethan's twenty-four days clean and sober to the day. In four days' time, he'll have completed his one-month of rehab. It's Sunday, visiting day, and I'm on my way to visit him, zooming along in the new loan car. I haven't seen Ethan since his admission morning. His counsellor isn't objecting to my visit, nor has he been advised that we call it a day. But it's come to light, in Ethan's therapy, that he's had co-dependency issues for most of his life, with his family, friends, girlfriends, partners, AA sponsors, AA members, all his relationships in fact, even with people he barely knows. He latches onto people. I know he hates his own company, and from what I learned, he gets fixated on people for different reasons: sexual attraction, to boost his ego, for financial gain or favours. Ethan sees relationships as insurance, or currency, to reap benefits; he's not choosy who he targets.

I arrive five minutes early. Ethan appears at the car door, squinting and shading his eyes from the sunshine. He looks suspiciously around the loan car and sees the kata guru gave me.

'You got a kata from lama,' he says. 'So you've met Loday!'

'Yes. I'll tell you all about it.'

His eyes aren't glassy. His dark-purple eye sockets have turned lilac, and he stands steady. He looks happy. His acid reflux has gone. He's squeaky clean and alert. How different he looks from the way he did on his admission morning.

He opens my door for me to get out of the car and hugs me briefly, then delves into his pocket for his tobacco pouch and proceeds to roll a cigarette. 'Come. Follow me.'

This rehab isn't as upmarket as the last residential rehab. He shows me the upstairs dormitory; it's tidy and Spartan. He shares it with other male clients. Once clients are detoxed in the medical room, they're moved into the dorm. At bedtime when they're hit with the sweats, night terrors and endless trips to the toilet with diarrhoea, a good night's sleep is impossible. Ethan shows me his timetable. The clients' breakfast bell is rung early followed by a full day's schedule. He's had a few warnings: one for smoking indoors and another for skipping group therapy while he took a nap.

Ethan likes group sessions, ever since he was praised and got a standing ovation for reading aloud his colourful life story in a feelings group. It's made him popular. He's the relapse hero, a badge of honour that he wears proudly.

Ethan shares a joke with a detoxed junkie, a heroin addict with whom he has bonded. Her name's Lita. It's common knowledge amongst the other clients that she copulates with a few guys in rehab; apparently, she's so charming that no one's grassed her up. Next, we rush to where the family meeting is being held.

Clients, their wives, husbands, partners, and loved ones, fill the brightly lit room full of chitter-chatter. Ethan and I sit at the back of several rows of plastic chairs.

A counsellor stands before a whiteboard and writes Triggers, Relapse, Relapse Prevention, Goals and Recovery on it with a marker pen. A smaller board has Twelve Step work on it. A hushed silence ripples through the room until you could hear a pin drop.

'Ninety-seven percent of you will relapse when you get out of here,' she says.

I try not to look alarmed. I glance to see Ethan's expression.

He briefly looks back at me and squeezes my hand. 'I'm never going to drink again. I promise. So marry me.' He's goofing around.

The woman continues to talk about the family disease and how addiction funding has been drastically slashed.

Someone raises a hand to ask a question. 'Should the whole family be teetotal to prevent a relapse?'

The counsellor thinks for a second, then says, 'In early recovery, support from loved ones isn't the key to sobriety, but it helps.' She pops the cap off her marker pen and writes: *One day at a time.* She goes on to talk about being patient; recovery is life-long.

Ethan loves me again. I believe every word. He'll never drink again. I think he might really like for us to settle down. For now, though, it's plain to see that recovery comes first and relationships second. Goals, the counsellor tells us, are more easily met when bitterness is replaced by forgiveness. Despite Ethan betraying me time and time again, I'm willing to bury the hatchet. It seems our relationship might be built on attachment, and I've yet to become acquainted with the real Ethan, the one who is willing to change. The talk continues, and the word 'enabler' is mentioned.

'Recently we had a client whose elderly mother scored heroin for her son. She called it kindness; we call it enabling. If you love the addict in your life, seek advice for you, not alcohol or drugs for them! There is help at hand. Don't be afraid.' The counsellor's final words are prudent.

By the end of the talk, Ethan is edgy, dying for a smoke. Visiting is almost over, and he becomes fidgety. Maybe it's the caffeine, or separation anxiety. We take a seat in the piano room where a man is in deep conversation with a heavily pregnant woman. Her head's down, while the guy holds her hands and does all the talking.

'Don't look now,' Ethan whispers, 'but that's Roy; he's in my group. He robbed an old lady of her life savings to fund this rehab. That's a junky for you! An alkie has principles. I confessed that I stole thousands from Koemi over the years. A junky never feels guilt.'

I'm intrigued as to why he identifies as an alcoholic. I know it's his drug of choice, but his drug addiction is almost as rampant as booze. Whatever it is, though, it's in the past. We can be normal from now on. We can get back to the way we were, only better, with our newly found hindsight.

The buzzer sounds to signal the end of visiting. Ethan and I exchange goodbye hugs, and clients and their loved ones share warm embraces in the lobby area. I notice the clients look cheery, and if I'm not mistaken, us visitors look worn to a frazzle.

Chapter Thirty-eiGht

When I arrive to collect Ethan from rehab, he's already in the lobby in a rush to leave. Rather than waiting for me to open the boot of the car, he risks scratching the rear door to use the backseat instead. Already I'm in a panic with a familiar feeling; he barks, I jump.

Aside from that, I can hardly believe he didn't sabotage rehab and stuck it out. The accomplishment is huge. It's a first for him to see something through to the end. Yesterday an after dinner 'clapping-out' ceremony was held for Ethan. He stood in the middle of a circle where clients clapped and sang a lucky rhyme, then recited compliments in turn while holding his hands to tell him, things like what an honour it was to have walked the journey of recovery with him. They presented him with a signed good-luck card along with one last rapturous applause.

'Sorry about the rush,' he says. 'I just had to see the back of that place.' He switches on his phone, the iPhone replacement, and sees he hasn't received one single voice message or text.

'Maybe everyone thinks you're still in rehab?' I ask.

'Whatever,' he replies.

'Misbah called to see how you're doing,' I add.

'He reminds me of my relapse,' he replies bluntly.

I feel a twinge of sadness for Misbah; he was one of the few who stood by him.

He lights a cigarette, blows a cloud of smoke out the window and looks out as if he is seeing the outside world for the first time since a long incarceration. Ethan's mood sways; he's glad to be out, but at the same time, he's not keen on the idea of moving into supported housing with other recovering addicts.

The supported housing, also known as a half-way house or dry house, is a terraced, four-bedroom property. Ethan is pleasantly surprised; his new key worker seems nice, and the dry house is newly refurbished. He is pleased with his allocated bedroom on the ground floor and sets about getting it looking homely. The dry house isn't monitored by on-site staff, as many others are, except for surprise visits or room searches to piss-test clients. There are pros and cons to the relaxed policy; every addict is different with the level of support needed.

Three other clients live in the dry house; two are junkies and a third who is a recreational user.

As far as dry houses go, Ethan's room is adequate, but he'd like me to be by his side until he settles, even though it exceeds the stated visiting hours.

The first week becomes two.

I dig out his AA books and start reading Bill W's *The Big Book*. I'm surprised Ethan's AA books are unread. Pages stick together where they've never been turned. I persuade him to start AA meetings, ferry him to closed meetings and join him attending open ones. Before long he has a new AA sponsor. Apparently, he is quite flashy, but he's got fifteen years clean and sober.

Ethan's so proud of his standing-ovation life story that he'd written in rehab that he asks me to read it. Rather than an honest account of his addiction, though, it's glossed over with tales of swashbuckling adventures that glamorize his addiction. He boasts of world travel, merry making, and women, especially those of means who've financed his addiction. He names all his favourite sweethearts, including Koemi and camping Trina. Bizarrely, he doesn't make any mention of my existence. It seems that all I've done for him counts for nothing, but I let it slide. He shows off his rehab good-luck card with messages; one says: *Don't forget to call me at my mum's number! Love Lita x.* I recognise the name; she's the junkie.

Thankfully, I manage to return the loan car without a scratch. My motor insurance payout is slow, so I have to borrow money from Sylvia to buy a used VW estate.

Ethan and his sponsor are getting along famously, and all's good until his mood turns foul. 'I can't wait for Lita to move into this dry house with me. She's a laugh, and an addict, so I've got more in common with her than with a lowlife like you. Me and Lita bonded. Why don't you fuck off?'

The abuse floors me; so much so, that I can't even speak. Without a word, I grab my backpack to leave. He chain-smokes and his stare fixes on me while I lace up my trainers. I think I will fuck off! Honest to God, I feel relieved to be getting away from him.

'Leave in the morning, not now,' he demands, standing to block the doorway.

I sigh. It's pointless to try and argue with him.

Ethan's morning mood is a one-eighty from the previous night. He makes mugs of breakfast tea, whistles, and warbles a happy tune. 'I'm so glad you didn't walk out. I'd pick up a drink without you. Take me to an AA meeting today?'

I do as he asks with the hope his new sponsor has the know-how to improve his mood swings. Little by little other addictions creep in. It starts with texting new AA friends, followed by continuous internet browsing and online shopping; after that, it's sugar, hypochondria, pornography, and a fixation with erectile dysfunction. He's possessive and whinges if I speak to Frida and Sylvia. He wants me all to himself and starts to jealously interrogate me, asking if I'm in contact with anyone who's male—which I am not, with the exception of Loday, who isn't on his forbidden list.

Ethan's other old habits resurface tenfold. He carries out random, regular, and multiple inspections of my emails, text messages, and my Facebook account. Not only does he go through each and every message thoroughly, but he also scrutinizes my computer with scrupulous attention, along with my small journal, in which he only finds jotted notes of his appointments and alcohol consumption. He isn't even red faced when caught reading it behind my back. It's like old times.

I grow used to his multiple searches of my pockets, backpack, and car. I've nothing to hide and dare not raise any objections—I'm as obedient as a well-trained dog. His extensive investigations produce no damning evidence because none exist. Nevertheless, this infuriates him even more, and although he hates me again, he doesn't permit me to leave his side.

Ethan's in a good mood. He read how nourishment is vital in recovery, so we're cooking a healthy meal together. I chop onions while Ethan peels potatoes.

He stops mid-peel, like he's just remembered something. 'Look at us. We get along nicely,' he declares. 'So I have to be honest with you and tell you something. Once I slept with a prostitute; it was a one off. The truth is so important.' He continues peeling.

I'm caught off guard by the confession; it's not the whole truth. He had revealed and retracted how his prostitute fetish started when he was a young teenager. Also, Vicky divulged his secret prostitute fetish to me. He, by saying he'd 'slept with a prostitute,' seems to be excusing, or even romanticising, his addiction to prostitutes.

'I know; your mum already told me,' I reply.

'Oh. She didn't, did she?' he says, and hastily changes the subject.

I let the matter slide.

When Ethan Skypes Vicky after dinner, I wait in his room and flick through a book. His phone pings a text message: *Let's keep going! Call me! Lita x*

It is the heroin addict from rehab. My mind races. It's clear he's in contact with her on the sly and has contacted her since rehab. They've swapped numbers; she's in his phone contacts. And yet it's him with the suspicious mind.

'How are your rehab friends? Have you heard from anyone?' I ask, offering him the chance to be open with me.

'No. Why would I want to be in contact with a bunch of junkies?'

So much for his new-found honesty.

Ethan hastily changes the subject and goes online shopping. 'These clothes will make me feel better,' he says. 'I'll pay you back, but you do owe me a favour, seeing as you lost my expensive watch. I'll forgive you if you lend me a few grand.'

His demands confounded me, and the accusation of losing his watch; that watch has nothing to do with me.

Koemi's given Ethan the taste for finer things; his orders mount to thousands of pounds. Regardless of what I say, he takes charge of my finances.

When Ethan gets his orders, he unwraps his hauls and they keep him happy for an hour or two, then he's in the doldrums. He wants more. He's already getting fed up with the dry house—

the feeling of being institutionalised. Try as I might to encourage Ethan to work the Twelve Steps, he constantly lapses into his old ways. He gets pumped up with enthusiasm when he speaks with his flashy sponsor, and then snipes at me soon as the call ends.

'Why don't you confess? You're a low-life. You hurt my eyes. You're disgusting,' is my morning greeting from Ethan.

'Confess? What am I have supposed to have done this time?' I ask.

'You've been having an affair with Cedric! You're a cheat!' he sneers. 'And admit it; in Wales you were driving back and forth to England for orgies.'

'What are you talking about? I haven't seen a soul, let alone had affairs! And in Wales I was driving all over the country because of you! Why are you doing this?' I'm completely floored.

'Stop talking,' he replies with a touch of Bertie.

I silently reach for my bag to go out and allow to him cool down. I need space, but he grabs my bag and makes a pointing sign to the floor with his hand. I sit, like a hated dog. My body is in an unbearable amount of stress pain. Ethan starts whistling a tune while he unpacks his new trainers and tries them on for size. I hold my breath, waiting for him to complain. He paces around, adjusts the laces, takes a few more steps and stops near to where I docilely sit.

'They're wonderful! Really comfortable. Thank you. I love you,' he exclaims. 'Let's make bacon and eggs and a lovely cup of tea.' He plonks a kiss on my cheek.

Later in the evening, I hear doors slamming and angry voices. It's a house raid by key workers. Ethan's name is shouted out. He dashes to the kitchen to find out what's going on.

'You've broken your curfew,' the furious key worker shrills. 'Since you arrived, three weeks ago, you've had a guest after visitor times. You'll get a written warning tomorrow!' We'd thought she'd busted the house to do random drug tests.

The recreational user snitched; he's smirking.

Ethan doesn't argue back. He bemoans how unfair it is that his family are content knowing he's in a dry house with hostile people, and how that doesn't help his recovery.

When a wave of tiredness hits me, I fall asleep on the backseat of my car while Ethan talks on. I wake to the sound of diesel engine and sense car movement. It's morning. I'm surprised to see Ethan at the steering wheel, driving my car without motor insurance. I sit up.

'Good morning!' he says.

'Where are we?' I ask, taken aback, not recognising where I am.

'We're half-way to Lyme Regis. We're going to view a flat. We have to be quick before it's taken. I have to get out of that dry house, or else I'll relapse!'

I take a minute to process what's happening. It's unlike me to sleep so soundly that the car starting didn't wake me.

He talks about the benefits of living on the coast. 'It's an ideal place for recovery. There isn't the temptation of drugs. It'll be a fresh start. I keep having these mood swings because I need to live somewhere beautiful.'

Quaint little shops are opening for trade. We buy coffee and sit on a bench that looks out to the English Channel. It's drizzling with rain and windy. With no time to lose, we attend the viewing. The property's manager shows us around. It's got great potential and is reasonably priced. Ethan thinks it's perfect.

'We'll take it,' he announces.

'Good. You'll have to pay a non-refundable deposit by the end of the day, and we'll draw up a tenancy contract,' the property manager says.

Ethan's wild with excitement. We find the local library where he can print out the paperwork. He has to provide a guarantor, so Ethan calls his mum to ask if she'll stand as guarantor. She's pleased to hear him so excited and agrees.

'Magda, I promise I'll pay you back the deposit!' he says.

I withdraw the large cash sum from my account and hand over the wad of notes.

'We need to book a room to finalise this and get the keys,' Ethan exclaims.

I withdraw another wad of notes for a guesthouse. After we check in, Ethan begins to calm down. Since we arrived at Lyme Regis, he hasn't tyrannized me. The surroundings must be helping.

He doesn't say much over breakfast. I'm none too pleased either. For me it's been an expensive flat viewing—over £500 with the deposit and guesthouse.

Much to Ethan's annoyance, we return to the dry house. Without a second's thought, he packs and loads his belongings into my VW, then returns his room key and quits the dry house.

'But you haven't even been with us a month,' his key worker says.

Ethan makes up an excuse, pretending he's going to stay with family.

Ethan's mum calls and says, 'I'm afraid I've had second thoughts. I'm not going to be your guarantor. If I go through with this, and you relapse, it'll be me who'll be saddled with one year's rent.'

Ethan hides his dismay. He even agrees with her, but he doesn't admit he's quit the dry house.

'That fucking sister of mine! She's stuck her nose in and talked my mum out of helping. I can't believe I've lost that flat!' he says in a rage. 'You see how I can only depend on you?'

'Yes, I mean maybe. But what now?' I ask.

'It'll be fine; we'll book a hotel for a while.'

Ethan and his sponsor arrange to have a Skype chat. Ethan glances at his wrist, out of habit, and remembers he doesn't have a watch.

He answers his Skype call, says, 'Pssst!' and makes a shooing sign to me.

I obediently leave the room, where I sit on the floor in the breezy hotel corridor, much to the disbelief of the cleaning staff.

When I'm allowed back in the room, I find Ethan's edgy. He's jealous that his sponsor is attending a fabulous event, while he's in a stew. He distracts himself over the next week with his usual behaviours—shopping for designer clothes and a replacement iPhone.

The new phone is shiny loveliness. He can't wait to set it up. I follow Ethan into McDonald's, where there's WiFi. He peels off the cellophane and prizes it out of the box, then to my dismay, he points to a table on the opposite side of McDonald's.

'Sit over there while I set up my phone. You get me?' he says.

It's a mystery to me why his activating the new iPhone is classified, and I don't know why I have to be sent away like this—not that I object, of course.

It takes a heck of a long time for him to set the thing up and install the updates and Apps. Eventually he takes a beaming selfie.

His good humour doesn't last long. He sneers at me again, accusing me of having a sexual relationship with Cedric and telling me he hates me.

Back in our hotel room, I feel trapped with him hurling more abuse, and by the time the verbal onslaught's done, I'm ready to throw in the towel.

He remembers something, and rummages through his bags. 'Here's what I'm looking for!' He waves a large envelope. 'It's a PIP application form. The state benefits are doing away with

DLA; it's PIP now. Personal Independence Allowance. The deadline date is soon. If I claim PIP, I can buy myself a new watch, and start paying you back. Sweetie, you'll have to do the form for me; I can't read it.'

He can read it—he just doesn't want to. He thrusts the thick envelope into my hands.

The PIP benefit is supposed to be awarded to people who suffer with mental and physical disabilities, to help them pay for physiotherapy, counselling, and other essentials. Ethan reminds me that addictions, like drink, drugs, sex, gambling, food, or shopping, are mental disabilities—which they are— and he believes the government should shell out and foot the bill for whatever the addict craves, whether relapsed or not. The government gambles many thousands of pounds every year when they place their trust in PIP claimants who are addicts.

The form looks like a nightmare. I try to concentrate to read it through, while Ethan entertains himself by sending me vicious text messages from his lovely new iPhone. It's his weapon of control and emotional abuse.

Ethan's admission date for another dry house is postponed, so we're holed up in the hotel room for longer than anticipated, and the costs are mounting, not that Ethan appreciates it. His mood swings could be blamed on his being dry drunk. Until I'd met Ethan, I'd never heard of dry drunk syndrome; it's a psychological phenomenon when the recovering addict, who is dry, continues to display toxic behaviours, as they did when in the throes of their drinking and using. Maybe I'm making up excuses for his unacceptable behaviour.

At long last, and after staying in the same hotel for over a month, the new dry house confirms that Ethan's got a room.

Chapter Thirty-nine

New town; new dry house. Ethan makes his room feel homely by pinning colourful fabric to the walls and placing rainbow lights on the shelves.

'You'll have to stay close, so I don't pick up a drink. Just until I settle,' he says.

My life's been on hold for so long that a little longer won't hurt. The dry-house rules are as rigid as the last—no guests outside visiting times—so I'll have to camp in my VW until Ethan's separation anxiety is better.

My next task is to list Ethan's unwanted clothes on eBay; he goads me while I do his listings, trying to get me to confess to an affair I never had. I concentrate on his computer screen. Unrelated photos plop into the eBay images folder as soon as Ethan's new iPhone connects with his computer—images of a smiling woman lying on a bed, naked except for blue, see-through undies. Ethan's computer's hard drive has been wiped recently, so these photos are new.

'Who's this naked woman?' I ask, guessing it's Trina.

Ethan takes a sharp intake of breath, stops his verbal tirade, and grabs the computer to look for himself. 'Who the hell's that?' he exclaims and smashes down the lid.

I shrug. 'Maybe someone else used your iPhone, took nudie photos, and guessed your iCloud password?'

Ethan hastily changes the subject. 'Errr, you deserve a nice cuppa.'

The photos mysteriously vanish soon after.

As luck would have it, Ethan's PIP assessor happens to have empathy towards addicts. He asks the standard questions and then tests Ethan's memory. He overplays having an abnormally low intelligence, just to tick the assessment's boxes.

I ferry him to another AA meeting. Afterwards, his sponsor calls to check if he'd attended.

Ethan slams the car door and jogs off to talk in secret. I wait in the darkness, sitting in the driver's seat while I know Ethan's lambasting me to his sponsor.

He returns to the car with a spring in his step. 'My sponsor has told me what I must do. I've got a surprise in store for you.'

My hands shake while I try and concentrate on the long drive back to the dry house.

Before I park, Ethan starts pulling at my sleeve. 'Quickly! Come inside with me!'

I can barely keep up with him because he's almost running.

Once in his room, he pulls out a chair, places my computer in front of me and opens it. 'My AA sponsor said you have to provide me with information; he said I should make you log into your mobile account so I can inspect your call history and check every call, text, and your contact numbers. I don't know why I didn't think of it before.'

Ethan breathes down my neck while the pages of my year's worth of phone history load. He grabs hold of my wrist so tightly that I can't move it and takes over my computer with his free hand. Over and over again, he pours over each number, call duration, time and date, while I tremble with fear. Unable to find anything incriminating, he eventually loosens his grip. I'm not sure why Ethan's sponsor felt assisted coercion would help recovery. This crime, against me, has awakened Ethan's new pastime.

'Time for a cuppa?' Ethan asks.

I'm so upset, I don't answer.

He gives a pat me on the head.

I guess he thinks that nasty tales about me takes the spotlight off his addiction. Intimacy between us, even talking feelings, get twisted and broadcast by him. He might just need more time to adjust to sobriety.

'It's my Koemi's birthday today, so I'm going to send her an email,' he declares. I'm a little surprised he even remembers her birthday, what with his poor memory. He types away, then pauses and starts to abuse me again—the same old accusations.

His tirade makes me feel so ill that I take ten steps back and lean against the wall furthest from him. My legs feel as if they're going to give way from under me, so I slide all the way down the wall.

Ethan happily hums a little ditty.

I slowly stand to leave.

'You can't walk out on me,' he says. 'I have mood swings. Just deal with it.'

Ethan's sponsor suggests a few days focusing on his Twelve Steps would be beneficial, so Ethan agrees to me visiting Frida at a weekend retreat.

I feel lucky to be invited to the retreat and that Ethan's allowed me time off. Throughout my long journey, he sends kind-hearted texts.

My coach pulls into Newcastle bus station. Frida spots me, waves, and smiles. The very sight of her lifts my heart. When we reach the same house where I'd stayed previously, it feels homely, warm, spotless, and tranquil with all the gold and burgundy. Frida and I chat over soup, while the other students busy themselves with ironing their ankle-length Buddhist burgundy skirts and t-shirts. There's a frisson of excitement in the air while preparations for the retreat get underway.

Wake up alarms and gongs sound at 5.30 am for morning-prayer practice. The retreat begins with the lama's procession; the students sing him in, until he sits crossed legged upon his elevated lama seat. In unison we, his guests, retreatants, and students, perform three prostrations before him, then sit cross-legged on our floor mats. He recites Tibetan prayers, and then his speeches begin. The packed shrine room of students and retreat attendees listen attentively, scribbling notes while he talks. A lot of what he says goes over my head, maybe because I'm new.

Lunch is a bowl of rice with overcooked, rubbery mushroom stew that squeaks when I chew. At every opportunity I call Ethan, just to make sure he's all right. At night, when it's too late to talk, we type Skype messages, and Ethan actually sends me pleasant messages.

On day two of the retreat, my leg and back pain cause a lot of discomfort and make it difficult to concentrate during the long periods of listening to lama's teachings. I'm not sure if I feel better or worse for being here.

At the start of day three, the last day of the retreat, Loday suggests I seek refuge with the lama. I hadn't given a thought to seeking refuge beforehand, and I know little to nothing about the relationship between Buddhist teacher and student, but I hastily agree, without thinking it over. It seems the proper thing to do. To join this spiritual family is surely wonderful because Frida has taken refuge, as has Ethan, and also Loday, who I trust entirely, was ordained by the lama years ago.

In a small room upstairs, the lama holds a private audience

during lunch break. Those in need of advice, blessings, and words of his wisdom book a slot to speak with him. I join the queue and when it's my turn, I enter the room and kneel before him. I offer him a kata and ask if I may seek refuge. He jovially waves his hand as a welcome to me to join this Buddhist family. When leaving the room, I bow my head, and walk backwards, careful not to turn my back to him, as is customary.

The ritual I'd attended when Frida had sought refuge with the lama a few months ago is repeated, this time with me. I kneel before the lama, in front of the crossed-legged students, and recite refuge vows to lama. He snips a few strands of hair, gives me blessings and my new Buddhist name, then hands me the photos of Buddha and himself, as well as a small metal pendant with an image of Buddha on it on thin red string. The pendant is identical to the ones his students and the ordained wear. They're meant to be worn at all times apart from when showering, and no other person is allowed to touch or handle it. Ethan rarely wears his one, but he still treasures it.

Straight after a dinner of soup, I tell Ethan I have taken refuge. He's pleased and has news of his own. He's decided to start house hunting for us, as he hates the dry house. Moving home will be expensive, so I find a quiet moment to go online and investigate my lack of finances. I discover Ethan's relapses, his designer shopping sprees, the numerous hotels, the times he'd frogmarched me to the bank for wads of cash, and miscellaneous spending add up to a tidy sum—around minus £20,000, plus interest is accruing every day. Even my car insurance pay-out where my Yaris got totalled is spent, and I've yet to repay Sylvia for my second-hand VW. I have my doubts about trusting Ethan when it comes to money. It's pointless to be angry or resentful, but if it were the other way around, he'd be furious. I look to the positives; Frida has some earnings put by, in case of a family emergency, and now that Ethan's getting better, we can both start to earn a living.

I have one day left in Newcastle. The lama asked one of the older nuns to take Frida and me out to one of his favourite coffee shops.

Frida sits opposite me, sipping her latte. I notice she's applied concealer to hide black rings around her eyes. She now survives on less than six-hours' sleep a night, and five months have passed since she first arrived at the sangha. She makes no mention of what her plans are after the retreat, and when I ask where she sees herself in the future, she explains that the lama makes decisions for all sangha and students.

It feels odd saying goodbye to Frida. The teachings have eaten up our time together. Frida and the younger nun drop me off at the coach station. Before my coach departs from Newcastle, I already miss her.

Ethan's due to meet me as soon as my coach reaches my destination. At regular intervals, I text him, so he knows my exact location. When I'm close, Ethan sends me a text: *I'm on my way but I'm stuck in a lot of traffic.* I'm flummoxed why he's running late; my journey's taken nine hours so far.

I step off the coach and look for Ethan, but he is nowhere to be seen. I hike around looking, but I can't find him. Around an hour passes before he calls me.

'I'm here, right outside!' he announces.

I dash outside before he disappears. He's driving his mother's car and doesn't look well, his face ashen grey. He's distracted and not happy to see me.

'Where've you been? Where's my car?' I ask.

'Long story. It's been impounded, by the police. I got done by the cops for driving while talking on my phone and driving with no insurance. Anyhow, I have to find someone; get in the car.'

He drives like a maniac and pulls up outside a block of flats where drug deals are going on in broad daylight. My heart sinks. Evidently, he was late meeting me because he was trying to score.

'Why don't we go and get food,' I suggest. 'If you eat and think this over, you'll feel better. The craving will pass after you've eaten!'

He ignores me, hops out of the car, and I watch helplessly while he rings on a buzzer, running his hands through his hair in desperation. To my relief, he can't score. But he dashes back, drives to a run-down part of town, and winds the window down to call out to a junky who's loitering on the street corner.

'Got any white?'

'Not on me, but I can get some good rocks,' the junky replies.

'What's happening?' I ask. 'Ethan, think this through. You know what they say in rehab; if you play the tape in your head of relapsing, you'll see the consequences. If you relapse, I've got to leave you to it! How will you explain a relapse to everyone?'

He buries his face in his hands, his craving eating away at him. I reach out to hold his hand and think of tips on what to do for relapse prevention: drink water, eat a meal, have sugar, deep breaths, talk to AA sponsor, go to an AA meeting, go for a run.

'Phone your sponsor!' I say.

'No, he's never gonna hear of this!'

'This craving will pass. Let's get out of the city; you can't risk your four months sobriety,' I say.

Without another word, Ethan steps on the gas to leave town. He lights a cigarette, and slows down after a few miles, half desperate to turn around and score. He starts counting to hundred out loud, then swerves in to park at a superstore, so we can buy sugary snacks. Whether it is the counting down, the sugar or Ethan's higher power, his craving slowly subsides. It's the worse craving I've seen Ethan experience since he got out of rehab. It's frightening to be reminded of its force.

His near relapse is our secret. The police will probably forget about his motoring offences, seeing as the paperwork's a faff; besides, where he's well known as a registered addict, the cops usually let him off with warnings. We collect my car from the vehicle pound, Ethan's relieved it's not been crushed, but not as relieved as I am. Outside the car pound, Ethan spots a retail park; he wants a pizza.

The very second I find a parking space, he says, 'The truth will set you free! So I want to tell you that there's nothing I enjoy more than getting my revenge by cheating on a cheater. I've done it loads of times!'

I can't understand where the black mood's come from this time; he's a mass of contradictions. A dark atmosphere descends; I wish I were anywhere but here.

At the next AA meeting, Ethan catches up with his friends; a good AA meeting usually helps a rattled addict. Afterwards, we return to the dry house and discover that the guy in the next room has relapsed; he's ex-army with PTSD. Before Ethan's even processed the bad news, he learns that his junkie friend from rehab has also fallen off the wagon. They're dropping like flies.

Ethan calls Roy and discovers that Lita's back on the brown as well, and six others from their group have slipped. The knowledge of the collective relapsers, all in the same week, greatly disturbs Ethan. It's not surprising why he wants out of this environment.

Chapter Forty

I have little time to pay attention to Sylvia and Frida, and with all my Ethan duties, none whatsoever for myself. It's been over a week with no word from Frida. If something were up, I know Loday would call me, but I decide to call her to see how she is doing.

'Hello,' Frida says upon answering her phone. 'I've been meaning to call, but I've always got so much to do. I've just got back from the Buddhist centre. I had to attend a long audio teaching. I don't like going to them anymore, but it's compulsory; it's a transgression to not attend.' Her voice sounds almost devoid of emotion.

'Why don't you explain to Loday how you feel?' I reply.

'I have already. He cranks up the volume to the max, to force me to listen,' she says. 'Let's talk another time? I'm tired. I'll feel better in a few days when Sylvia arrives. She's booked a train; she's allowed to come and visit me for the weekend.'

Our call ends, and I'm puzzled why Loday would force Frida attend obligatory audio teachings. I recall that when I'd visited the sangha, the audio teachings were at least an hour long and scheduled in the early evenings in the shrine room at the monks house/Buddhist centre. Listeners take notes while the lama's pre-recorded lecture booms from a loudspeaker.

Ethan finds a new listing for a one-bedroom flat, available in two weeks' time, and he arranges a viewing. He spends the whole journey talking about how to make it cosy with new throws, rugs, cushions, and lovely things. We arrive a few minutes early and Ethan walks ahead of me, along a footpath towards the entrance door. Climbing roses in full bloom, pink and dark red, adorn the outside of the building, giving it a country look. Plants in pots bloom in the June sunshine, and the garden shrubs blaze with colour. Ethan bangs the doorknocker, and we hear unlatching noises from the inside before it opens.

'Hi, I'm Gary,' the prospective landlord says. 'Nice to meet ya. Come on up.'

We follow him up a carpeted staircase to the first-floor apartment. The lounge feels light and airy. The windows give a fantastic view of the sky and a village in the near distance. It has a homely feel and is the best property we've seen advertised. It's not cheap at almost £1,000 a month, considering it's small.

Ethan can't contain himself. 'We really like it! Can we agree to take it?'

'I'd like to find tenants soon as possible. I have to go home to my family in Jakarta,' Gary replies.

Ethan turns on the charm. I'm conscious to speak only when spoken to, because I know Ethan prefers to do all the talking. As soon as we step foot outside to return to my car, Ethan's charm turns to spite.

'See how charming I was! You, on the other hand, have lost us that flat, because you're charmless. You hardly spoke a word. Fucking idiot! If we don't get offered it, I never want to see you or speak to you ever again.'

I don't know how to behave in front of people anymore, with

Ethan's criticisms, accusations, and contradicting himself. He reprimands me at every turn. As always, I soak up his venting.

To pass the time, Ethan cheers himself up with eBay shopping. He purchases a job lot of designer clothing and sweet-talks Vicky into loaning him £500. We go to collect his haul. Ethan's over the moon that he's buying lovely new things. I try to wait outside the seller's house, but Ethan insists I go with him while he tries on the glad rags and twirls in front of a mirror. When the transaction is complete, we leave.

Ethan's high buy suddenly plummets. 'Oi. Confess! You liked that bloke, didn't you?' he yells. 'You swopped phone numbers with him, you cheating troll!'

'I haven't done anything,' I protest. 'I tried to wait outside!'

He won't listen. 'You think you got one over on me? Eh?' he smirks. 'Well, I've got one over on you. I prefer the company of prostitutes than your company. I've had dozens of prostitutes, so many, that I've lost count!'

'Please let me go,' I say. 'I can't cope. I don't want to see you anymore!'

'Shut it,' he snaps.

The remainder of our journey's spent in a silence that's thick with hatred.

Ethan and his sponsor arrange a coffee morning while I wait outside until he's finished chin wagging. My phone unexpectedly pings a text message. It's Ethan: *Darling, sweetie! We've been offered the flat!* He loves me. On one hand, the news is good—it's great Gary's chosen us—but on the other, Ethan's merciless; he continues to torture me.

Ethan might be right; when his surroundings change, he'll change for the better. Somehow Ethan persuades his dad to loan some cash towards the deposit, and between us, and housing benefit, it's just affordable. Ethan plans to find employment and start paying back his IOUs to me—this time he swears blind that he will.

Ethan can't wait to move, and the way he denounces me as a lying, cheating cunt to his family, sponsor, friends, and strangers in AA becomes a little less frequent—though it puts a damper on my enthusiasm to move in together. The way he deflects the spotlight of his addiction behaviours onto me boosts his ego. No one's even guessed he's gaslighting me.

Apparently, Ethan's sponsor would like to see Ethan immerse himself with a paid job. Immersion by working is a distraction for some addicts in early recovery, so Ethan starts to think of what he'd like to do.

As luck would have it, Gary doesn't ask for employment references, proof of ID, nor proof of income or character references. But after we've signed the tenancy agreement, he sits forward in his chair, narrows his wrinkly eyes and says, 'Don't think that my living in Jakarta means you can fuck me around. I've got someone who's going to be keeping an eye on things for me. Don't breach this contract. If you dare fuck with me, I'll fuck with you! Get the picture?'

'Yes, yes. We do. I won't let you down!' Ethan replies earnestly.

I'm shocked by Gary's cussing; it's a bit scary.

Our moving date fast approaches and Ethan's pattern of loving and hating me changes more often than English weather.

I'm parked outside his dry house in a parking space, when out of the blue, I hear an enormous bang. My car shakes and more bangs follow. I look around and see Ethan's face, contorted with anger as he kicks my car doors with all his might in a furious temper. I discover that his hissy fit is because my phone signal dropped, and he couldn't get through. He assumed I was speaking to someone without his consent.

'I feel bad I damaged your car doors and that I have these

mood swings. As soon as we move, they'll go. We'll have a fresh start,' he says. 'Mum says we'll be okay. She thinks jealousy isn't attractive, and that I shouldn't get upset by your dalliances with Cedric behind my back, that I should get over them. Isn't that wonderful advice from my mum?'

'Dalliances?' I feel so nettled by his gaslighting that I can hardly bear it for another second. Ethan's deflecting his own sexual misconduct to everyone is becoming insane.

I feel so confused and dither over whether we should move in together right up until the morning of moving day when we pack and quietly leave his dry house for good.

At our new home, Ethan becomes deliriously happy. He dashes from one room to the next, opens and closes cupboard doors, peeks inside the washing machine, flops on the bed and bounces on the sofa. While the kettle boils to make tea, he races up the staircase, two steps at a time, singing, whistling, and throwing his arms in the air with triumph.

'I'm so happy to be here,' he says, 'and do you know what's even better? The next time I relapse, I'll be in this lovely, cosy flat.'

I look at him in dismay.

'No, I'm not going to relapse,' he reassures me. 'This is my recovery flat.'

We make breakfast together and sit at the table where we eat while gazing at the view out the window. The usual undercurrent of tension between us decreases. I feel a surge of hope that Ethan's recovery will begin from this day on. When things are good between us, it's like there's nothing better, when they're bad, there's nothing worse. It's been four chaotic months since he left rehab, during which time he's mostly neglected AA and fed his other addictions.

Busy days of cleaning and sorting follow relaxed, cosy

evenings. Over the next few days, we collect Ethan's worldly goods from Pearl's house, and do the paperwork for housing benefit. We buy splendid paint to freshen up the place, and it feels like the start of better times. I can't completely blank out Ethan's testiness, feeling I have to keep up my guard, but the good life is ahead. I'm sure I'll regain my faith in him.

Chapter Forty-one

One of Ethan's rules is that I must not contact or speak with Vicky or any of Ethan's people. It's an effective way for him to play everyone off against each other, and guarantees I remain isolated, without support.

Ethan becomes irritable when his contact with his AA sponsor becomes erratic. Not only has he stopped helping Ethan with his Twelve Steps, but also, he wants Ethan to mentor Baz, the relapser.

'Baz is making you unwell. Do you think you should detach?' I ask Ethan while he plucks at his eyebrows.

'Maybe, but I know how it feels when everyone drops us addicts when we relapse!' He decides not to listen to me and becomes cantankerous. His jubilant mood, since moving in only one week ago, diminishes. While Ethan's in the kitchen talking to Baz on the phone, I flick through TV channels. I don't hear the lounge door open.

Ethan appears suddenly, making me jump. 'Where's your phone?'

'I think it's in my coat pocket!'

He hastily searches under the sofa and cushions. 'On your

feet! Stand!' He checks my empty pockets, then marches out to the coat hook to inspect my phone. He times my visits to the bathroom and bursts in when I take a shower or use the toilet. I accept I'm not allowed privacy; it's degrading to be his suspect.

The housing benefit applications for new rent claims take ages to process now that the benefit is Universal Credit—it's renowned for dreadful delays. But I know Frida will help with the rent that is due. The opening of the two-month summer retreat is imminent, so that's probably why I can't contact her.

Ethan seems compelled to lecture me at midnight with the usual put-downs. He even disparages my ancestors. At 4 am he finishes yelling and stomps off to bed. Before long he's dead to the world.

Terrified of moving in case he wakes, I wait for sunrise, then soundlessly leave our happy new home and close the door behind me. When I reach a safe distance away, I call Loday, knowing he'll already be up for morning-prayer practice.

'We have calm minds here,' he says in response. 'Don't worry. For now, I'll see the money is paid into your account. I think you'd benefit from attending a week of teaching here while the retreat is on.'

I'm so relieved. I shouldn't get another bollocking today over money, so I feel safe returning. I speak before Ethan can start on me. 'I'll pay our next rent later. I've sorted everything out,' I stammer.

'That's amazing. Just forget all that stuff I said to you last night. I'm happy now,' Ethan replies. He welcomes me with open arms and hugs me.

All's well again, and when Baz calls, he decides not to pick up, for fear of a mental tumble. Today we're like old friends, young lovers, soul mates, partners and companions; we're side by side, shoulder to shoulder; we go hand in hand and fit like a glove. All those things rolled into one.

'I'm going back to AA tomorrow. I know that'll make you happy,' he says.

I'm on the edge of my seat and nervously watch my phone the second Ethan leaves for the AA meeting. It's strange not to be monitored, and I half expect him to call with a drama. Remarkably, when he returns, he's happy as a clam. He feels great and answers his phone when Baz calls. By the end of the call, though, Ethan's mood has changed.

'There must be an easier way to make money,' he says.

'Whenever you speak to Baz, you get wound up. We'll be all right,' I reply.

He becomes engrossed with his phone, and a short while later, he tells me he's advertised for a lodger.

'No, don't do it,' I say. 'We're not allowed to sublet. We haven't been here a fortnight, and you want to breach the tenancy agreement already. Gary will be furious. There isn't even space here. We've only got one bedroom. And it'd be housing benefit fraud!' The web of deceit is dangerous for both of us.

Ethan looks at his advert. 'It's done!'

'You never listen to me,' I murmur. The subject is not open to discussion; my voice is a whisper in the wind.

Ethan flicks off the TV and lights and trots off to bed. As soon as his head touches the pillow, he's snoring. I'm careful not to wake him when I go to bed and wait for sleep. I can't see the wood for the trees. I don't know where I am. I'm alone; I've lost my bearings in the darkness and can't see where I'm going. I stumble and fall over a ledge into the blackness below. I'm free falling. Just before I hit the bottom, I wake with a jolt. It's just a nightmare, but my jolt wakes Ethan. He flicks on the lamp, lunges towards me, grabs hold of my face and squeezes my jaw hard in his right hand.

'Dreaming? Nice dream, was it? You fucking woke me up! Don't get any ideas about sneaking out for an orgy while I'm asleep, if you know what's good for you!' he says before switching off the lamp and resuming his sleep.

My clenched palms feel sweaty. My heart's pounding. I remind myself to breathe.

The next morning, he sweeps what happened during the night under the carpet. He answers his phone, shoos me out of the lounge and shuts the door. I'm not sure where I'm allowed to wait that won't cause offence. I hazard a guess that if I listen to music in the bedroom at the far end of the hallway, I shouldn't get a bollocking. I know Ethan's call has ended when he saunters into the bedroom and whistles. His sponsor told him to write a gratitude list.

On the face of it, everything might seem all right. I'm in a catch-22 situation. Sylvia needs more support from me, and something's up with Frida. She's wandered off her career path, and I'd like to know why. It's impossible for me to keep Ethan happy. Maybe if I spend one week in Newcastle, I might get my head together and see what's the matter with Frida. Together, we can all help Sylvia.

'We could both go,' I say to Ethan. 'You could see Loday. Wouldn't that make a change?'

'No thanks. You can visit, though,' he replies.

I can't believe he's letting me out of his sight for a week.

One week will fly by; Ethan won't be left to his own devices for long. He might even realise his abuse needs to stop. He's fine when I book my coach ticket but becomes sulky just before I leave. I pack light; my Nikon camera takes up half the space, and I've barely enough clothes for a week. The rest I leave in the airing cupboard, and I place a box that belongs to me in the lounge alongside Ethan's many.

Ethan drops me off at the bus station for my coach. I'm running late and can't find the right bus terminal. Out of nowhere, Ethan reappears, looking tense.

'Oh, you're back. Did I forget something?' I ask.

'No. I'm checking you're getting on the Newcastle coach. That's where you're definitely going, right?' he asks.

'Watch me get on the coach, and call Loday. You can catch up with him,' I say.

The last passengers are getting on my coach, so I join the line. I hug Ethan, and he limply hugs me back—so limp it's not really a hug. He doesn't stay to wave me off while my coach pulls away.

Chapter Forty-tWo

I finally reach Newcastle at 10 pm. Were it not for my incertitude as to what's going on with Frida, I wouldn't be making this visit to Pathgate. A young nun meets me and plays chanting music while driving back to the sangha.

Perhaps it's the thought of seeing Frida, or the rhythmic monotonous chanting of many voices, or the spicy smell of potpourri that pervades the red car that reminds me, I'm away from home. In a way I feel like I've been driven away from my new home. It isn't a safe sanctuary, like a home should be.

The nun opens the front door where we slip off our shoes in the porch. The footwear rack is full of boots, shoes, and Crocs, so I wedge my trainers at the end of the rack. It's quiet indoors. Evening prayer practice that started at 10 pm is underway in the loft shrine room. I tiptoe to the downstairs dorm bedroom, so I can plonk down my heavy backpack beside my bed on the lowest bunk. I wasn't expecting to see so many suitcases, bags, bath towels and toiletry bags. There are more beds than last time— eight bunk beds in the cramped room. Soup is simmering on the kitchen stove; I serve myself a ladle full and bring it into the lounge. To my surprise there's a little girl in a world of her own doing colouring in. The voices from the stairway break the silence, indicating that prayer practice is over. The little girl's mother is first to appear. She cuddles her child and admires the picture. Frida enters the lounge with an Australian student who is around her age. She beams a beautiful smile.

'How are you doing?' I ask Frida.

'Really good! At least I am now the retreat has started,' she replies.

I'm not sure what she means.

'It's so much better here now that the other students have arrived,' she adds, then wanders off to the kitchen for soup with her new friend.

The female sangha house is full to capacity—twenty-two female students in one modest-size terrace house with only one shower-room and loo between us. The male student house is just as full. Around seventy people are attending the retreat.

Ethan's on my mind. He hasn't phoned so he might be in a mood, but when I log into Skype, I see he's sent me a message only three minutes ago: *Hope you arrived safely! Hope you have a wonderful retreat!* We send messages to each other with him sounding upbeat.

Around midnight, the downstairs lights and lamps dim one by one while we students climb into our bunk beds and turn in for five hours' sleep. Frida's bunk bed is the row adjacent to mine; she drifts off to sleep and the other students soon follow. I snuggle down under the burgundy duvet. It's some consolation that Ethan won't be shaking me awake with a bollocking; nevertheless, I feel displaced, and at the same time, I'm where I need to be. It's a conflicted feeling. Horribly confusing.

The gongs and alarms sound at 5 am on the dot. Some students are early birds; others are oohing with achy bodies. A queue quickly forms outside the bathroom for the loo; then it's a quick change into loungewear. It's not until I enter the loft shrine room that I see how many female retreatants are in attendance. Three long rows of students sit crossed legged, each with a spiral bound Tibetan-text prayer book on portable, low tables. Before I take my place in the back row, I remember the ritual of three kowtow prostrations facing the statue of Buddha and portraits of the sacred ones. Prayers begin when a nun strikes a gong and leads us into Tibetan chants that I find hard to follow.

When practice ends at 7 am, it's time for breakfast. I'm not used to such an early breakfast, but it's another six hours until lunch, so I opt for toast and coffee. The kitchen is a hive of activity while everyone finishes their breakfast and washes the dishes. To ease the morning queue for the bathroom, some students have their showers before bedtime, others after breakfast. By 7.45 am students have changed into the sangha uniform of burgundy colours and leave for a Tai Chi lesson, which is held in the park opposite the Buddhist centre.

Directly after Tai Chi, it's back to the Buddhist centre where all students stack their shoes in the hallway cupboard and don their long, ironed, burgundy skirts for Tara practice at 9 am, which is followed by a short break before the lama's day of teaching begins.

The entrance ritual is as before, and after the lama takes his elevated seat, we jostle into crossed-legged positions on our mats on the cramped floor space. Cameras and microphones record every second of our lama's teachings for posterity. Loday presses record, and the teachings begin. We bow our heads and scribble away to catch as many words as we can in our notebooks. He speaks so fast, I can't keep up.

The nuns, who cook meals instead of attending the morning teachings, deliver the lunch they'd prepared in the morning. Lama's long-term devoted student serves his meal first. She raises his lunch above her head with one hand and uses burgundy fabric to cover her mouth with the other. The donations ritual begins, and a paper tower of sealed white envelopes forms.

Lunch upsets my stomach, making me feel nauseous. Maybe it's nerves. The lama has instructed the diet to be low protein, consisting of rice with stewed vegetables or rehydrated, squeaky mushrooms for lunch, followed by a carbohydrate snack of biscuits or cake for dessert, and vegetable soup for dinner. I'm used to a diet that's not nutritious, considering my neglected dietary requirements for the past year. All the same, I find the squeaky rice stew is not stomach friendly.

The afternoon teaching starts with the lama reminiscing at length about his childhood, and how his mother recognised how, at an early age, she knew he was a perfect, gifted genius. It doesn't seem relevant to Buddhism, but we continue to take notes until teaching ends at 5 pm.

I learn that the end of lama's teaching is not the end of the day. A new itinerary has been devised, and students must follow the demanding programme lama has planned. After teaching, an audio teaching follows, then there's a two-hour Puja, then one hour of prostration practice, closely followed by evening prayer practice. Puja or prostrations might be rescheduled at short notice. Altogether, including a one-hour lunch break, it's an eighteen-hour day.

Other new proposals lama has requested is for Facebook and all social networking to be deactivated, use of mobile phones to be kept to a minimum, no reading allowed, or books apart from the few available on his bookshelf in the upstairs lobby. No music can be played; internet use must be kept to a minimum; no newspapers or current news can be read, heard, or discussed, and contact with anyone outside the retreat must be kept to the bare minimum. The lama's restrictions aren't a lot different to what I'm used to with Ethan's controlling behaviour, so I'm not fazed.

By the end of the day, I'm exhausted. My body aches from sitting cross- legged, and it's even worse for my dharma sisters who aren't nimble. At 10 pm it's time for more sitting and evening-prayer practice, but I go outside to call Ethan instead.

While we speak, I imagine Ethan relaxing in the warm, using this time to unwind and focus on his recovery. Shivering with the cold, I walk a few streets down and crouch and stretch my legs while I tell him how the retreat has changed, how it's more full-on than ever before. He's not interested, talking of himself instead.

Day two is day one replayed, and day three the same again. I don't seem able to decipher my own notes because the content of lama's teaching is a mass of contradictions. A text message arrives from my phone provider informing me that my services have been restricted due to non-payment of my phone bill. I realise that all my direct debits must be getting declined, including my car insurance, everything. To add to my worries, Frida seems different.

In the breakfast rush, I manage to catch Frida while she folds laundry. 'Morning, Frida. How are you enjoying the retreat?' I ask.

'It's really good. But remember, don't call me Frida; you have to use my Buddhist name. That's what we're told.'

'Oh, okay, I keep forgetting … Have you thought about after the retreat, when everyone goes home? Would you like to move south? You can stay with me and Ethan,' I say.

'Thanks. But … I don't know.'

'Well, think it over. I'll have to book for a coach ticket tomorrow. My week's nearly up. My bank account is rinsed. What funds are available in the emergency account? Any idea?'

'Next to nothing. Lama has instructed his students to give him monetary offerings, so I've obeyed. He said we get merit by giving him money and working for the sangha. I'm lucky to earn merit and have to be thankful for bed and board, but I wasn't given permission to find employment or claim welfare. Lama's against anyone who claims welfare, and he says massage therapists absorb the client's demons, so he prohibits healers. He says he's our healer. And we mustn't question what the lama says,' she replies in a whisper with an almost vacant look.

That's not the response I was expecting. I'm dumbfounded to learn Frida's been sent on a guilt trip into giving cash donations in exchange for merit, as well as not being allowed financial independence.

It's been a mind-boggling five days since I arrived, made complete when Ethan dumps icing on the cake with a Skype message. It starts abruptly: *So strange! I've had a sick feeling all day. There's something not healthy between us. I asked my mum for money to repay you. It'll be in your account tomorrow. Hope you're okay! Good luck!*

The message is as clear as mud. It implies he's evicted me from my own home.

He knows my schedule and phones ten minutes before evening prayer practice. I walk towards the railway bridge to take his call.

'Take no notice of that message I sent, sweetie; I'm stressed,' Ethan says. 'I'm just busy; our lodger moves in tomorrow. She's renting the bedroom, and the lounge will be our room. She's paying a grand upfront for advance rent. It's easy income. Tax free! And Gary will never find out.'

'Okay. Have it your way, but I want to pay Gary's rent directly. Agreed?' I ask.

'Of course. Agreed.'

'What's happening about your PIP welfare application? Any news?' I ask.

'Oh yeah, it almost slipped my mind. The application was successful! I've been awarded PIP,' he reluctantly replies.

'Thanks for not telling me.'

He changes the subject to talk about how he's seen a yoga retreat in India that he wants to attend in the winter. From India, he'd like to do more travelling.

I return to my dormitory with my mind racing. A lodger's moving in; it's a breach of the tenancy lease. I check the time; it's 2 am. I've got to wake up in three-hours' time.

Chapter Forty-three

In the background of sleepiness, I hear the dormitory dharma sisters getting up with the 5 am alarms. I can't open my eyes, not until one of the nuns hammers on a gong right in my face, then I drag myself out of my bunk. While running upstairs to the shrine room, I fiddle with my hoodie zip and realise I've pulled it on inside out, but it'll have to do. I remember to do three prostrations facing the shrine of Buddha, then sidle towards the back row where I sit. The woman who sits next to me indicates where we're up to in the prayer book, but I get distracted by the beautiful pinky blue sky I can see through the skylight.

I'm taken aback when Loday suggests we go for a brisk walk in the park before morning teaching starts. 'I just spoke with Ethan,' he says. 'Great news! He's insisted you stay for longer. He thinks it will do you good.'

My stomach lurches with the unexpected bombshell. 'Oh, really? I've had a great week, but I should go home tomorrow.' Actually, it's been a challenge, mentally and physically.

'Let's compromise; just stay for one extra week. Did you know that being near your lama and chanting can cure Ethan's addiction?'

'So I heard, but—'

'No buts. You'll earn merit by attending teachings. And it's what Ethan wants—for you to stay.'

Without further ado, we head back to the sangha for the remaining day's schedule.

In the evening I walk towards the railway bridge and call Ethan.

'How was your day?' he says upon answering his phone.

'Not great. How come you've secretly interfered behind my back by telling Loday I have to stay here longer? And what happened to my money you were meant to transfer?'

'Oh! Yeah, change of plan,' he replies.

'But I want to come home. I can't take any more of this schedule, and I wanted Frida to stay with us. It's time she left here!'

'You can't come home, not until you confess your transgressions to me, such as being a cheating liar,' he replies.

'What did you just call me?' I ask in a voice so loud I don't know where it came from.

He hangs up and blocks me.

The gong smashes at 5 am. Morning practice is becoming more difficult, but I push myself through it. I arrive early for Tara practice, and Loday asks if I'd accompany him for one of his brisk walks in the park.

'How are you today?' he asks, before we reach the gates.

'I can't focus. Ethan's tormenting me daily. He's demanding that I confess to infidelity, but I'm not guilty!' I reply.

'With a chaotic mind like Ethan's, do you expect anything but chaos? You must ask your lama for guidance. Ethan's difficult. When he joined us as a resident student, he was thrilled that lama accepted him. His father phoned me several times when Ethan applied, begging me to ensure he got accepted, because none of his family wanted him. Even when he had a two-day relapse, shortly after arriving here, our lama gave him a second chance. His family are not what they seem; they're not good for his recovery,' Loday replies.

At lunchtime I kneel before the lama, asking for his advice about Ethan.

'Simple!' Lama barks out. 'You're two broken links of a chain. By coming together, you think you can make the chain strong. You can't. My student Ethan has the condition called addiction. You knew one another in a previous life; karmic debt is being repaid between you. So be grateful. And remember you can't fix him.'

Lama claps his hands twice, signalling the end of my audience with him. Even a stopped clock tells the right time twice a day. A slow, frightfully boring afternoon's teaching resumes, followed by the remaining schedule.

Ethan calls in a foul mood before evening prayer practice.

Karmic debt's working out just dandy.

'My sponsor said I must start making amends,' he tells me. 'Howard's at the top of my amends list of persons I've harmed, so I've written to him. I spilled my guts out and begged for his forgiveness.' Ethan doesn't want to relate what he has written, but at least he's trying.

I'm getting the hang of Tara practice. I don't understand any of the Tibetan, but at least I can follow the text more easily, which makes me feel slightly less of a fish out of water. Straight after Tara, we scurry around and arrange the shrine room for the day's teaching—burgundy rugs and floor cushions neatly arranged in rows and prayer books placed on every cushion. Each student deposits their notebooks and pens beneath their prayer book. Just like school pupils, we sit in orderly rows and in the same space every day. A few more students have arrived for the retreat, and one has taken my usual mat spot. I don't mind in the least; there's room in the back row.

Loday notices I've moved myself to the back. 'You need to move closer,' he says. 'Please, move forward, so you can see and hear better. Your wise lama loves to have his students as near to him as possible.'

'Come, sit with us,' another monk insists, picking up my notebook and pens to move me forward.

'Please, I'm fine here,' I reply. I prefer sitting further back because our lama's loud; he shouts a lot.

'No buts,' Loday says.

I reluctantly do as I'm asked and squeeze between two monks in the front row.

Our lama enters with the usual ritual, then sits upon his elevated seat and, with a smile, surveys his burgundy herd of students.

He catches my eye, and his smile becomes a grimace. He points his finger directly at me. 'Who do you think you are? YOU are sitting in my monk's space! I want my monks near me! NOT YOU! YOU have transgressed me and shown disrespect to my ordained monks with your selfish EGO.'

He shouts at the very top of his voice, and he's miked up for the filming of his dharma-lama-drama movie, so the loudspeakers amplify the sound of his tyrannical temper even further. He shakes his long-nailed index finger at me, which makes his batwing arm flab wobble. I feel humiliated getting a public bollocking from following the monks' request to move. All eyes are on me in shocked silence, and dozens of stares freeze while my face reddens in shame.

'Everyone. Stand up! I move you all! NOW!' the lama rages. One by one, he points at us and indicates who swaps spaces with who, signalling his monks to stay in their usual row. It takes the entire morning's teaching for our lama to re-seat his favourite students nearest him and row-by-row, in order of his preference of likability, we're all reassigned new designated floor spaces. He's not happy first time round and repeats the entire re-seating a second time.

'From now on you all must be seated in the spaces I have given you,' he shouts.

Once we've settled, he flashes a satisfied smirk, folds his flabby arms, and suddenly breaks into song, getting really into a Disney ditty to make everyone chuckle. Most do, perhaps more out of fear than amusement. It doesn't make me laugh; I'm still in shock from the bollocking.

I keep peeping at my watch, wishing the morning teaching to be over. When our lama finally calls for lunchtime, all students rise and gently tap their foreheads with their envelopes of cash donations before placing them upon our lama's table to form his daily money tower. A graceful dash for the only loo forms a long line, and the nuns arrive to deliver squeaky soup for lunch. I, however, hastily head for the shoe cupboard in the hallway, pull on my jacket and trainers and run outside. I keep on running, hot tears stinging my eyes, until I reach an oak tree where I fall to my knees and weep uncontrollably. I've managed to hide my shame all morning, but my stoical self lets me down by allowing my tears to flow, and I blow my streaming nose with yesterday's tissue from my jacket pocket. The tirade of verbal abuse was unexpected. Now I want to go home more than ever, even though Ethan has a vicious temper. It's better the devil you know than the one you don't.

'Please God, please help me,' I whimper out loud in between sobs.

If our lama can read minds, as is claimed by the ordained, I'm going to get another transgression bollocking for praying to God instead of his holy, tyrannical self. Our lama likes his students to offer their prayers to Buddha and himself, who, he says, is a living Buddha and has been one prior to when he self-appointed himself as a lama.

My hands shake while I anxiously light a cigarette. Our lama said smoking attracts demons, so it's banned anywhere near the sangha. The ciggie demon most likely will earn me another dressing down, but I don't care. I don't want to return for the afternoon teaching. But I'm damned if I do and damned if I don't, so I pick myself up off my knees and return to face the music.

Lunchtime is almost over. I've missed squeaky soup. Lucky me. One dharma sister noticed I'd disappeared and kindly saved me a piece of carrot cake. I force myself to nibble it, but I can't taste it. I feel sick. Each mouthful is a struggle to get down.

When evening soup is ready, the dharma sister persuades me to eat a serving. Much to my surprise, four of my dharma sisters give me a brief half-hug, even though it's a transgression to comfort a sangha sinner who deserves karmic retribution dished out by one's lama.

Ethan phones at his usual time before evening prayer practice, so I head for the railway bridge to speak. His amends letter to Howard has bombed.

'That fucker, Howard! I spent all that time on my letter to him, and all I get is a few words as a reply in an email. Not even a sentence that makes sense,' he rages. 'Guess what he wrote back? *You're forgiven. Released!* I mean, WTF!'

'I'm sorry to hear it's not what you wanted as a reply. I've had a rough day myself!' I respond.

'Oh, so we have to talk about you, do we? You've got our lama and the sangha's support. I've lost my family! They've cut me off!' he snaps back.

I don't know what he means by my having support here.

He rages for the next two hours about how Howard has hijacked his family's attention, claiming he's the Holy Trinity, when he led Ethan astray with prostitutes, drink, and drugs when he was young and vulnerable. According to Ethan, it's all Howard's fault; Ethan believes he's blameless.

He drones on, turning to his familiar vulgarity littered with jealousy, name-calling, and lewd obscenities. I stupidly defend myself, which fan the flames right up until after midnight when my phone battery runs out.

I hurry back to the sangha and unlock the front door soundlessly, so not to wake my dharma sisters. Maybe I should have been less harsh, shown Ethan pity with his resentments about Howard, who most likely wasn't the best parental role model when Ethan was a boy. I call Ethan from the sangha landline phone with the intention to show humility, despite the fact he'd given me another earful of abuse, only to find he's blocked the sangha phone number. In a panic, hands shaking, I message Phoebe from my computer, asking if she's heard from him; she hasn't. I wait a while until she sends me a reply: *Just spoke to Ethan; he sounds fine.*

I'm not sure why he's blocked me and not Phoebe. I don't know what he's up to, and despite trying to get some sleep, I can't control my racing thoughts. I'm caught between the devil and the deep-blue sea.

The morning gong smashes. Our routine commences, and after Tara practice, Loday informs me that he and Ethan have had another one of their chats. They've decided between them that I'll have to stay until the end of the retreat, a month away. It's Ethan's instructions and Loday insists.

'You risk demons finding you if you leave the retreat before it ends, and you'll regret it,' Loday says. 'Once demons find you, it's impossible to get rid of them!'

'I haven't done anything wrong, though! And yesterday I only did as you asked, and our lama shouted at me! Can you tell him you made me sit there?' I ask.

He shakes his head. 'No, you must be thankful our lama singled you out. It's his way of speeding up karmic debt. Before I was ordained, I attended his Tai Chi retreat; my chakras were blocked, and our lama punched me in the stomach to unblock them. I was winded, but I felt jolly good after the punch!'

I'm slightly miffed to hear this.

Our lama is in a particularly volatile mood for the whole day's teaching. Today a male student is his target for public humiliation. Our lama speaks of merit, death, demons, karmic debt, hungry ghosts, and war.

'Refugees are victims of their own karma!' he shouts.

We, the burgundy flock, scribble his pontificating in our notebooks, but alarm bells ring in my head. I don't believe refugees deserve persecution, and I wonder if he is an anti-Semite and racist. How can he think a refugee's suffering evens the score in the bank of karma? Jesus Christ was a refugee, as well as the Dalai Lama. He wanders off point to speak about the forest of karma and how Robinson Crusoe was unable to bank his karma on a desert island. I have no idea why a fictional character is comparable to refugees. I'm lost in his method of teaching.

While I wait for the evening's noodle soup to cool, eight of my dharma sisters, who are tonight's chosen ones to dine out with our lama, rush around and excitedly get ready, dressing in pretty, floral-patterned dresses instead of our burgundy uniform. Our lama will probably don his civilian clothing of either Dior or Prada plucked from his vast wardrobe and bought with students' monetary offerings. He frequently treats his students to lavish dinners. In rotation he love-bombs up to a dozen students at a time and invites them to one of his favourite restaurants. He foots the bill in cash, courtesy of his lunchtime paper money tower—his leaning tower of karma.

I've learnt by watching that when seated at his dinner table, students are not permitted to speak unless spoken to. He does all the talking. What's more, when he ritually proffers food from his dinner plate to spoon-feed his student disciples, they have to open mouths wide, be fed and be thankful. Fortunately, I've managed to avoid being spoon-fed. When he over-orders food, his students are expected to polish off the banquet, regardless of how full they are; it would be a transgression to disobey. Almost everything is a transgression, except the worshipping of him.

A handful of students are not worthy of his retreat dinner invitations, me being one of them, which is a godsend. I'm thankful to be eliminated from his shopping extravaganzas, where he showers various students with cash or costly gifts, and free flights to attend retreats. His love-bombing makes these recipients feel loved and indebted to him. His income is obtained from students' donations, and he likes to remind us that our donated cash generates good karma in return.

After our soup supper, the rest of the sangha complete the day's schedule. One of the young nuns I've grown to like won't be attending; she's suspiciously disappeared into thin air. I skip evening-prayer practice and trudge to the railway bridge. My phone rings. Ethan's unblocked me.

'Darling. Sweetie. I didn't block you,' he lies. 'I was so tired I slept like a log. I just woke up.'

'Is that so?' I remark.

He keeps up the pretence. 'I … I had to switch off my phone. I had cravings,' he stammers. 'I wondered if you'd transfer money to me. I haven't eaten all day. I'll admit I had a teeny slip yesterday. Now I feel a bit guilty.'

'Are you kidding me?'

'It's not my fault! My friend at yesterday's AA meeting offered me a few crack rocks at a bargain price!' He rambles on, trying to excuse using. Relapsing.

Five months of being clean and sober has gone in a puff of smoke. It's never dawned on me that a drug dealer touting for business would attend AA meetings. At the time Phoebe called him, he would've been high on crack, but he'd managed to cover it up.

I feel betrayed, but I manage to compose myself. A quote by Confucius springs to mind: 'Don't do unto others what you don't want done unto you.' In my way of thinking, I feel it's better if I show humility and not let him go hungry, even though he should face the consequences of his actions.

'I'll transfer enough for food, but I've hardly got any money left. Why not be honest with your sponsor and ask for his guidance and support?' I ask. Ethan might be exempt from the Confucius quote, seeing as his using and drinking career has the upper hand. I'm clueless what to do for the best.

'Darling, thank you. You have my word that I'll tell my sponsor, and I'll repay you,' he says with heartfelt thanks.

'It's a slip, Ethan. It's not unusual to have cravings and relapses. Relapse is part of recovery. You have to focus on sobriety. Be careful who you befriend, and more importantly, take care of yourself.' I'm treading on eggshells.

'Yes, you're right,' he responds. 'I was thinking you could send me thirty quid, for food.'

I don't know if he's listening to me. 'Ethan? Are you hearing me?' I ask. I'm worried what will happen now that using crack cocaine after his five months clean and sober has disrupted his brain's neurotransmitters.

'Yes. Umm. Promise me that this is our secret? I don't want

my mum to find out I had a slip!' He sounds more concerned about Vicky's judgment than his mistake.

'All right. I won't tell her this time. But I can't keep lying for you! I'll see what I can afford to transfer, thirty pounds seems a lot.'

'Thank you! See how I've only got you. Look at how in love we are,' he says, all lovey-dovey and reeling me in with affection.

I manage to increase my overdraft and transfer funds to Ethan for him to buy food.

I'm becoming accustomed to not having enough sleep and waking to the sound of the 5 am gong. It's not until prayer practice has ended and breakfast time begins that I notice Frida looks concerned while she butters her toast.

'Is everything okay?' I ask in hushed tones.

'I'm not sure if I should say!' she whispers.

I know what she means; our lama has implemented further new transgressions. Students mustn't speak to each other unless it's dharma related, as it 'disturbs the minds' of others. 'Don't think! Don't speak!' he reminds us every day. His efforts to enforce a mostly silent retreat is not straightforward. When we're not under his eagle eye, our adrenaline builds during our measly amount of unsupervised time, because we have to muster the energy for the next day, so relinquishing our speech is not feasible for everyone. However, for most of us the lion's share of being literally speechless and our psychological solitary confinement guarantees paranoia and distrust. Attending retreat teachings is meant to help 'things to come up' emotionally, but the only thing I feel coming up is my squeaky soup. Our communication restrictions with one another make us strangely isolated despite not having physical space from each other in our overcrowded living conditions. Regardless of the rules, it's impossible for me to quit communicating with my own daughter.

'What's happened?' I ask.

She looks around the kitchen to check if the coast is clear. 'Last night was terrible. Bella was crying all night long and couldn't get to sleep. I asked what had upset her, and she told me an incident happened during the meal with our lama. He was in a temper and lashed out. He beat her! Started hitting her around her head, right there in front of the other students sitting at the restaurant's dinner table! Apparently, she owes karmic debt from a previous life, and that's why he hit her. Imagine that.' Frida looks perplexed.

I envisage Bella getting walloped with our lama's large, martial-arts fists. We hear footsteps and stop speaking while silently pressing on with breakfast.

A young nun swishes into the kitchen and murmurs the Buddhist greeting, '*Amituofo.*'

A senior nun follows her, sulking. A house full of students is disrupting her routine, and she can't hide her annoyance. She eyes us with contempt. It seems we're under surveillance. She'll most likely rat on us now that she's spotted us talking unnecessarily.

'*Amituofo,*' we reply in unison, and our hectic morning routine commences, tinged with sadness over Bella's traumatic beating.

Our lama is in fine form when teaching starts; he laughs, sings Disney numbers, and speaks of when he was recruited by the Royal Ballet after taking one ballet lesson in their rehearsal room. He says they proclaimed him a ballet prodigy and asked him to join the Royal Ballet teaching staff to train principal dancers. His tales are becoming more farfetched. Eventually, squeaky lunch is delivered, and I check my phone to see if Ethan's messaged me. He has sent a text: *Please call when you read this.*

I hurriedly pull on my trainers and run outside to call him.

I'd like to hear something positive today. I sense Ethan might thank me for transferring money that I can ill afford, as well as remaining calm when he told me he had relapsed.

'Oh, it's you,' he says nonchalantly when he picks up my call.

'Yes, of course. How are you? Did you eat?' I ask.

'Eh? Eat? Oh. Yeah, I did,' he replies. I'm listening for him to say a thank you, but all I get is, 'I just wanted to tell you something; you're a lying, secretive, cheating troll! You make me want to throw up.'

My heart sinks. I instantly regret sending him money. Hopefully, I'll remember not to do that ever again. I head back for the afternoon teaching to hear our lama's drivel for the remainder of the day. It's hard to concentrate on an average day, but now, because of Ethan's relapse and his vitriolic outburst, it's impossible. His brain chemistry might be affected by the reintroduction of crack and booze, but he shouldn't be taking it out on me. His choice to relapse was his decision.

After teaching, Loday twigs something's up. He makes coffee and suggests a brisk walk in the park. 'You seem troubled; is it Ethan again?' he asks as we enter the park gates.

'Actually. Yes. I can't cope. He's not doing well without me.'

'It's karma. It's meant to be,' he replies.

He's so disconnected from reality that he may as well be on another planet. I'm not convinced it's a karma thing, but he goes on to sing our lama's praises by speaking of his extraordinary powers. Apparently, he can bring roadkill back to life, change the weather, heal the sick, make people fly, as well as limitless other supernatural feats. We dash back to the sangha and to our day's frantic schedule. When it's time for evening prayer practice, I slip away to call Ethan from the railway bridge. He doesn't pick up for the first few rings, then he answers.

"Allo! Who's this?' he yells in a broad cockney accent.

'It's me,' I reply.

'Who's me?'

'Magda.'

'Oh. Hi. I think I blocked you,' he says.

'What's going on? You're slurring!'

'I … well … I don't know!' he replies.

'What have you relapsed on?' I ask with a sigh.

The line goes dead. When I call him back, I find he's blocked me.

After Tara practice I ask Loday if he's got time for a quick chat.

'I've got bad news, Loday, Ethan's relapsed,' I blurt out.

'Of course, he's relapsed. He doesn't practice chanting,' Loday replies. 'At least you're here; he'll have to face the consequence.'

'I need to go home before it gets worse,' I reply.

'You can't. You have to stay. If Ethan hurts you, your daughters will be emotionally harmed, and you'll create negative karma. The demons will enter into all your lives.'

Ethan makes a half-hearted attempt at going cold turkey, only to slip again. He calls me from a crack den.

'What are you doing? Are you mad?' I ask. There's loud music, singing and giggling in the background. I can barely hear him.

'Don't nag me! It was too hard to white knuckle it. I can't stop. And I've just lost my mum's car. Forgotten where I parked it!'

As quick as you can say Jack Daniels, he's alcohol dependent again.

At first Ethan's dad disbelieves me when I relay the bad news of another relapse, and that he's lost his mum's car. Also, the new lodger has to be told.

'Hello?' the new lodger says upon answering her phone.

'Hi, it's Magda here. I need to tell you something. Unfortunately, Ethan hasn't been well for some time. He's a drug addict, and an alcoholic, and he's relapsed. Have you ever heard of blackout drinkers?' I ask.

'No. No, what's that?' she stammers.

'A blackout drinker might hurt someone and have no recollection of it while under the influence. Ethan's one. You're not safe around him. His relapse could last weeks, months or even longer,' I explain. All the cash she's given Ethan has gone up in smoke at the crack den.

She sounds like she's going to cry.

Moments later, Ethan calls me. 'What the fuck have you done?' he shouts down the phone. 'My dad's just phoned me, and my lodger's packing to move out. My relapse's a secret, and you told on me! I've lost my family and lodger because of you! My dad's told my mum!'

'Phone your sponsor, Ethan,' I reply, and switch off my phone.

Chapter Forty-four

'Today's told me that Ethan relapsed!' Frida says.

'Yes. Two weeks ago. He's full blown now. I don't know what to do,' I reply.

We exchange glances for a matter of seconds before a senior nun appears in the dormitory. She needs our help to make soup for the sangha, because she's got to write and submit her weekly personal journal to our lama. All the ordained are required to write their weekly reflections for our lama's inquisitive mind. I suspect the journals feed him information he can use to make them think he can read minds.

We see four of our dharma sisters in the kitchen, chopping and peeling. Dharma music blares out of the CD player; it's the only music allowed in the sangha.

'There aren't enough chopping boards. Why don't you go for a walk and have some space?' Frida whispers.

The library's banned, as are reading books, save for the ones on lama's bookshelf, but the library is where I want to go. There's a hushed silence while I browse the new releases. I look around the room, and someone catches my eye. She sits at a computer desk, staring at the screen. She looks familiar; then the penny drops. I tiptoe towards her.

'Hi! Where have you been? How are you?' I ask.

Her gaze meets mine, which gives me a shock. Her eyes are red and swollen from crying. I didn't recognise her at first, but she's the nun who suspiciously disappeared. Her shaved head has grown out into a brown pixie style, and she's wearing civilian clothing— meaning she's been disrobed, so now she's an ex-nun. Either she's walked out or been thrown out of the sangha.

'I'm fine. I needed to use the library WiFi. How are you?' she nervously replies.

If she'd left the sangha on good terms, I wonder why she isn't using the WiFi at one of the sangha properties.

'I'm fine,' I reply.

'How's Ethan?' she asks.

I'm touched by her concern. 'He's not very well at the moment.'

'If you need guidance, you know who to ask.'

She means our lama, so I nod. 'Have you asked him for guidance?' I blurt out.

'Yes. He's all knowing.' She answers with a cryptic riddle— the same method Ethan uses to answer questions when he wants to be evasive.

I can tell she wants to be alone. Now that she's disrobed, I can, and do, hug her goodbye. Since her taboo disappearance, her dharma sisters have been worried about her—apart from the ordained, who practice non-attachment, except for guru. Things don't add up; something's amiss at our sangha. For the life of me, I don't know what.

Frida's wide-eyed when I put her in the picture about my bumping into the ex-ani.

'I wonder what happened,' she whispers, 'and if you think that's odd, Ethan's sozzled, and he's been calling me. He's weird;

he told me he'd just yanked his floppy dick out and was playing with it! That's creepy, so I hung up. I'm not taking any more calls from him.'

'Oh God! I don't know if he'll remember making an obscene phone-call. He's not well,' I say.

Ethan's drunken depravity was directed at Frida, but I'm his real target.

My phone rings. It's Ethan. 'Something terrible just happened!' he exclaims.

'What now!' I reply.

'My dad and Phoebe made me angry. I found an iron bar and smashed your car up. It was an accident!'

'What the fuck? This is a wind-up … Right?' I shriek.

'Didn't mean it … I just …'

'You had so many cars to choose from, but you just HAD to pick mine! Didn't you?' To my dismay, Phoebe's left me in the lurch by not reporting him to the police for vehicle criminal damage. I can't make an insurance claim, and I still owe Sylvia for the car loan. It's highly unlikely any member of his family will cover the car repairs.

I end the call and dial Phoebe.

'Me and Dad paid Ethan a visit only to find him swaying and swigging from a bottle,' she tells me. 'He's off his head. He chased Dad with an iron bar. I thought he was going to kill him! But he couldn't catch him, so he vandalised your car instead. The wing mirror and windscreen's gone, and the there's other damage. We confiscated the car keys, so he won't be able to drive. I'm finished with him this time!'

As soon as we end the call Vicky calls me. 'Thanks for trying to help,' she says. 'I want to let you know that I won't be helping Ethan ever again. Let him drink himself to death. I wish he'd die! He always says he wishes he were dead, so I'll see you at his funeral. I suggest you step back and detach as well. Any future contact is through my niece, Tansy.'

It's not easy to hear her talk about his funeral, but some people do drink themselves to death.

She's calling for his final curtain, consumed with hatred, because it's gruelling for any of us to love Ethan, and that, in itself, is mournful.

When I was young, my mother told that me throughout her childhood in Ireland, she wished and prayed that her sadistic alkie stepfather would drop dead. Her mother, Mammy, abandoned and lied to her, even made my mother believe, for her first seven years, that her mother was her sister. Then she reclaimed her, like lost baggage, from the loving home my mother shared with her 'parents,' who were, in fact, her grandparents. They had raised her since the death of my mother's real father.

Mammy abducted my mother from her granny when she felt her daughter was old enough to help raise her half-siblings— who Mammy and her alkie despot husband treated well due to their 'pure' bloodline. My mother's early memories, after her abduction, were grisly, like the time the stepfather, in a drunken rage, scooped up my mother's new kitten and strangled it right in front of her, then threw it at her feet and hollered at her to bury it. When Mammy gave birth to a stillborn baby, while the stepfather was out drunk somewhere, it was my mother, a tiny child herself, who cradled her dead half-brother, swaddled and placed him in a little box for a pauper's burial. When my mother was nineteen, she escaped to London and met my father. A few years later, her stepfather, a devil incarnate, drank himself off this mortal coil.

The stories of my mother's childhood trauma seeped out gradually over the years, like a poisonous gas. I became accustomed to its smell. I sat, and listened, like a mute child.

Little wonder that, after my birth, she had a nervous breakdown and succumbed to prescription-drug use. When I was small, she became too ill to mother me, often fatigued or bed-ridden, frequently in a volatile temper or comatose, and sporadically sectioned in a psych ward where my father and I visited her. Me, watching, soaking it all in. Mute.

As an adult I recall being given sage advice: don't hold onto resentment towards your mother; she might not be here much longer. We talked things out. I forgave her for my childhood, and she forgave me for her health problems—that arrived after my birth.

Addiction is a progressive disease, and I see how Ethan has manipulated me into pitying him. Partly because I don't want him feeling like an outcast, I've allowed myself to get suckered in. Before now, I've prevented Ethan from hitting rock bottom, but by doing so I've prolonged his drinking and using and unconsciously fanned the flames of his family's resentment. It seems his terrible legacy is to be wished a dead man, six feet under, by his own mother. By chance, our lama chose 'filial piety' for the retreat topic—in short, this means to be good, courteous, respectful, and loving to one's parents and ancestors. But how is this feasible when there's an addict or fiend in the family?

Loday hears what's happened to my car and reckons he's got a solution. 'Your lama will sort this out. He'll buy you a car, one that's better!'

'That's a nice offer, Loday. But I couldn't accept.' I just want my own car. Besides, I know promises never come to fruition; they're white lies or emotional blackmail.

'Rubbish! I shan't hear another word! Forget about Ethan and his demons,' Loday says. His interfering in my life is questionable.

Ethan's using and drinking continues to escalate. His co-dependency and vitriolic Skype messages, emails, and text messages increase tenfold. Vulgarities or empty suicide threats down the phone are commonplace. When he's in the company of strangers, or addicts, he blocks me. He entertains for as long as booze, drugs, and our money last. Only oblivion will do.

Our retreat moves closer to its end; I count down the days. My head is fogged with our lama's naff teaching methods, his scaremongering, hunger for power, and cash, and his un-Buddhist ways of practicing dharma.

The Puja ceremony we do is meant to purify all and sundry. During the rituals we make offerings to Buddha to earn merit. Maybe this evening's Puja will balance the karma. The lengthy ceremonies are held in the Buddhist centre's shrine room, and I always sense a devilish atmosphere, as if ghosts have joined us.

The ordained used to throw our Puja food and flower offerings in the river for Buddha, but the river got bunged up with our copious flower bouquets, cheese straws, and cakes, so now they leave it by the bushes on the riverbank.

An impromptu bash is announced. Our lama has decided to hold an audience with himself as guest of honour. His holy self interrupts a tai chi class in the shrine room. He leaps around for a bit, demonstrating a few karate high kicks, but he can't kick very high. He's strong for an out-of-shape man of his age, and he can manage a powerful karate push that can make us lose our balance and be flung ten feet back. As well as our lama's gift of stomach punches to unblock chakras, sometimes he has winded guests and students with right hooks to their abdomens—all in the name of karma.

Tonight he's bent on basking in more spotlight. He strides centre stage and waves elaborate gestures to his best, devoted students and ordained. One by one, each take to the floor where they twirl, hop, jump, arabesque, spinning like planets, until the room resembles a mini rave. His selected favourites from the burgundy flock deliver a performance that resembles a homage to Houdini.

When the evening performance of magic tricks ends, I'm keen to tell Ethan all about it, but he's too pissed to listen. He makes a load of strange noises down the phone and hangs up. I need to get home and make him see the light.

The last day of the retreat is a grand affair: photos, celebration cakes and a long line of students bearing expensive gifts that they proudly present to our lama. In turn, we bow and offer him a white, satin kata to bid farewell, and he drapes the katas around our necks with a muttered blessing. After the last teaching of the retreat, he sashays out of the shrine room with the walk of a leisurely bride, while students sing a slow Tibetan song with a mournful melody—everyone knows the words, apart from me. I notice a few students shed tears of emotion, or lama separation anxiety, or both; for the life of me I can't think why. The next retreat is in mid-December, where all of his blurb will be repeated, retold and regurgitated.

To my dismay, I'm still not allowed to go home. Ethan's fully immersed in his relapse, and our lama has decided he wants a number of students to extend their stay to volunteer with a few renovations in two out of four sangha properties—one being the Buddhist centre, the other the female house. He's too sacred to get his hands dirty by grafting himself, and it's out of the question to raise objections to our lama.

Not surprisingly, at our lama's request, the renovations develop into a large-scale refurbishment project. He wants walls knocked down in the main shrine room, and one large shower-room converted into six compact ones in the female house. He desires a monster amount of decorating in both houses, as well as plastering, plumbing, new flooring, and more besides, all paid with student donations from Pathgate's coffers and free labour provided by students. In exchange we'll reap the karma rewards for good merit, or so he reminds us. As far as I'm concerned, the manual work beats our 5 am - 11 pm retreat schedule. The bulk of the work, however, falls upon the shoulders of a young Australian student, who happens to be a plumber with construction work experience. Although he's missing his wife and small child back home and has to hold down his job in Sydney, he gives his time without batting an eyelid.

Meanwhile, Ethan has had a change of heart. 'I don't give a fuck about the shrine refurb!' he rages when he calls while I'm in the middle of sweeping up brick dust. When he calms down, he continues with, 'Darling, I've decided I need your help now, and I'll allow you to come back. It's your job to get me clean and sober; I can't do it alone. I've asked Tansy to send me to rehab at least a hundred times. She won't. And she's got tons of cash.'

But I can't forget his violence. 'It's not my job, Ethan! What can I do? I can't stop you using and drinking. Only you can. It has to come from within.'

At that moment I hear a crash coming from the kitchen. I rush to see what's caused the racket, only to be confronted by a pair of wriggling legs that have come through the ceiling. Judging by the trainers in mid-air, they belong to a Dutch student.

'You okay up there?' I call out.

'*Amitoufo!*' he yells back. His struggle to free himself causes most of the remaining ceiling to drop to the kitchen floor, exposing the upstairs floorboards.

A different chaos ensues. Day in and day out we work, attend regular morning and evening prayer practice, dash around like headless chickens, and in-between I answer Ethan's endless vulgar phone calls. He slurs, accuses, swears, abuses, blames, brags, reminisces, complains, or goes missing when he's busy entertaining his chums or junkies. By the sound of him, and with my past experience of when he's relapsed, I know it's pointless for me to run back to him just to slip back into my enabler role, also it's problematic to break free from the sangha. On one hand I feel guilty from detaching with love, on the other hand, I'm trapped and might be better off where I am, as bad as it is. The melting pot of opinions has created a mare's nest which Ethan fans with his deflecting and lies. A compromise springs to mind; I might be able to return to my hometown if I find a domestic violence refuge for women, but when I probe these options, I doubt I meet the criteria.

There's a delay with the sangha's building materials delivery. We wait patiently all morning until Frida and I are taken aback when a monk and nun invite us to go for a walk with them. They want to try out a few kites they'd bought. It makes a change to be doing something normal to pass the time, and we relish the breeze as the wind takes them up into the blueness of sky. It feels strange to not breathe oxygen laced with brick dust. When the wind eventually dies down, the ordained reel in the kites and briskly head back to the sangha. Frida and I dawdle behind until they are out of sight.

'Walls have ears; it's impossible to talk back there. Surveillance!' Frida says.

'Yes, I noticed,' I say. 'Do you think that you've been here long enough? I can make a plan to get us out of here. What do you say?'

'I'm scared to leave. I know I'm not doing well here. When I run errands, I take a detour through the park; there's a bench under a tree where I sit down and cry. The truth is … I'm miserable! Our lama scares me. All he seems to do is bawl abuse. Even when Loday told me to show you around Newcastle when you first visited, the lama admonished me for neglecting my sangha duties! Even though I had permission to take the afternoon off! I didn't take the same vows as the ordained, but I have to follow the same vows. I'm not allowed to be myself. The restrictions are crazy.' She doesn't meet my gaze, as if she feels confiding in me is a transgression.

I think back to how I had entrusted Loday with Frida for a short spell of respite. It's turned out to be anything but. My heart beats a mile a minute while I compute her despair. 'Listen carefully,' I say. 'Leave everything to me. All I'll say for now is your time here is almost at an end.'

Frida's huge, sad eyes fill with tears. She sobs, great heaving sobs where she can't even catch her breath. I hug her petite frame tightly, an attempt to hug away some misery; it does little to ease her sorrow.

'Ahhh! To be sure bejeezus we have tears flowin'!' I recite my late mother's saying in my best Irish lilt. She remembers it, and with this, she manages a smile at the Irish-ness of it. If I'm not mistaken, the more I remind her of life before Pathgate, the more it brings her closer back to her true self. We muster the get-up-and-go and return to the sangha full of rubble.

It's almost beyond belief when Ethan calls; he sounds proud as a peacock. 'Guess what? I'm sober. I did it! I got prescribed Valium yesterday; I haven't touched booze for twelve hours.'

'That's amazing! You see; you can do it.'

'Yes. And I've even listed a new advert for a subtenant. Got a viewing tomorrow. Not only that, I'm getting my AA one-day sober chip this evening.' He waffles on about sobriety and how easy-peasy it is to get sober.

I half believe him and bide my time until he calls next.

'I'm still sober. Are you proud of me?' he asks. 'And the viewing went well. I've let the room to a nice Irish bloke. He's signed a lodger tenancy and paid me a grand upfront. What a doddle! I'll transfer the money to you, so I don't get tempted to blow it.'

This time I don't even bother to check my bank account. I now know dishonesty is inherently part of his character. Over the next three days, he calls with regular sober updates, until the fourth day when he calls at midnight.

"Allo? Who's this?' Ethan slurs the question in a mock cockney accent. He's clearly three sheets to the wind, shit-faced.

'Ethan? You phoned me. Why are you slurring?' I reply, knowing full well why.

'I'm not slurring! It's my Valium! Shane's moved in. We ate dinner together; everything's cool.' After blaming his garble on prescribed benzos, he suspects I've guessed he's fallen off the wagon and abruptly hangs up.

Chapter Forty-five

I'm at my wits end. Despite Ethan getting his own way by securing Shane as his replacement lodger, it's done more harm than good. Shane's now entangled in the relapse. Ethan proceeds to entertain himself with his brutal calls and messages. It's fine for him; he's numbed with substances, so he remembers little to nothing from one minute to the next, or so he claims. The hours I waste on the phone with him, giving inspirational pep talks are ludicrous, but well intended in the hope he might listen and find his way back to sobriety. It's futile, though. He always reverts to the same old song, with him voicing his regrets, whys, and what ifs. My denial and inability to let go doesn't help either of us.

Addiction to crack is expensive. His all-nighters at his crack house make him a favoured customer, until the cash is spent, and he's no longer welcome. He doesn't care; he just drinks to oblivion.

Just before bedtime my phone vibrates. It's not Ethan's number; my first thought is that he's OD'd.

'Hi, it's me, Ethan. I'm using Twitch's phone.'

'Who's Twitch?' I reply.

'My new best buddy. Now listen; I've got news. Tansy's offered to pay for rehab! She's already found the best rehab, and I'm getting booked in for three months. She's fronting twenty-five grand! I'm being admitted in a few days' time. How about that?' 'That's … that's amazing. You're sure, right?'

He hangs up, and I can't help feeling sceptical about whether this is truth or lie. It's unexpected news. Tansy believes detachment is essential; she's all for disengaging with him.

A discussion's underway in the rubbly kitchen next door to my dormitory. I hear my name being called out, so I hastily present myself. When I reach the doorway, everyone looks up.

The nun continues speaking, 'Please, can all of you pack a bag. We've been told to stay at the male sangha house for a while, just until the refurb's complete.'

No one asks any questions. We nod as if we know what's going on. Frida rinses grit from two cups and pours coffee that we bring into my dormitory.

'Why do we have to move out?' I ask quietly.

Frida shrugs. 'We just do as they say. Nothing makes any sense here.'

'My head's spinning. Ethan called last night. He says he's got rehab booked, but I don't know if it's really happening,' I whisper.

'Weird. If that's the case, you need to do stuff,' Frida replies.

I know what she means. The dormitory door bursts open.

A senior ani strides in and says, 'Hurry up you two, please; there's work to be done. You have to pack your things, then help me with sewing and preparing lunch.' Her smile becomes a sneer.

'*Amituofo,* Ani. We'll be with you in five minutes,' Frida replies.

With such little notice, we pack enough for a few nights to

260

tide us over. We don our coats and shoes, pick up our backpacks and head out. A freezing wind stings our eyes as we briskly walk to the male house that's a few streets away. Newcastle's bitter winter is on its way, even though it's still September.

It's the first time I've set foot inside the male sangha house. The property is one in a long row of modest Victorian terraced properties, many of which look run down, but this house has a modern front door and new double-glazed windows. Indoors it's similar to the female sangha house. Of course, it's spotless, as was the female house before the refurb started, and it has the same colour scheme and identical fireplace portraits. The newly fitted kitchen is smaller than the one at the female house, but the rooms are bigger, including the loft shrine room. In peak season, during retreats, the house accommodates twenty to thirty people. We're shown to the downstairs guest-room-cum-dormitory that's next door to the kitchen. This is the female students' sleeping quarters for our five hours in bed. I pick the bottom bunk from eight. Frida has the bottom bunk at the opposite side of the room. We feel displaced.

A tall man wearing a pinny stops at the dormitory doorway. 'Hello. We've been expecting you. I'm Eric.'

He seems to think we know of him. Like many other guests who pass through for visits, he's just appeared.

'Hello,' Frida says. 'Nice to meet you. Do you need help with lunch?'

'No, I've almost finished. Thank you.'

At that moment, the older nun skulks by. 'Ah! There you are Eric!' she trills—it appears Eric's made a good impression already. She looks at us. 'Eric's busy cooking. That means you two can come with me and help with sewing.'

We follow her into the lounge where the sewing machine is set up. Burgundy skirts in different stages of making are piled neatly on an ironing board. Her mobile phone rings, and she glides out of the room to answer the call. It seems fitting to proceed with the unfinished sewing, so I measure and cut the fabric while Frida sews and stitches.

When the nun returns, she's delighted to find we've finished. 'Oh, I see you're all done. *Amituofo*. Time for a herbal tea!' she declares and plops herself down on the plump sofa.

Frida dutifully dashes to the kitchen to make the requested tea. There's just enough time for me to pop outside. I walk towards the block of grim flats at the end of the street where there's shelter from the wind. I retrieve my phone from my pocket and see the missed calls from Ethan.

He answers on the first ring. 'Oh, Sweetie, guess who I'm with? That pillock Twitch. He won't go home. Oy! Bruvva! Say 'Allo! Oy, Twitch!' He switches to speakerphone,

'Howdy doody! Twitch here! Everything's ace!' Twitch replies.

A Bob Marley track blasts out, and they join in, warbling out of tune, then howl with laughter.

It's pointless to try and speak to Ethan when he's like this, especially with Twitch for company, so I tell them I have to go for lunch. I end the call, feeling useless.

On returning to the house, I see the Australian man lying flat on his back in the hallway, exhausted. Other students and the ordained are sitting in the lounge, eating in silence. The student who fell through the ceiling sits on the stairs, engrossed with his iPad. He's smiling, watching something funny. The WiFi ban must have been lifted.

A small mirror has appeared on the windowsill in the bathroom with a clean razor next to it—a sign that a face or a head has been shaved earlier. I peer up close to see my reflection. Dark circles ring my eyes. I look ill, pale, and drawn. The locked door suddenly rattles and startles me. There's not a minute's peace to be had in this place.

In the kitchen Frida's drying the dishes. I see she has saved me a portion of lunch.

'It's good,' she says.

'Thanks. I thought our lama was coming here for lunch today,' I whisper.

'So did I, but he's busy packing. He's leaving for the airport later, to give teachings in Greece. He'll be gone for a few days.'

My heart skips a beat. 'Really? You sure?'

Frida nods quizzically. 'Sure I'm sure.'

The ordained and students leave to resume their day's chores and duties, going off in different directions, either to the Buddhist centre or to the female house of rubble. Surveillance is reduced. Because the ordained are preoccupied, they're not on watch duty, and now that lama is leaving England, no derogatory reports written by the ordained about other students will be submitted until his return. Furthermore, we'll have a break without lama dishing out bollockings.

I daren't waste a single second. I find my jacket that hangs in the dormitory and rummage in the pocket for my phone to make my call.

Ethan answers his phone and blows a long, loud raspberry.

'Ethan?' I say in a panic.

'That was my bum! Oh, hi, sweetie, honey, it's you. Twitch's tootled out to buy us some more booze and cigars. Did you want to have a chat?' he asks.

'Ethan. What's happening about rehab? Are you going?' I ask.

'Of course, honey! In a few days' time. Shhh. I'm treating myself to one last ever blow out. Why don't you come home? After my detox, I'll be admitted into secondary rehab, and I'll be allowed to spend weekends at home.'

'How can I afford to get home? You haven't paid anything

into my account! I haven't even got a door-key to let myself in, and I'm worried about my car that you've vandalised. Remember?'

The line suddenly goes dead. *Shit! Not again!*

I stare in disbelief at my shitty handset. Thankfully, it rings.

'Darling, my phone went funny. Twitch'll be back any minute. Oh, and sorry about my phone. I did my iPhone thumbprint thingy to get into my banking app, and our call cut off. I've just paid money into your account for your train ticket home. That's almost rinsed me out. Can we chat later? I'm so lucky to have Twitch. I called my sponsor and told him he's a useless tosser. And I told Loday he's a prick,' he declares.

'Hang on … are you telling the truth? About my fare?' I ask.

'Yes, I know I tell the odd lie, but not this time! Oh. Hey. Twitch is back! I love you. Bye!'

It's with familiar dread that I log into my online banking to check if he's spun another yarn. I brace myself, but when my eyes focus on my available balance, I'm gobsmacked to see Ethan's transferred £200. It's the first time he's ever kept his word.

I hurriedly track Frida down and find her in the Buddhist centre's shrine room, standing on a ladder and painting the ceiling with a roller. She's wearing dusty Crocs, a mask, huge gloves, a white paper coverall over her clothes and DIY goggles. She looks a bit like a spaceman.

'Hi! Where is everyone?' I enquire.

She removes the paint splattered goggles and mask. 'Ani and Eric have dropped lama off at the airport. I think Loday went to buy DIY stuff with Ghita, I don't know where everyone else's gone.' She climbs down the ladder.

'That's good. I need to tell you something. Let's head back to the dormitory.'

Frida steps out of the coveralls and slips on her jacket and shoes. We make it back to the dormitory before anyone returns.

'We're leaving!' I announce.

Frida looks alarmed. 'What do you mean?'

'Ethan's transferred money for the train fare home. We'll leave together,' I reply.

'Are you sure?' Frida answers nervously.

Before she asks more questions, I open my Macbook and look up Trainline for tickets. 'Holy shit! Look at that. A single fare is a hundred and fifty quid! I've only got two hundred.'

We look at one another.

'What'll we do?' she asks.

'There's only one thing we can do,' I reply. 'I'll go back alone, sort everything out, see Ethan gets into rehab, and get my car repaired. God knows how much it will cost and how I'll pay! But when I drive back to Newcastle, I'll get you out of here.'

She wrings her hands.

'I'll be back. Don't worry,' I reassure her. 'Now that lama is flying to Greece, it's easier for me to leave here and deal with the mess at home. Thank God we've got a home to go back to in the south. Once Ethan has detoxed, he'll be allowed home every weekend. Things are going to work out just fine.'

'You're right. Ethan could do with some support. And getting the car repaired is way overdue. I can't wait to escape from here, and for us to live like a family. It'll be great when Ethan's in recovery. And I'll see Sylvia again!'

'Yes, it's going to be amazing,' I reply.

'Here goes.' I select one single-journey ticket. A train departs from Newcastle in twenty-four hours' time. My train booking is confirmed. Being forced to leave Frida like this, for any length of time, pains me; after all, she's been trapped in the sangha for nearly nine months. I'm anxious to return and get her out of this terrible place.

In the meantime, it's best I do not mention to Ethan that I've booked my ticket home. I'm scared he'll put the kibosh on my travel plans and snitch to Loday as he's done in the past. Ethan's addiction has thwarted the development of all the good things in our relationship, including trust and emotional intimacy— which is non-existent. Loday would definitely forbid my leaving the sangha without lama's consent. Loday and Ethan being in cahoots has to be prevented.

I busy myself packing my backpack with the little clothes I arrived with, my Macbook, Nikon and wash bag. Evening prayers seem short—led by the senior nun, who sings through the prayers so fast that no one can keep up with her while she wildly beats the hand-held drum like a wild thing, as if there's no tomorrow.

Tomorrow … hurry up tomorrow.

Chapter Forty-six

Permission has been granted to the student who has the bulk of the building work to skip morning prayers, but he still drags himself out of bed at the ungodly hour and attends. His eyes are bloodshot from tiredness. The prayers commence with the students and nuns in attendance. The construction work screeches to a halt because a plasterer has to fix the walls. With lunchtime fast approaching, I feel a sense of dread.

In our dormitory, Frida's learning Tibetan texts; she stops for a second and whispers, 'You'll have to tell them you're leaving today. It's best to get it over with.'

I doubt she's heard, but at that moment, the senior nun bursts into our dorm. The nuns don't warn with a door knock. '*Amituofo!* Who wants to offer me some help? There's much to do today. I'm going to the food market. I take it you're not busy?'

I get the feeling I know exactly what Frida would like to tell the nun she can do with another day spent browsing vegetables at the food market. She's renowned for wasting a good half an hour choosing between a broccoli or a cauliflower.

'*Amituofo*, Ani,' I say. 'Actually, I haven't got the time for the market. I'm leaving. I've booked a train for five o'clock.' There.

I blurted it out.

'Oh! But … *amituofo*. I didn't know this,' she replies, looking alarmed.

'Ani, could we please give her a lift to the train station?' Frida asks.

'Err … certainly. Let me see; we can leave at four.' She's so taken aback; she doesn't know how to react. I reckon she doesn't know if she's glad to see the back of me or not, so she simply says, '*Amituofo.*'

Our lama has spent the entire summer telling all of us, 'Don't speak; don't think,' in an effort to ban speaking to one another—unless it's dharma related—but even the ordained can't get the hang of that instruction. Frida and I know the nun will disclose my travel plans to the ordained faster than a hare. Sure enough, within the hour Loday turns up.

'Oh! Hi Loday,' Frida says, opening the door so he can wander in.

'Thought I'd say hello; I heard you're leaving today?' He looks in my direction.

'Yes, I'm catching a train at five.'

'That must have been expensive,' he says.

'Yeah, a-hundred-and-fifty quid, one way. Ethan paid me back a little of the money he owes me.'

'What's the hurry?' he asks.

'She's not hurrying at all,' Frida says. 'She should have left when her car got vandalised.'

'I have to go home and sort things out,' I say. 'Ethan's going to rehab in a few days. His cousin's paying twenty-five grand for his treatment. So I have to see he's okay and sort out other stuff, like my car repairs and contacting our landlord to give him an update.'

'His cousin's funding his treatment? Why?' Loday's face

flushes and turns an angry red. 'What a waste of money!' He frowns, his expression changes from puzzled to furious and he starts to pace around, shaking his head in disbelief.

'Well, it's a last-minute thing,' I say. 'I don't know the details. She wants to help him get better, and he wants to beat it this time.'

He shrugs. '*Amituofo*. I hope you have a safe journey back.'

'*Amituofo*. Thank you.'

He glides out of the room, still red faced, and slams the door shut.

'Wow! Loday's truly raging,' Frida whispers.

'You can say that again. I wasn't expecting that reaction,' I reply.

Frida shakes her head; she wasn't either.

I'm paranoid in case I forget my train ticket reference number, so I'm careful not to misplace it. I figure I'll be back in a few days' time to collect Frida, so I skip saying goodbyes to the others.

Frida hands me a paper bag. 'Here's a few snacks and a bottle of water.'

I just manage to squeeze it in my backpack.

The senior nun fires up the little red car and dharma music blares out. Frida sits in the front passenger seat; I sit in the back. We've given ourselves plenty of time to catch my train. I gaze out of the window watching Newcastle whiz by. The signs to the station are in sight, and rush hour traffic's starting to build. Suddenly the nun swerves off the road without indicating and takes a side road. She picks up speed and zigzags up and down side streets.

'Deary me. *Amituofo!* We seem to be lost,' she declares.

'But you left the dual carriageway and started driving in the opposite direction!' Frida exclaims. 'We can't be lost. You've been driving to Newcastle station for the past ten years. We have to turn around!'

She grins. 'All in good time. *Amituofo.*'

'Please turn around, Ani!' Frida pleads.

The nun drives around in circles until we join the carriageway. 'Dear, dear me. *Amituofo.* We're lost again!' she says.

'Follow the sign!' Frida shrieks.

My phone rings. I'm in such a panic I don't answer.

'There!' Frida points to the entrance of the train station.

I check my watch; my train departs in five minutes. The nun pulls into a parking space. 'Thanks for the lift, Ani. *Amituofo.*' I call out as I scramble from the car.

'*Amituofo,*' the nun replies.

Frida and I run to the ticket-collection machine. I hold my breath while I enter my reference number. Thankfully my ticket hasn't expired, and it prints out. We can't see my train on the board, so we dash towards the gate where a guard's chatting to a colleague.

'Please, can you help? I have to catch this train!' I show him my ticket, hoping there's been a delay.

'Yes. You need this gate, pet. You've missed it. But your ticket is good for the next one,' he replies in a broad Geordie accent and opens the gate to let me through. Frida untangles herself from my backpack and hands it to me. I sling it over my shoulder and hug her as tightly as I can, not wanting to let go. The nun was out of luck by hoping she'd scupper my travel plans.

'I'll drive back as soon as I can,' I say over the noise of Geordie accented public address announcements. I tidy flyaway strands of Frida's hair.

'I can't wait to see you. Hurry back and take me home,' she says.

'For sure,' I reply.

Frida pulls up her big hood and turns to walk back to the

irate nun. She turns briefly with one last wave. I wave back with both arms, then make my way to the platform where I plonk myself down on a metal seat. The platform's so cold and windy it blows my hair in all directions. According to the board, I've an hour to wait for the next train. It feels weird to be free, in a public space, with no sangha surveillance. There's noise: jostling, kerfuffle, and crowds all around me. It's surreal. I've been trapped in the sangha bubble for so long that I'd almost forgotten how the outside world feels. Just as I glance at the board for the umpteenth time and see that my train's delayed, my phone vibrates in my pocket.

'Hello?' I say, straining to hear.

'What time do you call this? I thought you'd phone. I'll be dead in a minute!' Ethan snaps.

'Ethan,' I reply as another loud Geordie announcement belts out of the platform speaker.

'What's that noise? Sounds like you're at the airport,' he hollers.

'No, I'm not at an airport.'

'Where are you then?'

'I'm waiting for my train. I'm on the platform, on my way home.'

'Really? I'm so pleased. What time will you be back?' he asks.

'There's a delay; by midnight, I hope.'

'That's wonderful news!'

I walk towards the refreshments area, where it's quieter. 'Listen, I'll text you from the train. I might lose my signal on the way.'

'Okay. Great!'

Finally, my train arrives. I manage to get a grubby seat on the busy carriage. My thoughts turn to Frida; I wonder what's she doing now? I send her a text to say I'm on the train. Cold, smelly air escapes from the vents. Commuters snooze soundly, and a few read today's newspapers. My phone pings every few minutes with Ethan's texts asking for updates.

A uniformed guard walks along the aisle with a rattling trolley of refreshments. A hot drink would be welcome, but I'm scared to spend two quid. I catch glimpses of shadowy trees that whiz by in the blur of darkness. The train stops at its calling points, edging further south. When my station's four stops away, I prepare to disembark, half afraid of missing my station. When I have two stops to go, I discover I'm going to miss my interchange train by a matter of minutes. It's the final leg of my journey and the last train of the day. I'll have to hail a station taxi to finish my journey.

My body aches. All the stress and months of uncomfortable sitting in the sangha have taken its toll. I'm relieved to disembark and find the taxi rank outside.

My phone rings in the cab. Ethan wants me to stop on the way and find an all-night booze shop. 'I've almost run out, and I'm going into withdrawal,' he says. 'I forgot to go to the shop earlier.'

This is all I need after eight hours of traveling, but I tell him I'll try.

I spend the next forty minutes looking out the window, the stretch of motorway zooming by. With just a mile to go, I ask the cabbie to stop at the petrol station, where I withdraw fifty quid from the ATM and buy a cheap quart bottle of vodka for Ethan. I don't give any thought about enabling or ask myself why he didn't get his own booze. At this stage, I just want to get home. To my immense relief, the cabbie finally pulls up outside our home. I send Frida a text to let her know I'm home. Within seconds she texts me back: *Thank goodness! I was getting worried! I love you! Speak tomorrow!*

I'm not expecting a fanfare, but I am taken aback to find the front door wide open. 'Ethan! I'm home!' I call out.

'I'm upstairs!' he hollers back.

A woman's jacket lies over the upstairs banister, and my box of stuff I'd left at the top of the stairs, on the landing, is gone. In addition, I can't see any of my mail, so I quickly check the drawer where it might be. There's no mail, and I don't recognise the new, half-empty boxes of Viagra and birth control that's been bunged in the drawer. I let it slide.

I find Ethan in his pyjamas, tucked up in bed, propped up with six pillows. The setting looks staged, with the patient in his sick bed waiting to receive well-wishers; although, frankly, he does look sickly. He looks at me with purple eyes that I know from times past. Beads of sweat trickle down his face, and his drenched hair's stuck to his clammy forehead. His belly's bloated, which is why he needs so many pillows—sitting up eases the bloating. It looks like he's aged at least ten years in as many weeks.

He opens his arms feebly, and I suspiciously hug him a hello, still not knowing for sure if rehab is really happening or if shit's going to hit the fan.

'Did you buy booze?' he asks.

'Yes. Vodka.' I retrieve it from my backpack.

'Thank fuck! I'll pay you back, right now this minute.' He picks up his iPhone to use his banking app. 'Oh. I forgot. My thumbprint doesn't work anymore because I ruined it. Look!' He holds up his thumb. It's one, huge blister, a burn from his prolonged use of crack pipes and upside-down lighters.

'Maybe you can log in to online banking later?' I suggest.

'Ahh. No. I'm locked out of online banking as well. Anyhow, I don't want you to see how much of our cash I've spent,' he jokes, or is he serious?

'Sorry. I should ask how are you? I missed you. I'm happy you're home,' he says, changing the subject of money, or the lack of it. He sits forwards and starts to roll a cigarette. Halfway through, he unscrews the cap off the vodka bottle and pours a moderate measure into a china mug. He notices me watching him. There's a distance between us, like we're strangers and at the same time not.

'Oh,' he exclaims and jumps off his sickbed to tug at my battered trainers and pull them off. 'You're home. So take your shoes off!' Then off he dashes to the other side of the lounge towards the CD player, where he proceeds to play his current favourite track. He starts warbling out of tune, grabs my hand to dance and pulls me around. I humour him for the first verse, until I free myself from his grip to turn the volume down.

'I've had a long day, and I'm bursting for the bathroom,' I say.

'Of course,' he agrees.

The large burn holes in the bathroom linoleum catch my eye and reveal how Ethan, and his companions, have been cooking heroin on metal spoons that were dropped on the bathroom floor while they were using. It's an effort to remind myself to be calm, and I go to the kitchen to put the kettle on. Dirty dishes are piled high; the cooker is filthy, and there's splashed tea, sticky beer puddles and crumbs all over the floor. I thought Ethan would have tidied up. The rare times I've seen him sober, he'd been a little OCD in the kitchen. Actual evidence of his drinking is minimal. He's got rid of his empties. More teaspoon-sized scorch marks over the white worktop where the kettle stands. When I open the cutlery drawer, I see several ruined, blackened teaspoons that have been carelessly thrown back. In view of what's been going on here during his relapse, the place could be a lot worse. It looks like Ethan has done a good job clearing away a lot of evidence, but some evidence is more difficult to erase than others.

Before the kettle boils, Ethan appears. He wants to show me the website of the rehab he's checking into, and he wants to dance, sing and be silly. He wants hugs, affection, and reassurance. He wants to be loved, trusted, and understood. But he can't give anything in return; he's too sick. He doesn't even love, understand or trust himself. He's in a wobbly mood, fearful of a detox one minute, and jovial the next.

'I haven't thought about cheating, my love,' he blurts out, then pauses. Before the atmosphere becomes more awkward between us, Ethan's iPhone dings phone messages. 'It's Tansy! She wants to know how I'm feeling.' He smiles, almost forgetting I'm there, and he gets distracted by typing lengthy replies into the early hours.

Chapter Forty-seven

Shafts of morning sunlight stream through the gap in the curtain. Ethan wakes as soon as he senses I've woken.

'I'll make some tea,' I say.

'Oh, yes! I've missed morning tea,' he replies.

But … when I make it, he manages to drink just one mouthful before he retches.

'I finished the vodka an hour ago. I'm going into withdrawal,' he explains. 'We have to go to the shop and buy more booze.'

So we rush like mad to get ready to go the local shop just around the corner. Ethan takes me by the hand and pulls me along the footpath, and that's when I see the full extent of the damage to my vandalised car. Smashed glass is scattered all over the dashboard and front seats, and my wing mirror is missing. Last night was too dark to properly see the damage. Flattened beer boxes that Ethan had placed over the windscreen has kept out the rain.

'You've made a right job of that, Ethan,' I remark.

'I'm sorry about that. I promise I'll pay for the damage. Every penny. You know you can trust me!'

Yeah. Sure.

He pulls his hood as far as it will go over his face and walks as fast as his feet will carry him while his fearful gaze darts around. Clearly, he's trying to hide from someone. It's unnerving not to be able to even pop out to our local shop without a lurking sense of trepidation. He hastily chooses his poison, a large case of beer and two bottles of wine. Unable to wait the short walk home without drinking, he opens the wine and knocks back gulps straight from the bottle, all while walking briskly and looking over his shoulder.

'Rehab said they'd call this morning,' he says as he fills our fridge with the beer.

While I rustle up omelettes, Ethan sits at our small kitchen table with a mug of wine. He lights a cigarette and gazes at the view yonder, then tucks into breakfast as if he hasn't eaten in ages.

'You shouldn't have gone there,' he says. 'To Pathgate. I relapsed because you went there.'

'It was meant to be for one week,' I reply. 'You wouldn't allow me home. Remember?'

He sighs. 'Sorry to blame you. I mean, yeah, I picked up a drink because I felt like it. I wanted to see what would happen ... When I stayed there, I had trouble. Rinpoche didn't allow AA meetings. My mum visited me there once and she said it's like a cult. She stayed a night in a hotel near the sangha and couldn't wait to abandon me and leave me to it. I know what they're like, them Buddhists. They're cultish. Brainwashed! A bit like some AA meetings which can be cultish, but with them Buddhists, it's in your face.'

I stare at him in disbelief. 'You knew all this and kept it secret! Why?'

'I wanted you to find out what they're like for yourself.'

I snort. 'That's just great. And Frida's still there.'

'She'll be okay. Loday will mind her. Anyhow, you're home now, so Frida can move in with us if she likes. We'll all get along just fine. We can book a train ticket for her.'

His shocking revelation about the cult is difficult to comprehend. But at least he can see Frida needs to get out and move in with us. Maybe he's trying to make amends. 'She'll like living here. I'll tell her later.'

'Of course, darling, this can be Frida's home too.' He polishes off the bottle of wine and belches. 'Umm, sweetie, I need your help with something ... that is ... I need you to speak to my phone company about my bill. They sent me a text about it. Please?'

'What the heck?' Then I sigh in resignation. 'Oh, okay.'

He dials his phone provider and switches to speakerphone, then passes his handset to me.

'We need to discuss Ethan's bill,' the man says, 'there's three-thousand, five-hundred pounds he needs to pay today to keep his services. The premium-rate numbers have made quite a large bill.'

Blimey!

Ethan looks sheepish. He's racked up thousands of pounds worth of phone charges calling sex lines.

I hold my breath for a few seconds to process this new debt. 'I, errr ... I'm afraid Ethan can't pay this bill. He's an addict and he's checking into rehab soon, and he's unemployed.' Classical music plays while I wait for his response.

'Sorry to keep you,' he says on his return. 'I've spoken to my colleague, and we've decided that the way forward is to waive the entire bill, this time. I'll update his account right away.'

The instant the call ends, an explicit text message arrives: *Hey baby, how do ya fancy a good hard f**k, I'm gagging for it!*

Ethan hides his face in his hands. 'What have I done?'

278

I can't respond.

'It was meaningless,' he coos.

I clear the table and start washing up. 'Okay. Forget it.'

The weird thing is, there are times, such as these, where Ethan manages to 'luck in' when it comes to the kindness of strangers or loved ones—be it for cash, unpaid loans, expensive gifts, free holidays, shelter, favours, having his debts written off, frequently getting off the hook with the police, and cadging funding for rehabs. Maybe it's his higher power or something.

I walk outside, stand by my vandalised car, and call Frida on the off chance she isn't snowed under with sangha errands. To my relief she picks up.

'Hello. Is everything alright? How's Ethan doing?' she asks.

'He's okay. It's a bit of the usual chaos; you know how it is.' It seems I've already switched on my autopilot, and survival mode has reactivated itself.

'That's good to hear. Do you think you'll be able to come and get me soon?'

'Yes, soon. I'll bring you home; you'll like it here. Ethan said you'd be welcome to move in, so it's plain sailing,' I reply.

'I can't wait! I'll tell Sylvia.'

I unlock my car to retrieve my SatNav to estimate how long the drive to Newcastle will take. But my SatNav isn't plugged in the cigarette lighter where I'd left it. I search the door pockets; it's nowhere to be seen.

'Ethan? Have you moved my SatNav?' I call out.

'Oh, yes. It's on the desk,' he replies.

All I see on the desk is a pile of messy papers and his mail. 'It's not!' How the hell will I manage to drive to Newcastle without a SatNav?

Ethan saunters over to the desk and casually moves around his paperwork.

'I said it's not there, Ethan!'

He doesn't even seem surprised. 'Oh, honey, it's disappeared. Maybe my mate Twitch stole it, or one of my other friends, couldn't say which one. Poor addicts! They need to get their gear somehow. What a shame. Don't worry; I'll replace it,' he says in slurry tones.

By the way he's acting, I reckon he's traded it for crack.

'You're upset,' he says.

'Well, I'll be happy when you're in rehab,' I reply. Perish the thought if he mucks it up.

'We'll be fine; won't we? You'll learn to trust me. A clean and sober me. And with Frida here, I'll be extra nice. And you'll both get along with Shane. His lodger rent will bring in good money while I'm in rehab.'

Seems his obscene phone call to Frida is water under the bridge.

'It might take a while … learning to trust you,' I reply, feeling optimistic by the very thought of it.

He pulls me in close and gives me a stinky-of-booze hug that's broken by his ringing iPhone. He lets go to answer it and walks to the other side of the lounge. 'Tansy! Tans, sweetie; I was just about to call you. Rehab rang me. Guess what? They'll take me in two days' time,' he gushes in his camped-up Bertie Wooster accent. He puts the call on speakerphone but thinks again and turns it off.

'Yes, Tans, I've spoken to her; actually, she's home. She caught a train back.'

I can't hear Tansy's reply, but I'm being discussed.

'I'm sorry you're unhappy she's come home, Tansy. But I think she had to come back because it's her home, and she has to sort her car out and other stuff.' He listens intently and with a guilty expression. 'Oh, I'm so sorry I didn't ask for your permission. … A contract? Sure. Okay. Email it to me. I love you. And I'm so, so sorry about her coming home.' He ends the call and fumbles for his lighter. 'Umm … that was Tansy.'

'I guessed,' I reply, waiting for some kind of explanation. I have no idea what interests Tansy so much about me. I've never even spoken to her, and I've had enough of being under surveillance. I reckon Ethan's been denouncing me to her.

'The thing is this,' he goes on, 'Tansy has a … what she calls a rehab deal. I have to sign a contract. She's drawing one up, and I have to agree, in writing, that I'll never see, speak or contact you ever again. In exchange she'll pay for my rehab. Twenty-five grand. She says all my focus from now on is rehab and recovery.'

'That's a peculiar kind of contract!' Her ultimatum sounds unreasonable to me. His phone pings before I've even finished my sentence.

'She's emailed me the contract already. I'm such a lucky boy. I got rehab!'

It seems she must have had one already drafted. He eagerly opens the message and reads it, which is an achievement in itself, judging by how much alcohol he's drunk this morning. Despite the fact I'm named in the rehab contract, he won't show me it. He reads it to himself, quietly … secretly … and replies without further ado.

'There. Sent. That was easy. I've agreed. I've promised her that I'll break all ties with you, and I'll never touch alcohol or drugs ever again after this detox.'

I haven't quite processed what just happened; it happened so fast. A few moments ago, we were discussing our future together, but without rehab he'll die. Recovery comes first, relationships second, or in our case not at all. If these are Tansy's strings attached, then so be it—besides, Ethan's wild about the idea.

One load of washing's going around, another's lined up.

Everything else is ready to pack in his rehab suitcase, but I can't get the stubborn red-wine stains out of his tops. I cook an early supper, a healthy pasta dish. It's kind of bizarre, acting this wifely role, be it a dysfunctional one, with our lifetime separation firmly signed away. Even while we eat our dinner, Ethan won't face up to how the contract is the end of us.

With the fridge refilled with a fresh supply of booze that will only last him until morning, Ethan is chipper. He's got nothing to nag about on his hazy horizon.

I make myself bedtime tea to relax, and Ethan lights up a fag when yet another message pings.

He stares at the iPhone screen for a few seconds and clears his throat with a rattling cough. 'Oh, something just happened.'

I dread it's Tansy cancelling rehab, and I look at him ready for whatever he's about to throw at me.

'We … we've sort of been evicted,' he continues.

'Evicted? What the hell are you talking about?' My heart starts beating a mile a minute.

'See for yourself. You're copied in the email!' He hands me his phone.

The email is from Gary and, sure enough, he's served us eviction notice, a Section 21 with a Section 8 attached. 'Ethan? This eviction notice says we're two months' rent in arrears. Holy shit! It says we're being kicked out in fourteen days' time. Is this a mistake?' I ask in disbelief.

'If that's what it says, it must be right,' he says nonchalantly.

It's fine for Ethan. He's anesthetized with alcohol, and he'll be in rehab for months. Afterwards some do-gooder or other is bound to mollycoddle him. I'm trying to get my head around this stone cold sober.

'You've made me homeless, Ethan! And what about Frida? Even Shane your lodger is homeless now, and he's only just moved in. You promised me you'd paid our rent from our rent account! You haven't even mentioned rent arrears, and we had over four grand in the rent account, including all the housing benefits. Where's it gone? And you had another two grand from your lodgers. Plus hundreds you cadged from your mum. What the fuck have you done with seven-thousand pounds in such a short space of time?' It's little wonder he wanted me out of the way for ten weeks.

He shrugs. 'Smoked it all off. Crack. And booze. This is the seventh home I've lost over the years because of my addiction. This time I lost our flat in record time. Two-and-a-half months!'

This is news to me. 'Oh my God! What have you done?'

He doesn't answer, or apologise, or try to explain, or attempt any words of comfort. He just says, 'I can't wait for rehab. I'll never drink or use again. Poor me. I've loved every second of this relapse. I've had a barrel of laughs!' He lights up a fag, happy as Larry.

'Have you really? Loved every minute? Well, what about you losing our home? As well as getting me up to my neck in debt! I am so not laughing, Ethan!' I retort.

'Oh, I forgot I've made you homeless. My relapse has been marvellous and terrible.'

If it is true that he's forgotten, it could mean his short-term memory has been impaired by his using. It seems I'm powerless over his addiction.

Chapter Forty-eight

Rain patters outside. I sit in just the glow of a lamp and watch from the window. The lights of the pretty village in the distance twinkle like a wintery scene that wouldn't be out of place on an old-fashioned style biscuit tin. It's such a stunning view, but it doesn't cheer me up. My mind races with a familiar sense of doom while Ethan snores like a walrus. His chest rattles, and he coughs and splutters, which wakes him. Bursting to pee, he stumbles to the bathroom. No sooner has he flushed the toilet than he's back, plopping down on the bed, pouring another drink.

'I can't work out why you look depressed,' he says. 'You should be happy. I'll die without rehab, and I'm about to be cured. Plus, we're over. That should please you. You only came home because you haven't got anywhere else to go. Well, you're free to fuck right off!'

'What did you say? Why the hell are you starting on me?' I ask in dismay.

'You heard.' He proceeds to relay graphic sex-for-cash tales that would make the Marquis de Sade blush.

'Please don't, Ethan,' I say. 'I think you've got a mood swing on the way.' By defending myself from his toxic deflecting, I play right into his hands.

The next morning, he's as happy as a lark. 'I was just thinking … why not let's part as friends? Forget what I said last night! We've both got happy times ahead of us.'

He might have a point. If we part ways on bad terms, it would be quite sad, especially after all we've been through; besides, forgiveness doesn't seem such a bad idea. 'I agree.'

'Tansy sent me a text! She's booked a taxi that'll take me all the way to rehab. Without stopping, obviously!' He looks around. 'Sorry about leaving you to deal with the eviction.'

Time's ticking. The taxi will be here in an hour. Ethan wanders to the fridge to count how many beers he's got left. He can't stand the thought of leaving any. While he waits, he plays Amy Winehouse's song *Rehab* on full blast and sings along out of tune, then he starts to boogie with the beat - waggling his index finger to the repeated no in the chorus—what a tragic irony. His clowning around makes me manage a smile, despite all the sadness: addiction and consequences, debt, poverty, betrayal, homelessness, the cult, us … and … everything.

'How do I look?' Ethan dashes off to the bathroom for a final preen in front of the mirror, flattening his hair this way and that, getting really close up to inspect his purplish eyes and sticking out his tongue. He rubs his reddened chin where he'd shaved with a blunt razor, and sticks pieces of toilet roll on bloody nicks.

'You look just fine. Hurry, your taxi will be here any minute!' I reply.

Ethan rushes to carry his baggage downstairs to the front door, so that none get left behind. He has a last look around. 'I think I've got everything.' He checks his phone and throws me a look. 'Oh, one last thing! Whatever you do, don't open the front door, and always keep it locked. Always.' He hands me our door keys to our soon-to-be not home.

'Always?' I reply.

'Don't ask. You don't wanna know.' He places a hand on my shoulder. 'Goodbye, and … thanks. You've been a good friend. See you in the next life.'

It's a queer farewell. I don't understand why he's being so blasé. He shows me no warmth; all he cares about is himself.

A sharp toot indicates the taxi's arrival. The driver hops out to open the car boot and looks astonished when he sees the mountain of luggage.

'I'll try and fit it all in,' Ethan mumbles while he wrestles with the load.

Once the luggage is stowed away, he settles in the passenger seat—and even fastens his seatbelt. Excited for his expensive rehab admission, he smiles, an ear-to- ear beamer, and waves, but he can't keep his eyes off his phone for longer than a few seconds. I remain standing there, like a lemon in the drizzling rain, waiting to wave him off. God help me if I were to turn my back.

Finally, the driver fires up the taxi. Ethan opens the window and sticks out his arm for one last wave. The cab pulls away, fast. Ethan's gone.

I return to our soon-to-be former home. Already it's losing its homely feel; maybe it's just me detaching myself. I double lock the front door from the inside, just like Ethan had instructed, then watch the kettle while it boils. It's only when I get the milk from the fridge that I realise I've made two mugs of tea, one for each of us. Silly really, considering Ethan always lets his tea go cold because of his gag reflux.

Suddenly I start to fret that he's feeling anxious, so I compose a text to send him—the last one I'll ever send him, because his

phone will be confiscated upon his admission: *Ethan! Good luck!*
I hope they have chocolate milkshake on the menu!

He'll understand the text; it's a nod, for old times' sake, about his love of milkshakes and how we'd shared them. I know for a fact he's holding his iPhone for dear life, but he blanks the message. An hour later, still no reply. I guess he's blocked me. I should be used to his heartlessness.

Chapter Forty-nine

The last thing I want to do is mope around or waste any time resenting, so I pack my Mac and walk to a nearby cafe that has WiFi so that I can look up garages and find someone who does mobile car repairs and replacement windscreens. Goodness knows how I'll pay.

The waitress takes my order of a pot of tea while cutlery clatters in the busy dining area where diners are tucking into hearty brunches. Upon logging into my email account, I see one that makes my heart skip a beat. It looks ominous. It's from Tansy. It begins friendly, though. She writes:

You have been a massive part of Ethan's life, and your help over such a long time has excused us, his family, allowing us to ignore him and his chronic addiction. We all owe you thanks, especially Ethan, despite his behaviour towards you. He needs specialist care in rehab to get well. Seeing as it's me who is financing this, I am asking you to give Ethan space. Promise me you shall cease all contact with him. Give me your word and honour it. If he gets in touch with you after his admission you MUST let me know, as he will be breaking the contract. Anyone going into rehab must not be involved in a relationship or have contact with someone who triggers them emotionally. You must respect me, and my money that I'm investing in this. It's your duty, and one of my absolute conditions. From Tansy.

At first, I feel a surge of annoyance from her condescending tone and demands. She's worried her cash isn't safe, yet my life isn't safe now that I'm soon to be homeless. I'm an adult and being told to sign an agreement with a stranger. Ethan's family's been out of the picture for ages, practising 'tough love' while they've prospered. I don't owe them a thing! No doubt by now they all know he's made me homeless and vandalised my car. Although it's doubtful they know the extent of the thousands of pounds worth of debt he's dug me into, nor the emotional turmoil he's caused.

I guess it's a case of 'eaten bread's soon forgotten.' I read her email a second time, and my outrage turns to apathy. I'm ready and willing to agree to her deal. I'm damned if I do and damned if I don't. It's best my response is affable, so I make my reply short and sweet:

Dear Tansy, Thank you for helping Ethan, I understand your terms, and so be it. Please email me what you would like me to do with Ethan's personal belongings that he has left behind.

It's a relief when I click send.

Now for my car repairs. The quotes are astronomical.

Frida answers her phone when I call. 'Did Ethan get off to rehab okay?' she asks.

'Yes. And I've got an update. It's not great news. Ethan's made us get evicted. If he cooperates, though, I might be able to turn it around and have the tenancy transferred over to me. I'll work something out.'

'Oh God! What a mess! I hate the thought of you all alone with everything to sort out without anyone's help,' she replies.

'I'm fine; don't worry.' I feel terrible for having to drop

another bombshell.

I realise she must be worried because Loday phones me a short while later. 'What's going on?' he asks. 'Frida's said you sound worried.'

'Don't ask! Ethan's managed to get us evicted. He's in rehab now. I'm trying to get my car fixed,' I reply.

'Don't worry; Ethan will be fine. Send me the car repair bill. I'll help you out.'

'Thanks, Loday, That's a huge help.' Frida and I donated plenty of cash towards our lama's coffers, but it's still a surprise to be offered financial help from the sangha.

The windscreen guy looks shocked when he sees the state of my car. Luckily the rain holds off while he replaces it. Next, I arrange the garage and replace my SatNav. All in all, it's expensive—just under a grand.

Chapter Fifty

Ethan's AA sponsor won't reach him if he tries contacting Ethan via his confiscated phone, so I drop him a short text with the update: *Ethan's been admitted into rehab, where he'll stay for treatment for many months. If he was rude to you while he was intoxicated, I'm sure he's sorry. Thanks for supporting him.* In my opinion his AA sponsor assisted Ethan's coercive and controlling behaviour, but I must let that go. For now, there's bigger fish to fry. His sponsor blanks my text. Charming!

Packing the boxes is tedious—wrapping breakables, packing, taping, and labelling—though it would be exciting if I were packing to move into a new home. The desk is a mass of paperwork that I hastily scoop up. One paper flutters to the floor; Ethan's handwriting's scrawled on both sides. I pick it up; it's an amends letter, written in rough: *Dear Howard, I'm sorry for my bad behaviour. I regret it now. You and me have always been like brothers, and I'm very sorry I forced all those women on you in the past. I feel quite bad. Do you think you can forgive me? I really love you a lot. From Ethan.*

It takes a few minutes for me to process the revelations. At first glance, it seems I'm not the only victim of Ethan's coercive and controlling behaviour; at some point Howard was too. On the other hand, Howard may have gone along with it; it's an open secret how he was a womaniser. Upon closer inspection of the pile of papers, I see other amends letters dated years back but never posted. His step work booklets reveal his regrets in his own shaky handwriting: his guilt over cheating, affairs, dishonesty, theft, and betrayals. Altogether they join erratic dots to make a hazy picture of his disturbed mind. I wonder if Ethan left all this evidence on purpose for me; I doubt it.

The front door downstairs slams.

'Hello, anyone home? Ethan! It's me,' a man's voice calls out.

Oh, God. It must be Shane the lodger. 'Shane?' I yell back.

I hear him run up the stairs. He bursts into the lounge. 'Hi. I'm Shane. Where's Ethan got to?'

'He's, well, umm, he's in rehab. You'd better sit down,' I reply.

He plops down on the sofa. 'What's the story?'

'I don't know where to begin. Ethan's drug and alcohol addiction has been a problem for years,' I explain. 'He's really sick, and his cousin's arranged rehab. He'll be in treatment for months. He's in primary rehab now, then he has to go onto secondary.'

'Oh. I see. Will he be okay?'

'Sure. They say they're the best rehab in the country. But, Shane, there's something else; we're in rent arrears. We've been evicted, and the landlord gave only two weeks' notice. Ethan stole our rent, smoked it off on crack and drunk the rest.'

His jaw drops and he shakes his head in dismay. 'Jayzeez, Mary and Joseph! I've only spent four days here! I gave him a grand and signed a contract! I should have known something was up.'

'How could you know?' I ask.

'The morning I viewed. Lita showed me around. Ethan and another bloke were drinking tea, and the three of them, sheepish like, kinda struck me as sketchy. They were really behaving odd,' he says. 'I think I woke them up. Sure, be jayzeez, if something seems too good to be true it usually isn't!'

'Oh. I see.' Another one of Ethan's little secrets comes to light. It appears that Lita, the junkie Ethan met in that rehab in February, may have spent more nights in my home than me. I wonder when she'd taken up residency in my bedroom.

'I'll rustle up something to eat for the two us,' Shane says. 'I'm gonna have to work something out. I'll have to save up another deposit. I don't expect HE will pay me back!' Shane looks upset, proper choked, but there's nothing I can say to ease his predicament. I'm in the shit myself.

He cooks sauté potatoes, and we eat at the table, talking of Ethan and his addiction. While we talk, his bitterness subsides. Ethan's lucky that Shane seems too nice a chap to hunt him down for justice.

I return to the lounge full of boxes to resume packing and sorting. Ethan's copy of *The Big Book* catches my eye; he's never bothered reading it. I start reading random chapters, but it makes my eyes smart with tears. It's an emotional read at the best of times. Strangely for this time night, my phone rings. I don't recognise the number, so I listen for the caller to speak first.

'I know you're there! You get me?' he snarls.

Oh my God. It's Ethan.

'Listen up good, bitch. Get outta my home. I want you outta there and on the streets pronto. Got it? And if you mention this call to Tansy, you're dead! I've tricked the receptionist for the office phone to call you, so no one will believe you anyhow. So fuck off!' The line goes dead.

It's bizarre how he's a controlling bully even when under lock and key in rehab—and subject to Tansy's contract to boot! The call lasts less than a minute, and yet it disturbs me for hours.

Shane gets up early and makes a pot of strong coffee. 'I'm off later today. Here, take this.' He holds out the door key in the palm of his hand. 'I'm staying with friends. There's no point dragging this out.'

No sooner has Shane left than my phone rings.

'Hi! I'm Gary's wife. I'll be there soon. I'm dropping over for a property inspection today. I'll see your eviction is swift. In fact, I've decided to bring it forward. Understand?'

I thought she was in Jakarta! I know her threat's illegal because she hasn't applied for or got an eviction court possession order. But by surrendering at least I'll distance myself from the mess.

Gary's wife arrives, notes the damages, and leaves after the inspection. I'm looking forward to unwinding, but my phone rings, and it's Ethan's mobile number,

'Thank God you picked up! Are you still at home?' he asks.

'Why are you calling?' I ask, really miffed seeing as he was nasty the last time we spoke.

'I'm in a tight spot. Rehab's thrown me out. So you can look after me. I'm on my way back,' he says in his cooing voice.

'You've got to be kidding!' I reply.

'Phone Tansy. She knows. See you soon.' He hangs up.

Just as I'm about to call Tansy, she calls me. 'Yes, it's true. He's been discharged over an incident. He was aggressive; threw a chair or something. I don't know, and I'm not getting a refund! What a waste of my money!'

'I don't understand,' I reply.

'Me neither. He's on his way back to you. There's no way I'm putting him up. I'm too busy. So you'll have to take over.

Otherwise, he's on the streets. Rip up that contract of mine; I need your help!'

'Yes, okay; I'll help.'

Oh no! I don't know why I agreed to this. I've enough on my plate being in the midst of eviction, and I need to rescue Frida. The last thing I need is more of Ethan, but within the hour, he's back, with his mountain of baggage, knocking on the door.

He greets me like he's just back from the shops, lunging at me and giving me a gigantic hug. I can smell a trace of alcohol. Before I get a chance to speak, he's putting on music, acting silly.

'Be serious,' I say. 'What's going on? What now?'

He shrugs, pulls out a cigarette and clings onto me so tightly that I can barely breathe. 'Dunno. It's kinda fun not knowing.'

I'm angry, 'No, it's not fun!'

'I'm sorry. I don't know. Tansy mentioned she might find me another rehab, but I mustn't relapse, so you have to keep my anxiety down. I promised her that I'd be nice to you.'

Between Tansy and Ethan, I don't know whether I'm coming or going. I know what's expected of me to try and keep Ethan's anxiety down, though. It entails switching to autopilot, being obedient and accepting all Ethan's unacceptable behaviour.

Thankfully, Tansy calls later in the evening with a plan of sorts. 'Great news! I've found another rehab. It's a secondary, and they'll admit you in a few days' time! It's near Crawley. So stay clean and sober; they'll pee test you on arrival. The deal's off if you relapse. We'll work through this as a family. Ethan, they'll teach you to grow up. I've decided to help with housing, too. We'll go flat hunting. It's going to be absolutely fine.'

'Thank you! I love you! I won't let you down!' Ethan exclaims.

'I'll hold you to that,' she replies.

Tansy has given us hope; everything's coming up roses. Ethan's so jazzed, his determination makes me see that he deserves another chance. Our future will be all things good. But first, we've still got things to do. Ethan calls Pearl to ask if he can store all his stuff there. She lives a few hours' drive away, so it'll take a few trips back and forth in my car—about twelve hours driving. The local removals company is expensive, and no one else can be bothered to offer help.

Once Ethan's gear is stored away at Pearl's, we return home and take our last look at what's now an empty home. As usual, he runs me ragged with his list of errands, but somehow that glimmer of light at the end of the tunnel spurs me forward. Tansy has booked us into a basic hotel for the night close to the rehab. Ethan's assessment is early in the following morning. I check my rear-view mirror as our ex-home disappears into the distance.

'Hang on a second,' Ethan says. 'Can you quickly drive me to my doctor's surgery? There's a vitamin prescription I need to collect!'

'Okay, but don't be long; we must miss rush hour.'

Ethan trots into the doctor's surgery while I wait in my car. Half an hour later, he returns, running towards me, saying he's got it. He's snoring in the passenger seat before we reach the motorway.

Finally, we arrive at the hotel. After so much driving, it's heavenly to stretch my legs. Ethan wakes, reaches into his pocket and fishes for something that he pops into his mouth and chews.

'What was that?' I ask.

'What was what?' he replies indignantly.

'You know what.'

'It's nothing. Just a vally. Y'know. Valium. My doctor said I need a couple, just to takes the edge off the old cravings.'

I frown. 'But what about your pee test tomorrow? You've got to test clean!'

'It'll be out of my system by tomorrow. You're such a worrier. Let's grab a milkshake.'

Our room is on the top floor, and there isn't a lift, so we climb the stairs. The moment Ethan opens the door to our room, he complains; it's too small, the view's not lovely and nothing's to his liking. He'll have to make do. Now he's starving. The hunger caused by Valium has surfaced, so he orders a take-away delivery, then holds out his hand and says, 'Phone.'

I realise it's phone inspection time and dutifully hand it over.

'So. I see you sent an apology to my sponsor! Are you trying to elope with him? You whore!' He finishes his meal and berates me for four hours solid, while my food goes uneaten.

Eventually, he hollers, 'You can get outta my sight now! I can manage from here. I'll be in my rehab tomorrow! Fuck off out of my room!' He marches to the bathroom and slams the door shut.

Before he flushes the chain, I shakily grab my bags, jacket, phone, and shoes. I'm gone. When I reach the bottom of the stairs, I hurriedly force my feet into my trainers and dash to my car parked in the unlit car park. The cold October wind whips my hair in my face, and it's a struggle to open my car door against the wind. It's midnight, too dangerous to drive all night alone.

I bed down on my car seats for the night, but I'm not wearing enough layers, and it's so cold I can't get comfortable for shivering. Many hours pass with me curled in a ball. Ethan doesn't bother calling.

Someone taps on the car window. A face I don't recognise peers in. I open the window a tad.

'Hello? Are you all right, miss?' The man asks. 'I'm the manager. I brought you this.' He offers me a mug of hot tea.

I open my window so he can pass it to me. 'Thank you;

that's so kind.' I blush with shame.

Just after he leaves, my phone rings. I dread to answer it in case it's Ethan about to dish out another bollocking, but then I see it's Tansy's number.

'What on earth's going on?' she asks. 'Ethan called me. Running you down again. Honestly, you deserve a medal putting up with that ungrateful jerk!'

'I know; I mean I don't know. I slept in the car park last night.'

'Don't stress. You'll get a break from him soon. His admission's a few hours away. Go and have some breakfast. I'll call you later.'

The last thing I feel like doing is eating breakfast, but I'm light-headed after Ethan not permitting me to eat yesterday, so I head inside to the breakfast room.

Ethan sticks out like a sore thumb; he's sitting at a table tucking into a hearty breakfast. Before I get the chance to turn back and leave, he spots me. 'Oi! There you are. Come and sit down.' He pulls out a chair. 'Sit down. What happened to you last night? I came outta the bathroom, and you'd disappeared! Tansy said I gotta say sorry. So I'm sorry. For whatever I've done this time.'

Without replying, I do as I'm told. He acts as if last night never happened.

Ethan's terrible time keeping ensures we arrive at the rehab treatment centre ten minutes late. He takes hold of my hand and leads the way. He's chilled out.

Unfortunately, he fails the piss test.

'I thought I'd get away with having traces of Valium in my system,' he says. 'What's Tansy gonna say!'

Bad news travels fast, Tansy calls. 'Guess who just called me?' she says. 'The rehab! Were you aware Ethan had taken Valium before his assessment? I don't know what to do with him now. Any ideas?'

Ethan snatches my phone. 'Tans,' he says, 'don't worry. That rehab was bang out of order. Anyhow, I don't need rehab. I'm clean and sober. I've decided I'm going to look for an old camper van and live in it. It'll be cool!'

This is news to me, but Ethan's mind is made up, so it's another wild goose chase to have a look at a clapped-out old banger for sale in Brighton.

The lengthy drive to Brighton's a nightmare with heavy traffic and roadworks en route. The camper van is parked up in all its rusty glory and the noisy engine coughs out black exhaust fumes.

'Shit, man. Look at the state of that! Let's split,' Ethan says.

He spots a bakery near the sea front and instructs me to park in a superstore's car park.

'You go, queue,' he says, pointing to the bakery. 'I'm just gonna pop off to buy fags. Won't be a minute!' He dashes off in a mad hurry.

The bakery shop floor looks grubby. Their loaves are burnt and the hot-food counter containing sausage rolls and pasties drips with grease. Without a second's thought, I walk outside to try and catch him, to tell him the food looks terrible. But there's no sign of him. I look around in dismay, standing outside the bakery like a lost soul, then I spot him in the doorway of the shop next door. He hastily bends down, then stands up again and looks furtively around. When he sees I've clocked him, he rushes towards me, takes my hand and pulls me across the busy road.

'Stop it. Let go!' I shake him off, backtrack to the doorway and see the evidence he'd dumped a few seconds beforehand: three empty cans of Smirnoff vodka and cola.

'Those aren't mine!' he lies. A hint of vodka wafts in the air.

After promising he won't drink again, he drags me to

Sainsbury's bakery shelves, which are full of freshly baked Danish pastries, Cornish pasties, savouries and rainbow-coloured cupcakes. I pick two croissants and think we're going to the kiosk to pay, but he heads towards the booze aisle.

'Don't, Ethan. You promised,' I plead.

'Honey, I have to take the edge off; just the one!'

I thought he meant one single lager. That would be fine, right? But no, he lifts an entire cardboard crate of bottled beer.

'Ethan! I can't be around you if you carry on drinking!'

He's like a thing possessed, hurtling along in a driverless express train. I may as well be invisible. He carries his beer haul to the checkout. The second he pays, and with the speechless cashier watching him, he rips the beer box open, grabs hold of one and flips off the cap with the end of his lighter. He downs it in one.

'You can't drink that in here,' she objects.

I feel so embarrassed I don't know where to look.

To my surprise Ethan shoves his wallet in my pocket. 'Look after my bankcard. Don't give my wallet back to me. Even if I beg. Remember, I've got a grand in my account; my welfare money's just been paid.'

I'm not sure if this is his way of telling me he's powerless over his drinking. He strains to lift the open beer box from the counter and races towards the exit to the car park. Two bottles fall out and smash onto the floor.

Rather than wait for security to tell me off for the breakages, I dash to my car with him close behind. I fire up my engine and drive out of the car park, while Ethan sits in the passenger seat cracking open another. I'm so anxious from the thought of him grabbing my steering wheel, the way he does when he's drunk, that I turn into the next side road and park. He pulls out his phone and calls his father, with the intention of pulling on his heartstrings for an invite to his father's home, over a hundred miles away.

His father hears Ethan's slurring words and knows he's drunk and that he'll be damned if he offers help or his spare bedroom. He hangs up.

By sundown Ethan has just one beer left. He staggers out of my car to pee up the car door while holding on to the roof to steady himself. I gather up his empties from the foot well to place them in someone's recycling box. All of a sudden, he punches my new windscreen, lets out a yelp of pain and starts kicking my car door.

'Stop it, Ethan!' I yell.

He staggers towards me, closes in, and starts tugging at my pocket. 'This beer ain't doing nothing! Gimme my wallet! I gotta score some crack or smack!' He hisses through clenched teeth.

'No! Remember what you said! We're trying to find you another rehab. Come on, Ethan, help me out here,' I plead.

'Cunt!' he shouts back. His tugging gets rougher, and he tears my jacket pocket.

I manage to break free and run from him, but he catches up, grabs a handful of my hair and pulls me to the ground. I look around for help. Young revellers out for the night rubberneck the assault and walk on by. While still trapped by him pulling my hair, I fumble in the darkness for his wallet in my pocket. Thankfully, I manage to retrieve the wallet and throw it as far as I can. Ethan instantly lets go of my hair. His gaze follows the flying wallet like a hungry Doberman would watch an airborne lamb chop. He gallops towards it and dives as soon as it lands.

Without a backward glance, I make my escape and sprint back to my car. I jump in the driver's seat and lock myself in. I can hear Ethan, a little way up the street, screaming obscenities. I think he could be having a psychosis. My hands shake while

I try to find the ignition, praying my car will start first time. Thankfully, after one turn of the key, it fires up first time. I accelerate and get the hell out of there.

A police car with sirens blaring overtakes me. My first thought is whether they're after Ethan. Regardless, I drive for a few miles until I'm out of town, then I find a residential street to park up and calm down. My head says abandon him, like everyone else has done, past and present. Leave him stranded. Right? But my heart says let him cool off; it's unlikely he'll find his own way to another rehab without my help. Ethan may have spun Tansy a yarn. She has no idea how things have escalated. I send her a text message: *Ethan's relapsed. Urgent! Please call. I've had to run for my life*. I wait in vain for a call back. She may have switched her phone off in anger.

I wonder where he is now. Has he been arrested again? Stabbed in a crack den? Or unconscious in a gutter? God knows. It looks like I'm in for another sleepless night in my car. At some point I doze off. The cold wakes me, and at first I don't know where I am. The road's quiet. It's still dark. Apart from a few dog walkers and cyclists, there is not a lot of activity.

I check my phone. A text from Tansy says: *I'll call you later on today. He's driving me around the bend! Keep yourself safe*. It's not what I wanted to hear. I want her to tell me she'll drive out to Brighton and take over with getting Ethan sorted out, or help me with him, at least. He must have cooled off by now, but when I call him, he doesn't pick up. I drive back to the scene of the crime where I'd left him. He's not there. I drive around in circles and still can't find him, so I head to the hospital. It's getting light, and the local hospital is well signposted. Before I find a parking spot, I spot a dishevelled Ethan, hair in all directions, puffing away on a fag.

'Ethan!' I holler out my car window.

He stops, mid-smoke, looks up and claps eyes on me. I wave frantically for fear he'll disappear again. He raises a hand high in the air and ambles towards me, one hand holding his fag, the other clutching his stomach. He doesn't look well.

'Thank God you found me. What happened? I don't remember,' he exclaims.

I think he's lying out of shame. 'You really don't remember?'

He hugs me tightly to distract me, or maybe he's scared. 'No,' he replies. 'All I remember is I got bumped trying to score. Took me ages to score some brown. It was weird shit, spun me out, thought I'd OD'd, so I called an ambulance. I've spent the last few hours in A&E.'

'That doesn't sound too good. Get in the car; we have to get out of this town. Tansy might call soon.'

He jumps in my car and, to my horror, whips a crack pipe from his pocket and lights crumbs of crack in full view and broad daylight.

'You better get out if you're going to do that! I'm not getting myself in trouble because of your crack,' I warn.

He moodily lobs it out of the car window as if the drug paraphernalia were an apple core. 'Happy now?'

I drive towards a garage that I'd spotted earlier to refuel. Half a tank of diesel should be enough. Ethan calls out to me while I'm filling the tank.

'Here, use my bankcard! I'm sorry about earlier. And sorry to ask, but I'm going into withdrawal, so can you pick up a few beers?'

I reluctantly agree. Even though I don't want him to drink, I think he has to; he's probably alcohol dependent already. I feel embarrassed while paying for the case of beer at this hour of the morning. What if the cashier thinks it's for me! I push the shame aside and go to pay for the booze, fuel, and bottles of water.

'Sorry. That card's been declined,' the cashier says.

Great! I should have known. I use my own bankcard, and to double-check the declined payment wasn't an error, I check his balance on the garage's ATM. Sure enough, his account is overdrawn. He has withdrawn large cash amounts before and after midnight to score. I return to my car.

I hand him the card. 'Here, take your bankcard. It's declined. How have you spent a grand in one night?'

'Err, I forgot! I mean … I don't know.' It's plain to see he's lying.

Ethan's starving again and wants fish and chips from a chippy near the sea front. I realise I'm letting myself in for more shame by his outlandish drunken behaviour in a public restaurant, but I risk it anyhow. He refuses to see the precariousness of his situation, and instead of keeping his alcohol levels steady, he guzzles the booze so fast that at this rate it will run out before nightfall. I can't stand feeling defeated and being in limbo again, yet the more I try to be pragmatic, the more Ethan rallies against me. I'm so low on funds I can only afford to pay for a fish supper for Ethan. He eats great hunks of battered cod with his greasy hands while sitting next to me in the car passenger seat. I call the rehab who'd rejected him to ask for their advice.

'Ah, you're calling about Ethan,' the man who answers says. 'We're not the right rehab for him. However, I can suggest a reputable primary rehab that will detox him. They charge around five-thousand pounds, for a two-week rehabilitation programme, but there might be a non-refundable deposit to pay. I know they refer their clients to a secondary rehab. Have you got a pen handy? I'll give you their number. The rehab's in Hertfordshire.'

After jotting down the number, I call the newly recommended rehab, a two- hour drive from where we are. A kindly receptionist answers the phone and puts me through to one of the admission staff. I explain the turn of events, and she listens sympathetically before starting his telephone assessment. It's the usual questions.

'Tomorrow we'll have a free bed, if you can get Ethan to us after breakfast. Shall we say by nine o'clock?' Then she speaks to Ethan as if she's talking to a toddler.

He talks back nonsense while hiccupping and tells her that his belly is bloated. He thinks he's dying and says it's unfair that he was born an addict. She agrees it's a terrible thing, which comforts him no end. He can't wait to be admitted and hands the phone back to me for talk of costs.

Right in the middle of my relaying the rehab message to Tansy, Ethan snatches the phone from me and starts to warble Bob Marley to her, but she's pissed off and wants to walk her pooches.

I'm uncertain if Tansy's good for her second round of funding and have to wait for a phone call to confirm. Eventually, it comes through. Tansy has settled the account for Ethan's treatment.

'I can confirm the funds have cleared,' the rehab woman says. 'We look forward to seeing Ethan tomorrow morning!'

'Are you sure? Definitely tomorrow? No hitches?'

'I'm positive. Don't worry. We'll see you in the morning.'

Ethan whoops with delight. It's plain sailing now, so long as I'm able to supervise Ethan and ensure he doesn't go missing or get arrested.

'Yippee! I'm going rehab,' Ethan yells. He jumps out of my car and unloads all his worldly goods to repack everything. There's no stopping him, and he draws more attention to us by chucking his bags and cases on the pavement, sniffing the armpits of his dirty clothes and separating them from the clean ones. He disposes of his empties in a nearby bin, mops his sweaty face with a baby-wipe, sprays himself with cologne and then settles back into the passenger seat to reward himself with beer. One can after another empties until finally, and in mid-sentence, he flops his head back and starts snoring. It's 10 pm.

A window of opportunity has presented itself. I gently reach over for his seatbelt, lift his dead-weight arm through the belt and fasten him in. His floppy head lies at a crooked angle, so I retrieve a cushion to support it, then enter the postcode for rehab into my SatNav. The two-hour drive will be safer with him asleep, so I fire up and pull away before picking up speed. I thank God I'm able to drive in peace without him running off or getting arrested.

The roads are clear, and I pray I'll get us to rehab before he wakes. Finally, my SatNav directs me to our destination.

It stands behind a huge brick entrance that is higher than the Edwardian house, which, with its replica battlements, reminds me of a castle—which is apt, considering the battle that goes on in rehabs.

The outdoor security lights are on, and the accommodation's twenty or so bedroom windows are in darkness. I pull into the driveway where two other cars are parked. With a sigh of relief I switch off my engine. I can't believe I managed it. The sudden sound of the engine getting switched off disturbs Ethan's sleep. He stirs. I hope he'll drift off again, but he rubs his eyes, disorientated.

'Where are we?' he groans.

'We're here. Rehab,' I reply.

He tries to focus his eyes. 'For real?'

Before I reply, a tap sounds on the car window. 'Everything all right?' a man from rehab asks.

'Sorry, yes. We're early. Ethan's being admitted at nine,' I reply.

'Oh, that's fine. You can stay parked here. I'm Liam; I'll see you tomorrow.'

When he's gone, Ethan hops out for a pee next to the

flowerpots while swaying and looking upwards at the CCTV. He lights a fag, fumbles around for another beer and reminisces about the good old days. I wish he'd shut up. I'm exhausted.

Chapter Fifty-One

Somehow, I manage to get relatively comfortable, despite the steering wheel, handbrake, and gearstick in my way. It's bitterly cold. Every time my eyelids droop, Ethan shakes me awake. He's got more to say, wants to tell me how much he misses the high life.

'Ethan, please let me rest? I hear you loud and clear, but now's the time you can turn a new leaf. Rehab begins in a few hours.'

He hiccups. 'I'm scared.'

'Don't be. I'm here,' I reply.

He moves his face close to mine. 'I might die in detox,' he slurs.

'Ethan. You're not going to die!' He won't die, not this time. But if his addiction continues, if he keeps relapsing, eventually he'll die, for sure. He plants a smacker kiss on my cheek, and I pat his cold hand to reassure him.

He sulkily pulls his hand away. 'Don't do that. That means goodbye.'

I don't know what he means.

He lights another fag and opens a beer.

'Come on, Ethan, shake a leg. Let's do this rehab. It's gone nine!'

It's no good, he's too scared to be admitted. He calls Tansy just to bad-mouth me, because he's not ready to say goodbye to his addiction, the constant companion that has been with him for so long. Tansy guesses he is causing chaos, and she is annoyed he's jeopardizing his treatment.

He faffs around all morning, and at lunchtime, Liam and two key workers appear in the car park and persuade Ethan to agree to treatment. But it's not until he swigs his last mouthful of beer that he eventually admits he needs help.

The key workers take an arm each; Liam takes his luggage, and together they assist him into the reception to sign the admission paperwork. It's done swiftly, before he changes his mind.

'You need to leave now; don't drag out saying goodbye,' Mara, the woman I spoke to on the phone tells me. 'We'll settle him. He'll be detoxing soon.'

I head for the exit doors and step into the courtyard near the car park. To my surprise I hear Ethan calling out to me. I turn around to see him being led by Liam and another man, walking with him with their arms linked.

I turn and look at his smiling face. He looks gaunt. I'm half expecting him to call out something pleasant, but I'm mistaken.

'I hate you, Magda!' he yells from the other side of the courtyard.

My heart sinks. It's like being struck down.

Liam calls out, 'Don't take any notice of him!' They bundle him through a door, and he is gone.

I return to my car, feeling absolute exhaustion, sadness, and relief. I compose a text to Tansy: *Ethan's been admitted. He was anxious but is in good hands. The rehab staff are very nice. He is keen to start his Valium detox later today. Thanks for your help.* I try to sound all calm and polite, hiding my hurt.

It's unlike her to reply promptly, but she does and says: *Thanks for the update. Anxious my foot! He was being a fucking jerk in my opinion. Of course he's keen for Valium, any old drug keeps him smiling! I hope you get rest and find somewhere safe!* It's not the reply I had expected. It sounds pretty harsh, considering he has to go through another detox.

She makes no mention of supporting Ethan together, the two of us, during and after rehab. She just sounds sick of him. Tansy's anger is not something I can process. I've got a long journey ahead of me. According to my SatNav, Newcastle is almost three hundred miles away, an estimated drive of four-and-a-half hours. I hastily call Frida.

She picks up on the second ring. 'I've been so worried,' she says. 'Are you okay?'

'Yeah, don't worry. I'll explain everything later. Listen. I'm on my way back to Newcastle, but don't tell anyone. I'm coming to get you out of there. Okay? See you in four or five hours, depending on traffic!'

'Really! Oh my God! I won't say a word. Call me when you get here. I love you!'

There's no time for chitchat; I want to be with Frida as soon as I possibly can. I find a can of Red Bull under my seat, as well as a bottle opener, beer caps, lighters, and horrible reminders of Ethan's relapse. My journey begins. I'm determined not to get lost by taking a wrong turn; I can't waste a drop of fuel. The motorway is packed with traffic, and it's not even rush hour. I drive through rain showers and sunshine, until dusk, then nightfall. The temperature plummets the further north I drive.

I call Frida as soon as I park outside the sangha. I've only just got out of the car when she runs towards me and greets me with a hug.

310

'You came back for me. You came back,' she says quietly and wipes her tears with her cuff.

'Of course I came back for you!' I reply, choking back my own tears.

'Come on, let's get the kettle on,' I say.

Frida helps me with my bags, and we exchange updates with the latest news since I left three weeks back. I keep it simple, although, the past few weeks have been anything but. Frida explains that she has coped quite well, supported by a close friend, an Australian girl, who's due to fly home in a few days' time.

The sangha no longer looks like a building site. The refurbishment is nearly complete, apart from finishing-off touches, so the dust-sheets and power tools are gone. Most students have left for home, but otherwise everything is as I remember, including the icy atmosphere.

After prayer practice at 11 pm, despite the cold weather, I sneak outside for a walk to the railway bridge. The street's quiet, and I'm free to stare at the night sky without Ethan yelling drunken abuse at me on the phone for hours on end. At this moment, I can just be me.

I'm glad when it's bedtime. It's a good feeling knowing I'd managed to get Ethan to rehab, and I love being back with Frida. The dormitories are almost empty, and it's easier to fall asleep without a ton of snoring in the same room that was overcrowded during retreat.

The morning gong sounds at 5 am. I'm too exhausted to get up, so I go right back to sleep for a few hours, until Frida wakes me with coffee. When I try to get up, I realise how much my body aches because of sleeping in my car, stress pain and the sitting position of last night.

'Guru has arranged a lunch. Everyone from the sangha has

to attend,' Frida says. 'We have to be ready by noon.'

'Sounds wonderful. Can't wait,' I reply.

We hear the front door slam, voices and *amituofo* greetings. I open the dorm door and see Loday standing in the hallway with his parents and brother. His mother is a student who has taken vows and refuge.

'Hi, Loday, I'm back,' I say.

He looks in my direction but doesn't make eye contact. '*Amituofo*. I didn't know you'd returned.'

'I got back late yesterday,' I say.

'Oh. Really,' he replies, then turns his back on me while he speaks to his parents.

His mother nods, while Loday bends down to do up his buckles, and he leaves without another word. I sense that the lama has forbidden him to speak to me.

His mother, on the other hand, is delighted to see me. 'How have you been? You've spent some time away, I hear?'

'Yes, I was away for a few weeks. Ethan relapsed in July. It's a long story. He's in another rehab now. But he's made us homeless.'

Her eyes widen. 'Oh, goodness me! If ever you need a place to stay, I've got tons of space. Hold on; I'll give you my email. We can keep in contact.'

'That's so good of you. Thank you,' I reply. 'Tansy's viewing new rentals for us. She's offered funding to get us accommodation close to the rehab, so he'll be nearby for follow up appointments.'

She smiles. 'That's kind of her.'

We all know the rules. When we're in the presence of the lama, we have to be showered, clean top to toe, changed into clean burgundy clothing or best outfit and ready on time. We wait in the hallway for one of the convoy of red sangha cars to take us to the restaurant for lunch.

Our driver is a female student, a favourite, and she plays a chanting CD on the car stereo. The car windows steam up inside from the breathing of so many of us crammed in the small hatchback. We follow the red convoy into the carpark of a Lebanese restaurant.

A kindly waiter offers to take our rain-soaked coats as soon as we enter the reception area. We're early diners; the restaurant isn't busy. It's dimly lit, and the décor is smart with oak flooring and wall hangings. Fifteen of us, students in burgundy and monks in robes, stand in formation awaiting the great lama's arrival. Loday stands as far away from me as possible. It feels like a long wait, but eventually a student opens the door and in walks lama. Despite the rain he is wearing Ray-Ban sunglasses and dressed head to toe in black Prada. We bow our heads with hands together. We're not expected to kowtow lama in public places.

We wait like children to be seated by guru. He points to our chosen seats, and I get lucky; he seats me at the far end of the table next to Frida, and we're both too far away from lama for him to force feed us from his plate. He sits himself in the centre of the long table with his head monk to his right and Loday, the one he loves, to his left. By the time he is finished with musical chairs, I can't help but notice how he always arranges the seating with himself in the centre, Jesus like.

We know the drill; no one speaks unless they are spoken to. Lama's quick off the mark to recite some facts about Lebanon that he must have looked up beforehand.

The waiter pours guru a sample of expensive wine. He holds his glass up to the candlelight, swirls it, takes a sniff, and gulps it down, then he signals for more; he is happy with the vintage.

'Anyone joining me for a glass?' he asks.

We don't know if it's a trick question, so everyone politely declines, except for Eric, who hasn't seen the wrath of Lama. He says, 'Cheers,' in German and sips the ruby vino. Lama orders a second bottle, apparently keen to impress Eric, who is a cert to bring Pathgate revenue. For the first time, I notice that Lama drinks wine like water—come to think of it, he often smells boozy.

The waiter takes Lama's order first: steak, side dishes and flat breads. Frida and I order two side dishes to share, and the monks make their choices—they are not allowed to eat after sundown. When our food arrives, Lama makes a sign for us to bow our heads, palms facing heavenwards, while he recites a food prayer. He voices his opinions while eating, until he turns his attention to a forgetful Dutch student, the one who fell through the ceiling.

'You haven't lost anything this week, have you?' Lama asks with a frown.

'I don't think so,' the student stammers.

'Ah. You must remember to address me as Rinpoche!' he hollers, then gives a big belly laugh.

'Sorry, Rinpoche. I don't think so, Rinpoche.' The student bites his nails.

'As for you,' he adds loudly.

We all look up; he is looking at me.

'Yes, you! No smoking outside the sangha! You'll bring demons to my sangha!'

The other students look at him in awe, impressed by his special powers allowing him to see us without being in our presence. The ordained, I guess, have snitched on me. They look down, in embarrassment maybe.

'And you better start rising at five for morning-prayer practice! Skipping prayer practice is a transgression! You hear me! This is my sangha. You work for dharma; you think dharma.

This is not a guesthouse!' he berates me.

I acknowledge with nod, even though I don't agree.

He changes the subject again, to his favourite topic. Himself. 'When I was a student of His Holiness, I was his most trusted bodyguard. I saved His Holiness from being crushed to death. With a wave of my hand, I drove away surging crowds of thousands who wanted his blessing.'

At the end of the meal, he settles the bill, in cash, naturally. The German looks stunned, either by the wad of enveloped cash just produced, or the miracle of taming of the crowd. The rest of us have heard the fable many times before.

Chapter Fifty-tWo

Lama is against friendships; they are attachments, as are
family, that is why he bans his students from forming new
friendships or keeping old ones. When Frida said farewell to her
Australian friend, they'd exchanged email addresses. Currently
there are no restrictions on email contact between students,
provided the content is dharma related and not personal. Guru
believes his students must not 'disturb the minds' of others with
sentiments. We must not think or feel, but we of the lower ranks,
we still think, and we still feel.

Ethan is one week clean and sober to the day. His rehab's
timetable keeps him busy, so he has no time to bombard me
with calls. The latest news is that a secondary rehab is lined up
for next week. The new rehab is one of the best, and it's in the
heart of London.

'Just imagine it! I'll be in AA meetings with the rich and
famous,' he says. 'Oh, and get this, Tansy's offered to pay for at
least three months more treatment.'

'That's wonderful, Ethan,' I reply. At the same time, I
sense how the lives of others outside the sangha are progressing
while Frida and I languish in this strange toxic bubble, a time-

warp, where every repetitive day that passes, we become less of our former selves, dehumanized. There's still no word from Tansy about future housing options when Ethan's treatment is completed.

I dread the upcoming retreat. There are better ways to spend three days, rather than listen to Lama's nonsense, but I'd be asking for trouble if I don't attend. Preparations at the sangha begin. Attendance pre-bookings are good for this time of year, which is just as well for Lama because he needs his coffers replenished with student donations. Apparently, it is all hush-hush tax-free cash-in-hand income. In the main, the rituals and Lama's pontificating from his elevated seat are the same. It's *déjà vu*, apart from the unwelcoming atmosphere, especially Loday's coldness. The weekend's teaching is littered with bitchy remarks about ciggy demons and how people with mental health issues can go be damned. I want to reach out to Frida and say *Don't listen! He's crazy!* But I can't.

I'm relieved when the third and last day of retreat arrives. In the outside world, it's Halloween, the day Ethan gets his two-weeks-clean-and-sober AA chip, and he's being transferred to his secondary rehab.

The one good thing about this retreat is that Frida and I have been seated with a wall behind us, which supports our aching backs during the long hours of cross-legged sitting.

Lama makes his final grand entrance. We students kowtow to the master of ceremonies and resume our positions. Tibetan prayers begin, followed by the teaching, where we learn zilch. In a matter of minutes, all eyes are on me; guru has decided he'll shame me today. I'm the topic of his entertainment.

It starts with his stare. 'Do you know what I call people who associate with addicts?' he yells out. 'Rotten pieces of worthless garbage! You hang out with garbage; you become garbage. No one like that should be in my sangha. Not in my company. You bring bad demons to me and my sangha!'

I lower my head, wishing for the bollocking to end. I close my eyes and tune out. Someone nudges me, but I stay in my darkness. When an enormous thud hits the wall, I open my eyes and see the other students staring in disbelief. The mad man is smiling. He has missed his target by a whisker. I realise he has thrown a heavy stick at my head; it has landed on my burgundy cushion. He claps his hands. Nervous students laugh. Frida doesn't; she's terrified.

Some students shed tears when teaching closes. They touch the kata that guru drapes around our necks just before being sung out with a Tibetan song. Frida and I walk back to the female sangha house, avoiding being chaperoned.

'Christmas is the next retreat here,' Frida says. 'Will we still be here?'

'No way,' I reply.

'I shouldn't have asked out loud. He knows what we're talking about, with his superpower's hearing ability.'

I shake my head. 'Bollocks to his superpower; he uses spies.'

She sighs. 'I hope you're right.'

I commit another transgression by not attending evening prayers before bedtime. I wait in my car to hear from Ethan.

'I'm tired,' he says. 'Tansy's meeting me for coffee tomorrow. She's gonna take my bankcard. She says it's relapse prevention. And she'll provide a daily cash allowance with the office. I can't speak long … I'm sharing a room with someone. Twelve grand a month this rehab's costing, and I haven't got my own room! I bet he snores,' he mutters.

'Maybe it'll help recovery, having a roomie; I don't know. Besides, you're lucky, I had to share a small dorm with loads of people the whole summer, remember?'

'Yeah, but I deserve my own space. I gotta go. I'll call you tomorrow morning,' he says before hanging up.

I sit and wonder if he'll always be a narcissist. Many addicts would give their right arm to have what his got—a chance to stay alive. My thoughts turn to our situation; mine and Frida's. A tap on my car window makes me jump. It's only the Dutch student, taking a midnight walk in the rain, without permission. He waves and walks on by. We know we won't snitch on each other.

The sangha house is asleep when I return; it's been a long day.

Ethan's morning call doesn't happen. I take this as a good sign that he's doing well. Loday's parents are almost packed and ready to return home.

'It's been lovely seeing you again,' Loday's mother says to Frida and me as she fastens her bag. 'Shame about Lama's new restrictions. Did you know he's not allowing the ordained any leave over Christmas anymore? They won't be allowed to leave the sangha to visit family ever again. Loday's nephews won't see him any time soon. I know he chose to be a monk, but his family would like to see him once a year! What can you do, eh?'

It's the first we've heard about tighter restrictions.

'It's a rum thing. That's what it is,' Loday's dad says as he tenderly places his arm around his wife. They both know that nothing can be said or done to change it. Loday arrives to collect his family, and they head off to the train station.

Once again, I see a favoured student leave for home, and I get the same gut feeling I've had before, that we, Frida and I, should be leaving too. But we haven't got a home anymore, thanks to Ethan's relapse, nor anyone's help—apart from the offer of shelter from Loday's mother.

I stew for two days before I send Loday's mum an email asking if she's well and if the offer for a stay-cation is still okay.

Either she has blocked me or been told not to contact me, because I don't hear back.

The good news is that Ethan likes rehab. He calls at bedtime, excited that his

roomie's gone away for a mini break to Paris to visit a friend.

'And I've made new friends myself,' he tells me. 'They're all trust-fund kids here. It's the best rehab. So far, I've been offered freebies, holidays, and designer clothes, and one's got a limited-edition Lamborghini! Taking me out for a spin, he is!'

'That's really great, Ethan, but what about rehab?' I reply. 'Did you go for group therapy today? You haven't mentioned rehab?'

'Oh, that's boring! I've got a counsellor who's nice, and I'm fitting in. I'm friendly with Verity. They're all stinking rich. Tansy reckons I can wangle myself in with the wealthy. I've reported my bankcard as stolen, so I've a replacement card on the way. I'm smart. That's our secret,' he adds in a whisper.

'Isn't that a bit dishonest?' I reply.

There's a pause. 'Nah! She knows what I'm like.'

'Oh, I see. Uh, Ethan, I'm really desperate for diesel, so can you transfer money for fuel, please?' I ask.

'Of course, I'll transfer some cash first thing tomorrow, my treasure. And I'll start paying you back what I owe you. I promise.'

Tomorrow comes and goes, however, and once again, Ethan's timetable's so busy he forgets all about me. Come bedtime, I'm too anxious to sleep, but at some point, I drift off. The 5 am gong wakes me for morning practice.

Ethan's got the afternoon free; seeing as he hasn't called, I phone him.

'I was just about to call you, my treasure! I've had such a wonderful morning. In group therapy I made everyone laugh with my past drinking antics. Don't panic. I know you need fuel today. I asked Tansy if it's right to give you fuel money, and she says I mustn't give you a penny, because my money's all for me. But I think it's only right to treat you to some fuel. I'm about to walk to the bank in a second before it closes. Is that okay?' he asks.

'Yes, Ethan, that's fine, but I don't understand why Tansy's interfering? Does she know how much you owe me?'

He replies with a riddle. 'Well, yes and no.'

Every hour, on the hour I check my bank balance, to no avail, and to add insult to injury, Ethan's gone missing. He calls at bedtime. At first, I hesitate to answer; I am so angry.

'What's wrong this time?' I ask.

'Don't be cross. You should be happy at the sangha. Just let me explain; when I got to the bank earlier, they shut the doors in my face. I'll try tomorrow. First thing. I promise!'

I want to hang up, before I say something I'll regret later.

I'm starting to feel that I've been duped, used and disregarded by Tansy and Ethan.

Another day begins with the 5 am gong. For me it is the same routine day in, day out. For Ethan, he's taken to this rehab like a duck to water, and he loves the social scene and shopping in the West End with the rehab trust-fund sons and daughters. If it were I, gadding around, bonding with new-found friends - he'd be outraged, eaten away with jealousy. I'd never hear the end of it. I remain hopeful that he'll mend his ways.

The gong sounds for an announcement. The nun has our attention. She beams at us as she speaks: 'Our guru is having lunch here with us today; we must all prepare the sangha for his arrival. The flowers, fruit, cakes, and chocolate deliveries are due. This a special lunch. Tonight, he leaves us for a week to give teachings overseas.'

Our being given such little notice is no surprise. It will be a busy morning, what with cleaning, cooking, and laundry. Everything must satisfy his critical eye. I haven't seen him since Halloween, the day he threw that stick at my head.

A chanting CD plays loudly in the kitchen where six of us prepare seasonal vegetables. The youngest nun reminds us of the countdown until Lama's arrival, although we don't need reminding; we can tell by the building atmosphere of tension he's due. Once all the chores are complete, before he arrives, I tiptoe upstairs unnoticed. It's best I keep out of his sight, to avoid another bollocking. I check to see if the shrine room in the loft is free; thankfully, it is, and the small book cupboard makes a good hiding place. If my absence is noticed, I can claim I was studying the Tibetan texts. I'm in for a three or four hour wait, without anything as a distraction, until he leaves. I know Lama's arrived when I hear *amituofo* greetings and the roar of his belly laugh from downstairs. Around half an hour later, the shrine door slowly opens. I'm startled at first, until I peep and see it's Frida holding a bowl of hot food.

'Eat, it'll do you good,' she whispers.

'Thanks. How's things downstairs?' I ask.

She knows what I mean. 'He's fine, excited to catch his flight.'

'Where's he going?'

'Greece,' she replies. 'I better go back before I'm missed.'

Once my lunch has cooled, I silently begin the food prayer, on autopilot, before stopping myself and trying a mouthful of squeaky mushrooms. I curl into a ball and gradually drift off to sleep.

Frida gently shakes me awake. 'He's gone. You can come downstairs now; the coast's clear.'

I uncurl my aching body to stretch.

Downstairs smells of cabbage, flowers, and Lama's perfume.

The same CD plays, and four students tackle the stacks of washing up. I head outside to the railway bridge; it's starting to rain. I look up at the cloudy sky and think of the times Lama has taken credit for them by claiming he forms the clouds, which he calls his *nagas*. My phone has no new messages. Even though I haven't got many contacts, I scroll anyhow and stop when I reach Vinnie's number. In an act of rebellion against guru's rules, I call my friend from my old life. To my surprise he picks up.

After the usual greetings, he asks about Ethan, and I fill him in, ending with my homelessness.

'I wish I could help,' he says. 'Is there anything I can do?'

'No, I'll be all right, thanks, Vinnie,' I reply, then without thinking, I blurt out, 'Actually there is something. I hate to ask, but is there any chance you could lend me money for half a tank of fuel? I'm sorry; I'm desperate.'

'Of course! Text me your PayPal details; I'll send money now,' he replies.

'Thanks, Vinnie. I can't thank you enough!'

'No worries. Call me back if you need anything else,' he says.

I sprint back to the sangha to check if the transfer has cleared. He is as true as his word; I see the transaction. He hasn't let me down.

The door to my dorm opens, Frida appears and looks at me quizzically, wondering where I'd gone.

'Shhh!' I say. She closes the door, concerned. I place my hand on her arm and whisper, 'It's time!'

'What? Now?'

'Tomorrow. My mate Vinnie, from that farm community, he's loaned money for fuel. Lama will be in Greece by midnight. It's our window to flee. We'll drive to London.' Tears of relief fill her eyes.

I reach for a tissue, half afraid her tears will give us away.

'We'll be fine, don't worry,' I reassure her.

We know our escape is risky. We'll have to be on guard. I can't tell Ethan. He sealed our fates by luring us here in the first place, and his mouth is like a foghorn; he'd snitch to Loday behind my back in a heartbeat, just to put a spanner in the works.

'Who can we contact in London?' I whisper.

'I don't know; I can't think,' Frida replies. 'Wait, I just thought of someone who might help; she gave me her number in the spring when she attended a retreat. One time I asked for permission to contact her, the head monk told me she had demons, so I wasn't allowed to call her. Let me see if I kept her number.' She hurriedly searches her bag and wallet, then unzips her make-up bag and retrieves a tiny piece of paper that she unfolds. 'I have it!' she whispers.

'Call her,' I reply. Walls have ears in this place, so I quietly check no one is loitering outside the dorm. I give Frida the thumbs up and keep watch.

'Hi, it's Frida. Can we talk?' She can't hold back her tears while she whispers down the phone, 'It's a long story. Are you free to meet? Tomorrow night, in London? … the day after. Are you sure? Really? You'd do that to help me?'

I can't hear what our new-found ally is saying.

'Thank you so much, bye.' Frida blows her nose. 'Pammy's said she'll help. I'm to call her when we reach London. She said she'd make a few calls, and we'll go from there.'

'Thank God for Pammy!' I reply.

After prayers, just before bedtime, I sneak outside to the railway bridge for a cigarette. I see the Dutch student walking towards me in the darkness. Usually he walks on by, but tonight he stops to chat.

'I want out of here,' he announces. 'One day, I'll be allowed to leave.'

'You okay?' I ask.

'You're gonna get the demons out here,' he says disapprovingly.

'If you say so.'

'Yeah, I'm scared of demons. When it's safe, I'll go. The Lama's good to me. I don't know when my karmic debt will be repaid to him, but when it is, I'll be gone. I mean, maybe I won't ever leave. But I think I will.' He scratches his shaved, befuddled head.

I wish I could save him, take him away with us, and see he gets the psychiatric help he needs. He can't be much older than Frida. 'Karmic debt, huh?'

'See ya tomorrow. *Amitufuo*.' He bows with his palms together before walking off.

Our conversation, and the fact that I couldn't say goodbye to him, plays in my head while I try to get to sleep.

At breakfast, my stomach is doing somersaults. My phone vibrates. It's Ethan. I dread to answer, but I do, while slipping on my jacket and trainers so I can take his call outside.

'This fucking rehab!' he says. 'I want to discharge myself. I've had enough.'

I badly need to keep my shit together, but Ethan's rant lasts over an hour before he decides to take back all the stuff he just said. It's hard to feel pity for him. He's being given another golden opportunity and wants to throw it all away. Again.

Finally, he hangs up, just as I hear footsteps running towards me. It's Frida.

'Mum, I was looking for you. You've been ages. Please don't scupper this. Was that Ethan on the phone again? If you let him, he'll keep you on the phone all day. He runs rings around you. He's a spoilt brat. Don't fuck this up because of him. He'll suspect something and snitch.'

325

She's right. I feel a surge of guilt allowing Ethan another crazy call because of my lack of boundaries. 'I'm sorry. I'll get focused.'

'You must. Before it's too late,' Frida replies.

I see how I allow my phone to be used by Ethan to exert his controlling behaviour and abuse. 'We've got a lot to do,' I say. 'Let's get on with it.'

We return to the sangha house and find it so quiet you could hear a pin drop. The nuns are either writing journals or doing errands. Frida opens the door to our dorm and points under her bunk bed. I take a peep; she's already packed our holdalls. She soundlessly opens her drawers, empties the contents and hastily packs her suitcase. We work like a ninja relay team, hearts pounding, while taking it in turns to keep watch while the other carries the suitcase and bags to my VW estate parked in the next side street, hidden from view. Had we been anywhere but the ground-floor dorm, we'd never manage this unnoticed. Once all the bags are loaded, I throw my sleeping bag over the load. Frida's fabric storage boxes and various books, most of which she hasn't been allowed to read, are next to be loaded. We're almost done. I open the front door, only to see the kitchen door open and Frida making tea.

'Tea?' I ask—strange question, but it's a strange time to be thinking about tea.

'Not for me; it's for ani. She's asked for tea. She's just got back from cleaning Lama's apartment. She asked where my shoes have gone,' Frida whispers.

Oh, God, I could kick myself! I shouldn't have moved our shoes from the porch. I've packed all but the ones we'll wear for the journey. 'What'd you say to her?'

'I told her I didn't know.'

I pour a cup of strong coffee from the cafetiere, while Frida bleach sprays the already spotlessly clean kitchen counter and rigorously wipes it down. We hear someone humming a tune.

The elder nun glides into the kitchen and stops humming. '*Amitufuo!*' she says.

We *amitufuo* her back.

She collects her tea and glides off to the burgundy lounge, holding the rattling cup and saucer in her bony hand.

I check our dorm; as far as I can tell we're very nearly finished packing. We just have to pack our laptops and last bits into our rucksacks before zipping them up.

'Frida, I'm popping outside; I'll be back in five,' I whisper.

I take my well-trodden path to the railway bridge. I've been so busy that I've forgotten to check my phone, but there's no messages. Ethan's obviously distracted. My battery is only half charged, though, so I switch it off and zip it inside my pocket to save the rest in case of emergencies.

I return to the sangha and find the door to our dorm ajar. Frida's almost finished changing the bedding so ours can be washed. We hear a tap on the door, and in walks the nun, looking shocked.

'So you're leaving,' she blurts out.

Someone has snitched about the shoes.

Frida doesn't answer.

The nun takes a few steps closer to Frida—so close, she's at arms' length.

Frida plops down on the bottom bunk bed.

The nun edges closer still. 'Think about it. You can't leave. If you want to go, it has to be with guru's blessing. Wait until he returns from abroad.' She looms over Frida, who remains silent.

I detach the sangha house key from my key ring and place it on the drawers. 'There's the key. We're going. If anyone asks, tell them I'm making Frida leave.' I pick up our backpacks and take them to the porch, while the nun persists in trying to coerce Frida to stay.

When I return to our dorm, the nun, still looming, looks at me and says, 'But aren't you happy here? I thought you were staying for good. The world outside is full of demons. Serving Rinpoche is surely better than leaving. Maybe you're upset because of the retreats. They always bring things up for students. It'll pass.'

'I've outstayed my welcome. I never intended to be here this long. And I'm not leaving Frida here,' I reply.

The nun still lingers.

Frida's trapped on the bottom bunk because the nun has blocked her in. She hugs herself and says nothing.

'Can you move out of the way,' I say to the nun. 'We have to go now! Chop, chop!'

The nun looks flabbergasted, but she moves enough for me to take Frida's hand and pull her up. 'Come on.' I lead the way to the porch.

'At least say goodbye to Loday?' the nun says.

'Of course we will,' I reply, while tying my laces.

'Well, come visit us sometime. Next retreat?'

'Maybe,' I lie.

Frida, who's still lost for words, ties her laces. It's not like she's prepared a goodbye speech. All this has happened in a frantic rush. We sling our backpacks over our shoulders.

'Thanks for everything; take care,' I say,

'*Amituofo,*' she replies.

Frida *amituofos* her back.

The nun stands at the front door and watches us leave the sangha for the last time.

We clamber into my car, fasten our seatbelts, and I fire up the engine.

'Are you really going to say goodbye to Loday?' Frida asks.

'Yeah, I'll try; that's if he'll speak to me, mind.'

It's almost dark. I park in a spot outside the monk's sangha house. The front door is open. Frida and I find Loday, dressed in robes, standing at the sink washing up.

'*Amituofo*, Loday,' I say.

He stops, dries his hands and gives me a knowing look. '*Amituofo*.'

'We've come to say goodbye,' I say.

Frida stands behind me.

He nods. 'I heard you were leaving us.'

Clearly, the nun didn't waste time phoning Loday.

'Yes, I've outstayed my welcome.'

'You mean you don't feel welcome?' he asks.

'No.' The way he's avoided me isn't exactly welcoming.

'I'm sorry you feel unwelcome, and Frida's going with you? Where will you go?'

'Maybe Bristol,' I lie. 'We'll live in my car, seeing as Ethan's made us homeless. It'll be fine. It's better if I've Frida to keep me company. She'd like to stay, but I'm making her leave.' I give away little info plus a red herring.

He looks at Frida.

She lowers her head, vaguely expressing that she has no say in the matter.

'I can see your mind's made up,' Loday says.

'Yes. It is.'

He sighs. '*Amituofo*.'

We *amituofo* him back, and he acknowledges with a nod, then we see ourselves out.

As soon as we get back in my car, Frida removes her Buddhist pendant noose from her neck—the one hanging on thin red cotton that Lama gifted at the time of taking refuge. I doff my one too, and we drop them in a paper bag for disposal.

'Is this really happening?' Frida asks as I pull into the garage for diesel.

'Yes, it's really happening. We've escaped.'

She checks to see if we're being followed, and I twig that she's paranoid.

A half-full tank is all I can afford, and when I go to pay, I offer her my car keys through the passenger window. 'Here, take the keys; lock yourself in while I pay. I won't be a minute.'

I can't afford to buy us hot drinks, so I help myself to two paper coffee cups, pocket them and buy a bottle of water and Harbio sweets for us to share. Frida unlocks my car to let me in, and just before I jump back in, I remember the guru's laminated portrait of himself that's in my backpack. I manage to retrieve it and place it on top of a large, overflowing trash can.

Once I'm back in the driver's seat, I take off my jacket, fasten my seatbelt, and make myself comfortable. Frida slides the passenger seat back as far as it'll go for more leg room. It dawns on me that I haven't looked at my phone all day, but I dread to check it. If Ethan's sent any abuse, it'll distract me. With the long drive ahead, I have to stay focused.

'You ready, lil fella?' I ask.

'I'm ready,' Frida replies. 'Let's get the hell out of this town.'

I tap Brentwood into my SatNav as our destination. It's roughly twenty odd miles from London with free parking outside the town centre—a bonus considering our lack of finances, or wonga as they say in Essex. My SatNav estimates we've got a five-hour journey. I have to stay alert and make sure I don't take a wrong turn; a mistake would waste our precious fuel.

I pull out of the garage, leaving the grinning Lama on top of the garbage.

Suddenly, we hear an almighty bang, and we're so anxious

we almost jump out of our skin. I brake to a halt. A huge shower of silver stars shoots into the sky. We'd forgotten it was Guy Fawkes Night. One explosion follows another. I carry on driving and focus on the road, while Frida gazes out of the window at the dazzling display. As a child she always loved the fifth of November fireworks, whereas Sylvia hated them. One touch of the CD and it disappears into the mouth of the stereo. Ironically Sia's album *Some People Have Real Problems* starts to play. It reminds us of better times of after dinner sing-a-alongs with Sylvia.

'We'll call Sylvia in the morning,' I say. 'What's she going to make of us Londoners? Back like homing pigeons!'

Frida laughs a little. 'I don't know!'

I grin. 'I think she'll say I stole the lama's skivvy.'

Frida laughs louder, uninhibited because she's allowed to be. We retell the joke, and it gets funnier every time.

'Mum, do you feel that?' she asks.

I know what she means. As well as the humour, we sense a tranquil rush of jubilance. Combined with our adrenaline, it's powerful, like it's a spiritual presence.

We motor on, driving through Durham.

'Jesus Christ! Look at the sky!' Frida exclaims.

The entire night sky is blood red. We've never seen a sky like it.

'Is it him? Lama? They must have told him! It's his anger, because you stole me, Lama's skivvy. He knows we've escaped,' Frida exclaims.

'Bullshit! It's not him. The sky's red, that's all. It's auspicious. Shepherd's delight,' I reply.

'So you're sure it's not his rage?'

'I'm sure, lil fella. You're safe now; stop worrying.'

'I love you, Mum,' Frida says.

I have to choke back tears. I don't cry easily, but right now, it's hard not to. 'I love you too, lil fella,' I reply.

Already we have ditched the Buddhist names Lama gave us; they'll never be spoken again.

Over a hundred miles later, in Leeds, we take a pit stop. We've covered enough distance for Frida to calm down; at least she's less paranoid that we're not being followed.

Just before we resume our journey, Frida says, 'Mum, do you need the music on while you're driving? Or can we switch it off?'

She's so used to the silence of the sangha, she can't cope with the background noise of music.

'You don't have to ask; switch it off, lil fella,' I say.

We motor on with just the reassuring growl my car's turbo diesel engine and the heater. From time to time, Frida discloses disturbing snippets of what went on there, things she had not mentioned previously. In my wildest dreams, I'd never have thought Frida's short stay for respite there would result in her being habitually indoctrinated, bullied and driven to tears following her first week of arriving. Sometimes when she needed medical treatment, she was denied Lama's permission. And the secrecy of the cult meant she wasn't registered there: not to vote, claim state benefits or be known to the local authority in any way.

I know the sangha's rules and regulations with its punishments and admonishments, so my biggest worry is how ten months of brain washing and abuse has affected Frida's mental health. If only it were possible for me to stop the car and hug her trauma away. I can't help checking my SatNav every few miles.

When Frida stays quiet for too long, I ask, 'You all right, lil fella?' to bring her back from whatever dark space her mind has wandered off to.

'Yes, I'm all right, Mum.'

My foot's been on the gas for so long my ankle hurts, as

well as my legs and back. Frida's body aches too, not that she complains. I stop for a stretch and some fresh air, then we're off again. At long last my SatNav announces we're a mile from the M25. I've been longing to reach this junction for ages. It's just as well we're driving by night because the motorway has roadworks that narrows traffic down to one lane. We've got about twenty miles to go, not all of it motorway, to reach our destination. Just as I signal to leave the M25, to join an A road, a dual carriageway, I hear a bleep sound, and the orange light on the dash lights up—a low fuel warning. *Oh my Lord, don't let us conk out.* I keep glancing at the fuel light. It's getting nearer to empty every time; I swear it is.

It feels weird, slowing down to thirty miles per hour after driving hundreds of miles at speed. The quaint, up-market village has a small church with a car park hidden behind evergreen shrubbery. I know someone local who lives close by, but it's too late to call her now. Maybe she'll be around in the morning.

'We made it. Home at last!'

'Mum. You did it,' Frida replies.

Not that we've got a proper home, but at least we're back in our hometown.

The car park's empty, but soon the Sunday morning worshippers will start filling it up. I park at the far end, and Frida opens the boot to get a sleeping bag and pillows. A dog barks in the pitch-dark distance. I lock us in, and we get as comfy as we can in our half-reclined car seats, taking a pillow each and sharing the sleeping bag. We're exhausted; Frida drifts off before me.

We wake before dawn—our body clock's probably still on sangha time. With lack of facilities, we have to take turns to pee, hiding in the overgrown shrubbery. It's still too early to call anyone.

'It's nice to not wake up with a gong being smashed in our faces,' Frida says.

'Never again,' I reply.

'They won't guess where we are?' she asks. 'They won't come looking for us?'

'There's no way they'll track us down; we're safe.'

'I'm scared,' she replies.

I reassure her that everything will be all right, and she forces a smile.

The sun makes an appearance, and the neighbourhood starts to wake up. Swanky cars vroom past on the road behind the shrubbery, and people walk by—on their way to buy croissants and Sunday papers, no doubt. Frida waits in the car while I smoke under the evergreens. I turn on my phone and call Ethan to tell him what's happened.

He picks up on the first ring and says, 'Yeah? What the fuck do you want?'

I'm stunned by his rudeness. 'Well, good morning to you too! I've been driving all night; I'm on the streets. We've got out!'

'You what?'

'You heard. We've escaped!' The bleeping sound of text messages and voicemails begins, one after another, so many I can't count them. 'Oh, hang on, I've got loads of messages coming through.'

'Oh, wait,' he says. 'Don't look at the messages. I'm sorry, but I sent you a load of abusive messages last night! Can you pretend I didn't send them?'

'Errr. All right. I thought you might have been worried; what a shame,' I reply.

'It'll never happen again. I promise! Where are you?'.

'Parked in a suburb; just outside central London,' I reply. 'I need to sort stuff out now, so we'll talk later.'

'London! That's great to hear. Maybe we can meet up. I go to AA meetings near Harrods. It's good you're out. Those Buddhists cut me off when I relapsed!' He tries to drag the conversation out, perhaps feeling some guilt or shame over the messages he'd sent.

'I'm standing out in the cold. Please, for once in your life let me go and get warm,' I say and end the call.

Although he'd told me not to look at the messages, of course I do. Most read things like, *You cheap cunt fucking whore! You're out fucking, you slag! Ugly fucking troll. How's Cedders? You're with him, you dirty slag! Don't ever speak to me again! Why's your phone off? Whore!* My heart pounds. It's not easy soaking up Ethan's abuse. It's making me ill, and the more of it I take, the worse I feel. It's hard to believe he's in another top rehab, supposedly studying the Twelve Steps. I hide my upset from Frida.

'Frida, wait in the car; I'll see if Judith's awake,' I say.

Fear of rejection follows me up the garden path to Judith's enormous house. I take a deep breath and ring on the doorbell. She doesn't answer, then just as I'm about to leave, she opens it.

'Sorry. Oh, Magda! Hi. I wasn't expecting anyone. Is everything all right?' she says.

'I'm sorry to turn up so early. I lost your number. I was wondering if I could ask you for a cup of coffee. I've been driving all night,' I reply.

'Of course. Come on in. Place is a mess; we had a dinner party last night.'

'Thanks, Judith. Frida's in the car, can I just—'

She doesn't let me finish. 'Bring her in. We'll catch up over breakfast. Here, I'll leave the door ajar for you; see you in the kitchen.'

I walk on air back to the car park, thanking the gods she's affable. Frida sees me smiling and nods her head in a way that

335

asks, 'Are we welcome?' I give the thumbs up.

'Come on, lil fella. Judith's offered us breakfast. We'll call Sylvia later; she'll still be sleeping now,' I say through the car window.

Tears pool in Frida's eyes, her emotions getting the better of her by the act of kindness.

When we enter the huge kitchen, we see Judith's already set our places at the breakfast bar. The so-called mess Judith mentioned is just one large saucepan soaking in suds, and the breadboard's got a few crumbs; apart from that, it could feature in *Ideal Home* magazine.

Breakfast is a full English: eggs, bacon, sausages, mushrooms, toast, and fresh coffee. We haven't seen so much protein on a plate in ages.

'Don't wait for me, please, eat,' Judith says.

We're so used to the ritual of food prayer, it's strange tucking into a meal without saying it.

Judith grabs some fresh orange juice from her blue Smeg fridge and plonks it beside the toast rack. 'Here you go. So what's new? I haven't heard from you in, what? Five years?'

'Five years! How time flies. You first, Judith, what's new with you?' I reply.

'Oh, let me see. I retired last year. And we've got a new grandchild. Lots of babysitting. And time to do my gardening. God is good.' She points towards the patio doors that show off the garden. 'The pond had to go, what with the baby toddling.'

After one hour of small talk, I feel I should take the plunge. 'Judith. I know this sounds weird, but we escaped from a cult yesterday. We're relocating. Things are a bit up in the air.'

'Goodness me! A cult! That's terrible. I mean, what you've been through. Don't be ashamed; the good Lord is watching,' she says.

336

'Thanks, Judith,' I reply.

'Well, you're welcome to have a nice hot bath or shower, and if you need a few days' rest, you can stay in our largest guest room. I can offer you three nights. Symon won't mind. From Wednesday, we have much of the Lord's work to do; sorry we can't offer longer.'

'Thank you, that's amazing! You're very kind. And Symon too,' I reply.

After my shower I go into the garden and sit on a bench with the Sunday paper, catching up on current affairs. I'm so behind in political news; it was banned in the cult. Judith's popped out for a bit; Symon's at the Sunday service, and Frida is taking a bath. It's so peaceful. This is what normal people take for granted. The newspaper supplements have celebrity news, happy faces, what's on telly this week and Dear Deirdre the agony aunt.

Suddenly, the patio door flies open. I look up, startled.

'Mum! Mum!' Frida runs towards me, wet hair, bare feet, in a dressing gown.

'What is it?' I ask.

She hugs me, crying her eyes out. 'I got scared! I was calling out for you. No one answered me! I thought you'd left me!' she says in between sobs. Her body shakes in my arms.

'Shhh, lil fella, you're safe!' I reply. She gradually calms down. 'Come on,' I say, 'let's go indoors or you'll catch cold. Get yourself dressed and we'll call Sylvia, and we need to make contact with Pammy. Okay?'

'I'd like that. Sorry, Mum; I just had a panic attack.'

Sylvia has Frida laughing in no time on the phone, just like old times. We've agreed to keep the traumatic events from Sylvia, because of her problems with depression. Her trauma from the past is still the untamed lion within. So for starters we haven't mentioned the sangha was a cult. Instead, we left, or so we say, because we didn't see eye to eye with the others. We tell Sylvia it won't be long, and we'll try and visit her soon. With Frida's spirit lifted by Sylvia, I offer to make a pot of tea while Frida calls Pammy.

Tea's brewing, ready to pour. I carry the tray to the TV lounge where a massive telly is mounted on the wall. Telly hasn't featured in my life for so long that the fascinating jumbo window of moving pictures takes a bit of getting used to.

Frida pops her head around the door. 'Oh, here you are!'

I didn't hear her footsteps approaching because she walks without making a sound—old habits and all that.

'This house has so many doors that I keep getting lost,' she continues. 'Is Judith back yet?' She sinks into the sumptuous leather settee next to me and picks up her mug of tea.

'Not yet. Did you speak to Pammy?' I ask.

'Yes, that's what I've come to tell you. She's spoken to a friend who's got an ashram in London, and Pammy says they're sound. As luck would have it, they just happen to have a space available from this Friday. Pammy's arranged an introduction interview for me tomorrow. And guess what? If they like me, they'll offer me part-time voluntary work in their café in exchange for my very own private, spacious room. And free daily meals in the café. And free accommodation. In London! Pammy said there are no crazy restrictions. I'm even allowed an income if I want to seek part-time paid work.'

'Blimey! That's a result!' I reply.

Frida nods. 'Yeah, Pammy's offered me her sofa if I need a few nights. There's a trial period of one month at the ashram, and if I get through the probation period, I've six whole months there, guaranteed. It's a start.'

'Six months,' I say. 'I wasn't expecting such good news. I've got a few old Oyster cards in the car; you can have them, so that's your train fare sorted.'

'Thanks; it's lucky you've kept them.'

How lucky indeed, Ethan still hasn't transferred me a single penny.

We do our best to keep out of Judith's space, and she makes the guest room comfortable for us. My phone signal is weak in the guest room, so Ethan's suspicious mind does overtime should his calls go to voicemail. Now I'm in the outside world, his controlling pattern has amped up.

Frida's already asleep, but she's left the bedside lamp on, so I'm able to get ready for bed with some light. Sleep doesn't come easily. At some point I drift off, until I'm startled awake by Frida crying out in her sleep.

'Mum! Help!'

The lamp is still on. I sit bolt upright to see what's going on.

'Mum!' She whimpers, turns on her tummy and settles down again.

Our internal alarm wakes us early. At this rate we might rise before dawn for the rest of our lives; I hope not.

After breakfast I drop Frida off at the train station. Pammy's offered her couch for tonight if Frida's interview is too tiring. All I need to do is focus on the countdown to Wednesday when we have to leave Judith's. Every time I try to do internet searches or make any calls to try to sort my life out, Ethan phones for a marathon conversation to check up on me. He doesn't allow any focus on me.

Wednesday morning dawns bittersweet. We thank Judith for the three nights' stay, then I drop Frida off at the train station. She managed to pass the ashram interview, and heads there with as much as she can carry in her backpack.

November's not an ideal time to be living in my car. At least I know where I can park for free. I've no money for diesel, so I can't switch my car engine on for the heater. My street begging is mostly unsuccessful, so I apply for welfare; with any luck I might get money in a month's time. The food bank won't help, because I don't meet their criteria of being in receipt of housing benefit. I try the church to ask for a sandwich, only for the Catholic priest to slam his door in my face. How humiliating. Survival is a challenge. This way of life is not made any easier by Ethan's non-stop calls and brainstorms.

'Don't be a prude! I'm not willing to repay any money to you, not yet. I think you should try out sex work. It'll be a great income. Easy money. I'm into sex workers. So you should do as I say,' he says one particularly cold night.

'Please leave me alone,' I reply. 'Don't phone me again.'

He won't listen, and calls until I pick up.

'Sorry!' he says. 'I didn't really mean that. I was kidding. I'm spun out; I should have told you before, but I've seen a Harley Street doctor. He's prescribed really strong meds to help with my cravings. It's even made me relapse with porn again. I've been going to local SAA meetings, you know, Sex Addicts Anonymous. My brain will be better in a week or two.'

'Meds? But that might cause an alcohol relapse, won't it?' I ask.

'Nah. Don't be daft. I'll get a train to where you are tomorrow. I'll buy you lunch, as an apology. We'll be fine together when I've finished rehab. I don't know why I'm so horrible to you. I know I'm controlling; I can't help myself.'

I arrive at the station before Ethan. His hair is much shorter, and he looks remarkably well. It's incredible how he puts his body through so much with his addiction and yet bounces back so quickly.

'Phone,' he says, holding out his hand for the inspection. He can't find anything incriminating. Next, he searches my pockets and pats down my body. Some things never change.

I pass the search.

He tells me that someone in rehab cut his hair for free, but I don't believe him. Trust-fund kids don't cut hair. The job's too professional. Every two minutes he secretly checks his iPhone. Message alerts keep beeping. Maybe I'm just tired, but things aren't the same between us.

'It's changed, Ethan,' I say.

'No, it hasn't. I'm getting better. You should be happy,' he replies.

'Better? But I think you're being secretive, and lying, like about your hair.'

'I'm working on my dishonesty. But you're right about my hair. It cost me a hundred quid, including tip. I got it cut at a salon near Harrods.'

'A hundred! Ethan! You won't pay me anything back, and I'm freezing without the car heater!'

'Yeah, well my rehab counsellor and family have told me to end it with you. You're a distraction for me. I've told everyone it's over between us,' he replies.

'Well, that's what we need to do, Ethan. You're dragging me down. All I've ever done is mollycoddle you. It's all a one-way street with you.'

Thankfully, he agrees. Until the following morning when he's changed his mind again. I'm so scared he'll walk out of rehab that I jump when he barks, but things are changing. I'm changing, especially since his demands grow more outlandish.

When the rain eases off, I root around in my car looking for stuff to sell on eBay, like burgundy clothing and unused soaps and smellies—old gifts from the sangha girls. I'm parked next to a box hedge which makes a good background support to drape or place the items for photographing. This earns me odd looks from passers-by.

Staff at Starbucks turn a blind eye while I use their WiFi to create my listings. It's a good place to use the loo, warm up and read the news online. One story catches my eye; it is about an English domestic violence law passed under a year ago. They use the term 'coercive control.' In an instant I recognise myself as a victim of this crime. I wonder if it'll be enforced?

My eBay sales give me the means for my train fare to London, where I've arranged to meet Frida and Pammy. We have an appointment to keep. Frida greets me at Holborne with a hurried hug, and we run all the way to LSE—the last time we'd been to the London School of Economics was for a book reading some years ago. Frida rushes us through security, into the lift, through the very impressive library, until we reach an office that resembles a press office with an all-female staff.

I follow Frida towards a middle-aged woman who is sitting on a chair. 'This is Pammy,' she says.

'It's lovely to meet you and thank you so much for helping Frida.' I extend my hand to shake.

She accepts. 'She deserves help; if only I'd known sooner.'

A young woman calls out, 'Ahh, you just made it in time. Welcome to INFORM. Please follow me. She opens the door to an air-conditioned meeting room, and says, 'Take a seat!' She places highlighter pens and biros next to her writing pad and sits opposite the three of us. 'Okay. Let's begin.' (*note: Since 2018, INFORM has been based in the Department of Theology and Religious Studies at King's College, London).

Pammy goes first, reporting her experiences with Pathgate, how she, a woman with health problems, was once violently punched in the stomach by Lama as a karmic debt. She goes on to outline misconceptions within the sangha; she's an academic with a vast knowledge about Buddhism. The woman scribbles away, looking up every now and then. I'm next. I haven't even thought about what I want to say, so I speak with an open heart and answer questions, explaining how I got lured in, sent Frida there, and ended up homeless over it all. Basically, I tell her how it is. I name names, but not Ethan's. I refer to him as my partner who is a sick addict, still protecting him. Frida begins her report after me. It takes the longest of the three; ten months is a lot of telling.

'Thank you for your statements; I'll type them up,' she says. 'I'll tell you this. Pathgate have been flagged to us already. There've been others who've escaped and given statements to us.'

We're pretty taken aback by this. All this time, we were not aware that other survivors—those who'd escaped the so-called Rinpoche before us—refer to him as PY. We can't think of any other way, apart from reporting PY and his accomplices, to help those still trapped there. Pammy goes home, while Frida and I step outside into the sun. Flat broke and hungry. I spot beg and barely make enough for a coffee.

Back home—in my car—the temperature drops quickly. By night-time, my breath steams up my car windows creating a self-made privacy screen. I can't see out, and no one can see in. According to my car dashboard reading, which is never wrong, outside is minus six. The sleeping bag feels kind of damp because it's so cold. It smells too, or that might be me because I haven't showered in nearly a month. Finally, despite shivering, I get sort of comfortable. I hope Ethan isn't in a nasty mood when he calls. I've charged my phone, as usual, in the cigarette lighter. It never charges properly. I know it's him calling when it rings this late.

'Looks cold outside tonight. I've just had a wonderful hot shower. I bet you're freezing!' He laughs.

My heart sinks. 'Yeah, it's so funny you made me homeless.'

He sneers. 'I don't believe you're homeless and outside.'

'What?'

'Open and close your car door, so I know you're in the car,' he demands.

'No, I can't move, I'm so cold.'

'Do it,' he says.

I dutifully move from my comfort, climb into the front seat, unlock my doors, and try to open the driver's door. It's so frozen it's stuck. I kick the door panel with both feet, and it takes a few goes before I crack through the ice outside. My empty fuel tank beeps and I open and close the doors until I'm allowed to stop. I've just let in the freezing air.

'Okay. I believe you now,' he says. And so begins Ethan's new game of control.

His prescription dose increases. Tansy offers funding for him to see a few Harley Street psychiatrists, three-hundred quid per visit, to determine if he suffers from a mental condition, other than his self-diagnosis of anxiety, or if his addiction can be treated without prescription meds.

We meet for a bag of chips. We're like lost souls, trying to salvage our relationship.

'My counsellor said I mustn't see you ever again. He knows we sometimes meet for chips,' he says.

So I'm forbidden to be in his life—new rules set by his rehab and Tansy. He, on the other hand, won't let me go. His dishonesty of the double life is unhealthy for his recovery. Whenever he says he loves me, really, he loves me not. He reads me his newest version of his life story, the one for his rehab group. Of course, he omits the darker parts of his sketchy past, and chronicles his previous relationships, not that he's realised his co-dependency. Unsurprisingly, he erases me from his newest life story, not that it matters to me.

Ethan sends me an email saying he's leaving rehab. He's

relapsed on cocaine, and they've kicked him out. He's already got his bags packed to leave. In a familiar, mad panic, I call Ethan to see what's gone wrong.

'Ha ha! I gotcha! It was a joke. I haven't relapsed. I was kidding.' He laughs.

'That's really sick, Ethan. It's not a laughing matter,' I reply.

'You are soooo boring. Boring. Boring!' He slams the phone down.

The rehab doesn't tell Tansy, who's named as his next of kin, about Ethan swerving his therapy group sessions. Even the counsellors are secretive. Ethan receives another warning over this, despite him knowing that Tansy is trying to persuade the rehab to consider an extended three months of treatment, as a freebie, naturally.

Christmas is looming. He knows, through Tansy, that a marvellous family dinner gathering is planned, and he's not invited. His new rehab friends of means are all checking out of rehab for the festive season, and none are willing to adopt Ethan for Christmas at their family mansions either. He feels sorry for himself; his charm rarely lets him down. Try as I might to remind him it's not for long and what a gift it is to be in rehab, he sulks.

It's against Ethan's orders that I leave my car for daily walks to stretch my legs, but I do it anyhow. The high street is decorated with festive lights. Boozy night revellers pass me by, not noticing me sitting on the bench. I look at my feet so not to catch their attention. The street-sweeper vehicle approaches, brushing up butts and rubbish. Something glints in the cobblestones next to my trainer. I take a closer look and ease it out of the crack. It's some kind of ring, worthless probably. It's too dark to see if it's real. I pocket it anyhow before the sweeper sucks it up.

The following morning, I hesitate outside the pawn shop,

afraid my smell will make me seem dodgy. Smell be damned! I open the door and a bell above tinkles.

He's friendly, for a pawn broker, and he has a good look at the ring with a magnifier that he pops into his right eye socket. 'It's not copper. No. This is real. Hold on, and I'll weigh it.'

I walk out of there with a hundred pounds in my pocket. Cash! Enough for me to blow on Christmas presents I can send to Sylvia and Frida. Maybe a gift to cheer Ethan up too. What a result! Pavement spotting can bring a little extra income; I was half afraid of becoming a prolific shoplifter.

The worst thing about Christmas morning is not being with Sylvia and Frida. We speak on the phone instead. They're delighted with their gifts—diaries, crafty bits, books and treats. I try to sound bright. Next Christmas will be better, after all. Everywhere is closed for days, so I can't buy a hot drink or food with my welfare money that's just been awarded. At least I've got diesel for heat.

Frida and I meet on Boxing Day in a pub just off Bond Street. We're frugal, ordering a pot of coffee and a cake to share. Neither of us have heard from INFORM, we discover, but the police left a voicemail with Frida about the cult. They might follow up with a call back, but the MET police are swamped right now, so don't hold your breath. Frida's made lots of new friends. She loves her room, and her job; everything's good.

'No support from Ethan or his useless family, then?' Frida asks.

'Nah. They're all so busy, too important for the likes of me.'

'Thought as much. How about a New Year's treat, a shower at Pammy's? I'll arrange something.'

I smile. 'After nearly two months without a shower, I wouldn't say no!' Before I make my way back to my car, I call Ethan to arrange coffee. He suggests the Starbucks in South Kensington.

'You pay for your own coffee,' he says while we stand in the queue. He carries his tray of refreshments to a window table.

I order my latte and follow him. Once seated I hand him the wrapped gift.

'Oh, sorry, I didn't bother getting you anything.' He tears off the blue paper and says, 'I love sharks and penguins, thanks,' then he stuffs the gift in his pocket and starts to roll a fag.

His phone on the table rings, displaying a contact called Colette, but he dismisses it and suggests we drink outside so he can smoke. It makes a change not to be publicly searched.

'Who was that calling?' I ask as we settle outside.

'Err. The rehab office,' he lies.

Our coffee cools quickly out in the cold dusk air.

'Follow me. Wanna show you something,' he says.

'I'd rather not, Ethan.'

'Come on.' He starts walking fast, seeming to know where he's heading. After a while he stops outside a large modern building. I follow him up the steps into a deserted foyer. Posters on the wall declare, THY SINNERS BE SAVED.

A young woman approaches us. 'Can I help?'

'Well, I think you can,' Ethan says. 'You see my poor friend is homeless. Could you take her in?'

My hands get hot and sweaty, anxiety building. I don't know what this place is, whether it's the Sci's or a cult or what.

'No, sadly we can't,' she replies, 'but I can give you some booklets about greatness.'

I want to leave, but Ethan agrees to sit through a very long film about bleak prophecies, with us the only audience in the projector room. It finally ends, so we can leave. Once outside the church, I realise they're Mormons. *But aren't they dead against alkies and junkies?*

'What are you playing at?' I ask, almost running towards the train station.

'Helping! It's for your own good,' he replies.

'Well, if it's such a great place to be, you enlist. Leave me out. Okay?' I reply.

He stops, takes my head firmly in his hands and starts shaking it. 'You start thinking about me. You sort out somewhere for me to live. And don't you dare cheat behind my back. That'll make me relapse. I'm dead if I pick up a drink.' He loosens his grip. We attract stares from passers-by carrying Christmassy gift bags.

'Understood!' he yells.

I nod. 'Understood,' I whisper.

For New Year's Eve, we've made a pact not to disagree. We'll watch fireworks and be kind to each other. This year is going to be the best one yet; he's sure of it. He's certain we'll find a new home, start a business, go on a holiday and put all this behind us. He gets so carried away talking about the future that he misses rehab curfew by one hour and gets another warning.

Everything I need for my shower is packed. Anyone would think I was going for a ritzy spa day instead of my first shower in two months at Pammy's. When I arrive, I'm greeted by Frida. The smell of cooking fills the modest apartment.

'We thought you'd enjoy a hot, home-cooked meal. And you can stay the night,' Frida says.

Although I feel dirty, my stomach grumbles for the hot meal, so I eat first. After three shampoos my hair starts to feel clean, and I wash head to toe so many times my fingers wrinkle. The hot water soothes my aching muscles, and I almost feel good as new. I join Frida and Pammy in the lounge for a warm, relaxing evening.

No sooner have I sat down than my phone rings. It's Ethan again.

'Sweetie, my love, I need to see you ASAP. If you say no, I'll relapse. Tell me where you are. I'll come to you.'

'I can't give you Pammy's address. Leave it until tomorrow,' I reply.

'Hear me out! Don't hang up!' He tearfully asks to meet me until I reluctantly agree and arrange to meet him by my parked car.

I pack up and head out into the cold again.

He's late. I'm about to give up on him, when I see him in the distance, one arm raised high, so I see him. As he gets closer, I notice he looks cagey; he won't make eye contact. Without warning he pulls my jacket and starts searching my pockets. I get a familiar whiff.

I'm horrified. 'Ethan? You smell of booze! Are you mad?'

He huffily lets me go to retrieve the fag behind his ear. 'That rehab lets everyone else relapse, and they all get allowed back in. What do I get? A final warning; if I'm not sober by tomorrow, I'm out. I promise I won't drink. I'll sober up tonight in your car and go back to rehab tomorrow.'

'All right. But this is the last time, Ethan. Get in the car.'

'I won't let you down.' It starts pouring with rain as we climb inside. 'Thank God I'm not out on the street in that.' He rummages in his backpack and pulls out a bottle of wine. 'Just the one to help me sleep,' he says and drains the bottle.

A short while later, he roughly tugs at my jacket.

'Please stop, just go to sleep,' I say.

With both hands, he grabs me by the jacket and shakes me like a rag doll. Then, *wallop*; he throws punches at my head.

'Get out of the car! Now!' I demand.

'No!' He sulkily retreats back into the passenger seat.

I think he might strangle me. I know I'm taking a risk when I start my car and drive to the train station where I know there'll be people about.

I pull into the taxi rank. 'Ethan, go back to rehab now; trains are still running.'

He calmly lights another fag and starts talking nonsense, then shouting. I'm his hostage. A taxi driver, who's parked next to me, can hear the commotion.

I jump out of my car to speak to him. 'I've been taken hostage; can you help me? I have to get him out of my car!'

'You should call the police,' he says.

'I can't!' I reply, then hop back in the driver's seat, leaving the door open.

Ethan continues shouting until something catches his eye. Straightaway he shuts up. Two police cars pull up, and blue flashing lights surround us. I can't even look at Ethan while they bundle him into a squad car. They lead me into the other and ask me what's going on, am I hurt, do I need an ambulance, what's his name, my name and all the usual questions.

'We're taking you to the station,' the cop says. 'We've arrested Ethan for assault and battery, and we need you to make a statement.'

At the station I think the policeman realises I'm in shock; visibly upset. He's not surprised when I keep asking to leave and say that I'd rather not press charges. Two officers offer to drive me back to my car; they say Ethan's spending the night in the cell.

As soon as Ethan gets released, he phones to thank me for not going ahead with pressing charges, even though the police had asked him not to contact me. He looks on the bright side; he's sober for his rehab readmission decision appointment this morning because he's been in the police cell all night. Tansy's mad as hell hearing what's happened. Apparently, she has disowned him, so another relative, an aunt who he'd lost touch with, is to attend the rehab meeting with him to argue his case and overturn his rehab discharge.

I hear no word from Ethan all day. Surely this means his aunt has charmed rehab into overturning their decision. Nightfall is accompanied by more rain and howling wind. I make up my car seat bed and snuggle down for the night. No sooner have I drifted off than my phone rings.

'I've got good news and bad news,' Ethan whispers. 'The good news is I think I've found us a rescue puppy. The bad news is rehab wouldn't allow me back. So my aunty is letting me stay in her swanky pad in London for one week, as long as I'm sober. She's told me to find myself a dry house, or a free rehab. But I like it here, so I'll talk her round into letting me move in.' He belches.

'You're drinking,' I say.

'Don't you dare tell her! She'll boot me out if she catches me drinking.'

'She's not daft,' I reply. It's true; he'll be hard pushed to manipulate her the way he does with everyone else, especially me.

'She'll never twig. You're spoiling my nightcap,' he retorts. Clearly, he intends to get blotto. Only oblivion will do.

After he hangs up, I feel betrayed again. It's become clear I must let go. All of us rescuers and enablers are a hindrance to him finding recovery. This merry-go-round is driving me insane. Identifying with an addict's feelings, or misplaced empathy, is reckless, foolish—it's dangerous; I must stop. Bygone times have taught me the bewildering feeling of encountering useless, unkind people. Malice makes one feel hopeless. But what hasn't registered with me, until now, is that Ethan's feelings are distorted, unreliable—he's 'out of it,' lost himself by drowning his sorrows. In AA they say, 'The good news about being sober is you get your feelings back, and the bad news about being sober is you get your feelings back.'

At first light I psych myself up. It's a shot in the dark, but I have to start putting some focus on myself. I have to take back my power and make amends to Frida and Sylvia. I start to call a few old contacts to put word out about my own precarious situation.

One call leads to a friend of a friend who answers my call. 'I hear you need housing,' she says. 'I'm looking for a house sitter. It's a ramshackle old place, roomy enough, with a barn conversion next door. If the trial period works out, you can stay on. Interested?'

'Sounds perfect, thank you!' I can hardly believe my luck.

I make a list of the stuff I'll need, like saucepans, a frying pan, and a chopping board and I drive into town. As I walk along, I notice a group of people entering a church hall that has a notice on the door. Out of curiosity I take a closer look to read the notice. It says *Welcome to Al-Anon*, a program of recovery for the families and friends of alcoholics.

It sounds like exactly what I need.

A smiling woman gives me a warm welcome, and I follow her into a room containing a circle of chairs. She hands me a bunch of leaflets from a large box, then lays wordy coloured cards, called Al-Anon slogans, on a table. The meeting opens, and to my surprise, I hear life stories from the group that echo my own. They share experiences of their addicted loved ones, or sadly their lost ones, battle with alcohol and substance abuse. They discuss the family disease of addiction: enabling, denial, detachment, survival, The Three C's, rock bottom, recovery, and serenity. The Twelve Steps are read aloud, as well as the Twelve Traditions, based on the Twelve Steps and Twelve Traditions of Alcoholics Anonymous. I feel less heartache by the end of the meeting and think I'll go back next week. The woman suggests some recommended reading from the Al-Anon bookstore to help clear the fog, and I go home with a copy of an Al-Anon book called *Courage to Change*. Once I understand more about addiction, only then will I see signs of betterment within—for recovery has to come from within. There is always hope; one day at a time.

EpiloGue

Magda created boundaries and, apart from a period of erratic phone contact, utilized them. She made a fresh start in her new home, with a new phone number, to recover and reflect. She admitted how she'd been powerless over Ethan's alcohol, as well as his coercive control, sexual coercion, verbal abuse, financial abuse, violence, manipulating and gaslighting. She understood she could not control or cure his addiction and left the merry-go-round.

Magda sought therapy with a therapist trained in counselling victims of coercive control, sexual coercion, and domestic abuse. She put her focus on her recovery and her daughters. She studied Al-Anon Conference Approved Literature with a reading group and went on to represent a Twelve Step self-help family group. They carry the message of the Twelve Step program to families and friends of addicts and alcoholics in active addiction, as well as addicts and alcoholics in recovery.

Frida spent six peaceful months in the ashram, then relocated to the Midlands where she secured a fulfilling job and made new friends. She found love, and lives with her fiancé in a quiet suburb. Magda and Frida helped Sylvia move to a quaint house close to Magda. Sylvia is managing her mental health with lots of support from her partner, as well as Frida, Magda, and various health professionals.

Bella escaped from Pathgate and made a new life with someone special. They live happily together along with a cat called Mimi. Frida and Magda remain close friends with her.

Ethan forgot about the rescue puppy, and his drinking career progressed without Magda enabling. His aunt cottoned on that he was drinking and detached by asking him to leave her home. He headed for a camping site in the countryside to live in a tent. Further rehab-admission attempts proved unsuccessful, followed by more arrests, police cautions, and having two cars impounded by police before being crushed. Convictions followed—driving under the influence, no car insurance, shoplifting and a conviction for being drunk and disorderly while walking on a highway.

In court, Ethan was sentenced to a nominal fine, a twelve-month driving ban, and one year's probation. His probation officer, who understood addiction, showed leniency when Ethan repeatedly breached his probation order.

Ethan found himself homeless and with no one to turn to. He decided to detox and asked for Magda's financial support to fund a tenancy in a halfway safe house, along with the taxi fare to take him there. In another attempt to help him find recovery, Magda agreed. At first, he was grateful for having a safe, new home. The following day, however, although sober, he became aggressive, cruel, ungrateful, narcissistic, and controlling by phone. This compelled Magda to let go and end the relationship.

Ethan found new companionship with an active alcoholic and ultimately relapsed himself. He became homeless again. Eventually, Ethan's key worker intervened and secured a room for him in a hostel for addicts in active addiction. He was granted government funding for a stint in rehab, where he was detoxed, after which he moved to a village in England.

In 2018 one of PY, the Rinpoche's, ex-students founded Pathgate Survivors (PGS). A number of students have since escaped and contacted PGS; most are making a good recovery. Ex-students have provided their personal testimonies to PGS. Some include sexually harmed survivors, who were manipulated and coerced into abusive, sexual relationships with PY. One revealed that PY used engineered sexual coercion and non-consensual sexual relations with her when she was a young, vulnerable woman. She has made a remarkable recovery. The exact number of hand-picked vulnerable female students who PY harmed sexually is unknown.

PY was denied entry into Australia by Australian Border Force in January 2019. His travel ban saved Australian Pathgate students and visitors further abuse, brain washing, and thousands of Australian dollars of cash gifts towards PY's coffers.

A Note from the Author

Did you enjoy my book?

If so, I would be very grateful if you could write a review and publish it at your point of purchase. Your review, even a brief one, will help other readers to decide whether or not they'll enjoy my work. Large numbers of reviews are vital for helping indie books find readers, so I appreciate every little one and thank you for your time.

You can follow me on Instagram at magdalambauthor

Do you want to be notified of new releases?

If so, please visit www.aiapublishing.com and click the button to subscribe to notifications of new publications. You'll receive a free ebook of *Worlds Within Worlds* by Tahlia Newland in exchange. Of course, your information will never be shared, and the publisher won't inundate you with emails, just let you know of new releases.

Further reaDinG & resources

Books:
Fallout, Recovering From Abuse in Tibetan Buddhism, Tahlia Newland. AIA Publishing, 2019.

Beautiful Boy, A Father's Journey Through His Son's Addiction. David Sheff. Scribner. 2018. First published in Great Britain by Simon & Schuster UK Ltd, 2008.

In the Realm of Hungry Ghosts: Close Encounters with Addiction, Gabor Maté. Knopf Canada; 1st edition. 2008. Vermillion; 1st edition. 2018.

Codependant No More. How to Stop Controlling Others and Start Caring for Yourself. Melody Beattie. Hazelden FIRM; 2nd Edition. 2018.

Just For Today. Narcotics Anonymous. Hazelden Distributed Titles. 1992.

Books by Al-Anon Family Group, available from Al-Anon Bookstore:
Courage to Change: One Day at a Time in Al-Anon II. Al-Anon. Al-Anon Family Group Headquarters Inc. 1968, 1972, 1973.

Paths to Recovery: Al-Anon's Steps, Traditions and Concepts. Al-Anon. Al-Anon Family Group Headquarters, Inc. 1997.

Al-Anon's Twelve Steps & Twelve Traditions Revised. Al-Anon. Al-Anon Family Group Headquarters, Inc. 1981, 2005.

Opening our Hearts, Transforming our Losses. Al-Anon. Al-Anon Family Group Headquarters, Inc. 2007.

Many Voices, One Journey. Al-Anon. Al-Anon Family Group Headquarters, Inc. 2011.

From Survival to Recovery. Growing Up in an Alcoholic Home. Al-Anon. Al-Anon Family Group Headquarters, Inc. 1994.

One Day at a Time in Al-Anon. Al-Anon. Al-Anon Family Group Headquarters, Inc. 2002.

How Al-Anon works. For Families and Friends of Alcoholics. Al-Anon Family Group Headquarters, Inc. 1995, 2008.

Lois Remembers. Lois B. Wilson. Al-Anon Family Group Headquarters Inc. 1979.

useful websites

ACA website - https://www.adultchildrenofalcoholics.co.uk/
Action on Addiction - https://www.actiononaddiction.org.uk/
Adfam - https://adfam.org.uk/
Al-Anon - https://al-anon.org/
Al-Ateen - https://www.al-anonuk.org.uk/alateen/
Alcoholics Anonymous - https://www.alcoholics-anonymous.org.uk/
Beyond the Temple - https://beyondthetemple.com/
Cocaine Anonymous - https://cocaineanonymous.org.uk/
CODA Co-dependents Anonymous - https://codauk.org/
Coercive control collective (Austin, Texas, USA)
https://coercivecontrolcollective.org/
End the Fear (domestic Abuse in the LGBT community) -
http://www.endthefear.co.uk/same-sex-domestic-abuse/
Families Anonymous http://famanon.org.uk/
Gamblers Anonymous - https://www.gamblersanonymous.org.uk/
GAMON Family Group -
http://www.gamblersanonymous.org/ga/content/gam-anon-help-family-friends
UK alcohol and drug abuse prevention and treatment guidance -
https://www.gov.uk/government/collections/alcohol-and-drug-misuse-prevention-and-treatment-guidance
https://amywinehousefoundation.org/
https://drgabormate.com/
https://www.beautifulboyfund.org/
INFORM - https://inform.ac/

Mankind Initiative (Domestic Violence for males)
https://www.mankind.org.uk/
MIND - https://www.mind.org.uk/
NARCON - https://www.narcononuk.org.uk/
National Domestic Abuse Helpline
https://www.nationaldahelpline.org.uk/
NHS Addiction Help -
https://www.nhs.uk/live-well/healthy-body/drug-addiction-getting-help/
Pathgate Survivors - https://pathgatesurvivors.com/about/
Refuge For women and Children against domestic violence -
https://www.refuge.org.uk/
Rights of Women - https://rightsofwomen.org.uk/
S_ANON, family group for families and friends of sex addicts -
https://sanon.org/
S-Ateen, family group for 12-19 years olds affected by a sex addict
close to them - https://sanon.org/teen-newcomers/what-is-s-ateen/
Sex Addicts Anonymous - https://saauk.info/en/
Sexual Assault Survivors Anonymous - https://www.sasaworldwide.org/
Survivors of Incest Anonymous - https://siawso.org/
Talktofrank - https://www.talktofrank.com/
Turning Point - https://www.turning-point.co.uk/
UKAT - https://www.ukat.co.uk/drugs/
Victim Focus - https://www.victimfocus.org.uk/
Victim Support - https://www.victimsupport.org.uk/
We Are With You (previously known as Addaction) -
https://www.wearewithyou.org.uk/
Womensaid - https://www.womensaid.org.uk/

Housing advice:
Shelter https://www.shelter.org.uk/
ACORN - https://www.acorntheunion.org.uk/
Citizens Advice - https://www.citizensadvice.org.uk/

Debt Advice:
Citizens Advice https://www.citizensadvice.org.uk/
National Debtline https://www.nationaldebtline.org/
Step Change https://www.stepchange.org/

CPSIA information can be obtained
at www.ICGtesting.com
Printed in the USA
BVHW081330150921
616792BV00006B/27